Modern Furniture

Printed by The Guinn Co., Inc.

U.S.A.

Modern Furniture

its

DESIGN and CONSTRUCTION

by

Mario Dal Fabbro

REINHOLD PUBLISHING CORPORATION

330 West 42nd Street   New York, U.S.A.

INTRODUCTION

Today, the design of equipment is again as important and just as much a part of the planning of a building as spatial arrangements, structure, materials, and enclosing walls. This happy state of affairs is due to the fact that contemporary architecture truly reflects the living habits and social organization of our own day and age.

In Grecian or Gothic times buildings were planned around their own equipment. No architect was ever satisfied to stop his work after completeing a plan, some facades, and a few structural details. In a Grecian temple the statue of the god and his ritual home furnishings were given space and structure for their protection. In a Gothic Cathedral, seats for the congregation, equipment for religious services, and space for circulation were of first importance—after that, the enclosure of space and equipment in a rich structure and fabric could be undertaken.

This logical approach to architecture was lost during the Nineteenth Century. Archeology—not architecture—became the concern of architects. When an architect was busily engaged in acclimating himself to the building habits and mental attitude of another age, he had neither time nor opportunity to logically design equipment that would satisfy both an archeological approach and the demands of current living. It proved impossible for any architect to design, let us say, a Roman rocking chair or a Grecian stove. Those who had the time and the temerity to try it clearly proved that equipment for contemporary living could not successfully imitate that of another age.

We are no longer restricted to the narrow Nineteenth Century archeological horizon. We have regained that old approach to a living architecture and the equipment of our buildings is once more an integral part of that architecture. As a result, our buildings are once more alive and have again become a part of our natural environment.

It follows that architects must know how to design today's equipment in realistic terms. It is just as necessary for them to master the design of a sofa as it is for them to know the basic engineering principles for a reinforced concrete structure. The design of storage units becomes as important as the design of a door or window. A comparative study of living equipment should be one of our most valuable manuals—as useful and far more fascinating than a handbook of mechanical equipment or a copy of a building code.

Mr. Dal Fabbro gives us, in drawings and photos, a unique bird's-eye view of current design trends in furniture and equipment. His book should prove a useful tool to every professional concerned with today's architecture. As well, he has taken care of the needs of the amateur craftsman with "exploded" drawings that act as a guide to those interested in furniture building as a hobby.

Morris Ketchum, Jr.

ACKNOWLEDGMENT

Architects, designers and manufacturers in many nations have understood the novelty and importance of this book and have not hesitated to give me their full support by permitting me to publish and illustrate with original drawings special characteristics of their furniture designs. To them I am deeply indebted, for their help has enabled me to give a clear and practical demonstration of such designs. The work of credited designers has been shown. Ideas, other than those credited to specific designers, are given freely for whatever useful purpose you may find.

It is impossible for me to acknowledge the work of all designers who may note any resemblance to their own creations. This can be explained, in part, by the coincidence that in a certain nation the characteristic final solution may have the name of one designer while in another nation you may find the same design with only a slight variance in line, but having the same basic conception, free for anyone to interpret. Having recently arrived in this country from Europe, I have been particularly conscious of this fact, for the United States has such vast international ramifications that ideas and solutions of the European countries are readily introduced here.

I would like to express my sincere thanks and deep appreciation to Dr. Rudolph Parola of New York City for his aid in translating the material used in this book and to Solomon M. Delevie who ably presented this book to the publisher.

Mario Dal Fabbro

PHOTOGRAPHS USED IN THIS BOOK WERE TAKEN
BY THE FOLLOWING PHOTOGRAPHERS:

EZRA STOLLER   G. BARROWS

ROY STEVENS   FOTO PORTA

NOVELLI FILM   COTTCHO SCHLEISNER

STUDIO FOTOGRAFICO TRIENNALE
DI MILANO ITALY

FOREWORD

In writing this book I have tried to present to architects, furniture designers, manufacturers, and amateur craftsmen the best work of various designers for their study and interpretation. The scope of the book is limited to the treatment of special ideas and solutions of furniture, therefor, I have not considered the importance of shape or style.

The book is composed primarily of technical material with brief, concise legends to explain the drawings, each of which is notable for its mechanical features. If the drawings were vague or the examples distorted, my negligence would become immediately apparent to authorities. To eliminate this possibility and to help solve many technical problems, I have simplified the presentation and clarified certain difficult design elements.

Craftsmen, decorators, and designers will be able to understand easily and quickly from this book the development of furniture with unusual characteristics: what has been produced before and what may be produced in the future.

It should be noted that both the study and realization of folding, convertible, or special solutions adaptable for multiple use have had their origin in ancient designs and construction.

Now a word for each group of furniture as presented in this book:

Stools: The simplest form of chair is the stool. Of those you will find various solutions adaptable to other uses aside from the normal such as the folding, and other types which may also be used as tables, highstools, stepladder, raised and circular stools. We notice the evolution of the simple stool to its various and complex solutions, but each solution responds to a specified scope. This same procedure is to be found in other pieces of furniture to meet the varied tastes of mankind.

Chairs: There are many solutions applied to the chair that involve special characteristics of design and quality of material for its construction. Although metal has made great strides in replacing wood in construction, the future may make possible further development by the use of plastic, metal, and wood, all blended in a single element.

Among the particular solutions for chairs, the best results are attained in the folding and stacking type. The stacking type, adaptable for manufacture in metal, has met with considerable demand for use in public places.

Armchair: What has been said about the basic concept of the chair also can be said about the armchair. Its characteristic side arms permit various solutions of chair movement.

Included in this group are the lounge chair, the folding armchair, and the rocker. The latter with its varied solutions for rocking has been more fully developed in America than in Europe. Many systems and types such as the rocking swing, rocking armchair, and the plain old-fashioned rocker—all with characteristic solutions—have the same basic principle.

Sofas: The feature of these are their convertability into beds. The sectional sofa or pieces may form a normal sofa, or may be arranged in many interesting angular and curved forms.

Tables: A number of solutions with special characteristics are shown in this group. Included in the description is the type of material used in their construction, such as metal, marble, wood, and other special compositions. The group consists of small folding tables in metal and wood, useful as bed-side tables, reading tables, or coffee tables. Their general characteristics are folding legs, reversible tops, removable trays, stacking type, and those which may be aligned to two or more elements.

The game tables with folding legs and stacking feature are very useful in homes, gardens, terraces. An interesting table type is one that can be folded to resemble a suitcase. In metal and wood, it is useful in traveling and outings.

The dining, kitchen, and ironing board tables have their characteristic solutions to provide maximum length.

Foreword Continued

Office Furniture: In this group are the varied pieces of office furniture including the typewriting table or stand, desks, secretaries, filing cabinets, bookcases, and office files.

Living room: Teawagon-service carts, magazine racks, and bookcases are included in this group.

Dining room: In these dining room furniture designs are various solutions for buffets.

Bed room: The bed room designs show excellent solutions for vanities, dressers, night tables and cribs.

Kitchen and bathroom: In this group are various solutions for cabinets, storage closets, hampers and medicine cabinets.

Wardrobe: You will note the normal type of wardrobe with two, three, or four doors. Other types include those which can be aligned together, the demountable type, the large wall wardrobe, the sectional, and the storeaway type.

Beds, Wardrobe Beds, the Sofa Beds: In this group are the normal and varied interpretation of the closing and stacking type of beds. The most practical use for the wardrobe bed is that it can be folded either horizontally or vertically, and when closed it resembles a wardrobe. The sofa beds have their characteristic of serving a dual purpose: sofa by day and bed by night.

The sixteen page supplement at the end of this book was designed to help the amateur and home craftsman to design, understand, build, and experiment with original furniture solutions of his own. By building some of the pieces suggested in this section he will gain experience and eventually graduate to some difficult pieces in the balance of the book.

In conclusion, may I say that I feel that these numerous examples of furniture design will be helpful to those interested in making new models, as they have before them a vast collection of special types from which to work. Thus the creation and production of modern furniture advance.

Mario Dal Fabbro

TABLE OF CONTENTS

THE AUTHOR

Mario Dal Fabbro was born in Cappella Maggiore in Treviso, Italy in 1913. He studied at the R. Superior Institute for Decorative and Industrial Arts of Venice, Italy. After completing his studies there, he attended the R. Magistero Artistico from which he was graduated with high honors in 1937.

The basic reason for his success in the technical and creative field of furniture was the fact that ever since childhood he has been able to combine the theoretical and the practical, for following tradition, he worked in the family furniture design shop. Later he became affiliated with a well-known furniture house in Milan.

For the ten years between 1938 and 1948, Dal Fabbro created designs for private individuals and did work for the furniture houses in Milan. During World War II, he served his country in its armed forces.

He participated in the Trienali International competition in Milan in 1939 and 1947. Besides contributing to the Italian magazines *Domus* and *Stile* and the French magazine *L'Architecture D'Aujourd'hui,* Dal Fabbro wrote several books on furniture which were published by Gorlich in Milan. He also won the Ganzanti contest for standardization of furniture.

In 1948 he transferred his activities to the United States. With this book, his first in this country, he returns to the field of design.

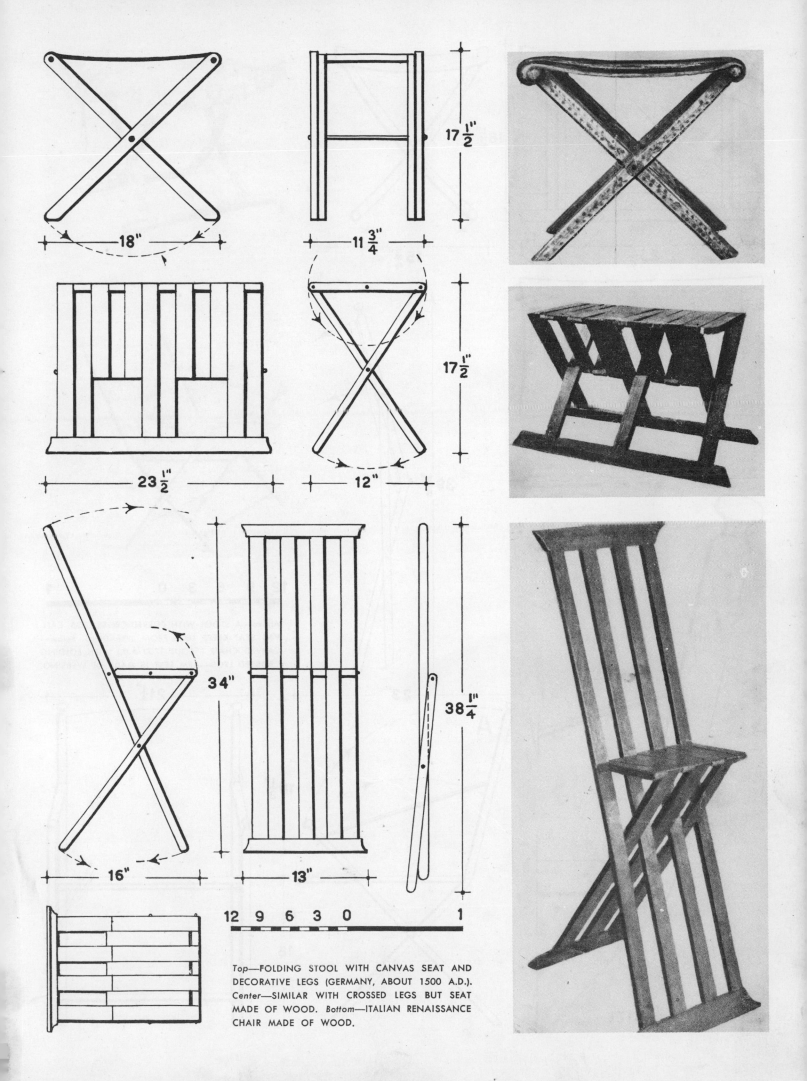

18"

17 1/2"

11 3/4"

23 1/2"

17 1/2"

12"

34"

38 1/4"

16"

13"

12 9 6 3 0   1

Top—FOLDING STOOL WITH CANVAS SEAT AND
DECORATIVE LEGS (GERMANY, ABOUT 1500 A.D.).
Center—SIMILAR WITH CROSSED LEGS BUT SEAT
MADE OF WOOD. *Bottom*—ITALIAN RENAISSANCE
CHAIR MADE OF WOOD.

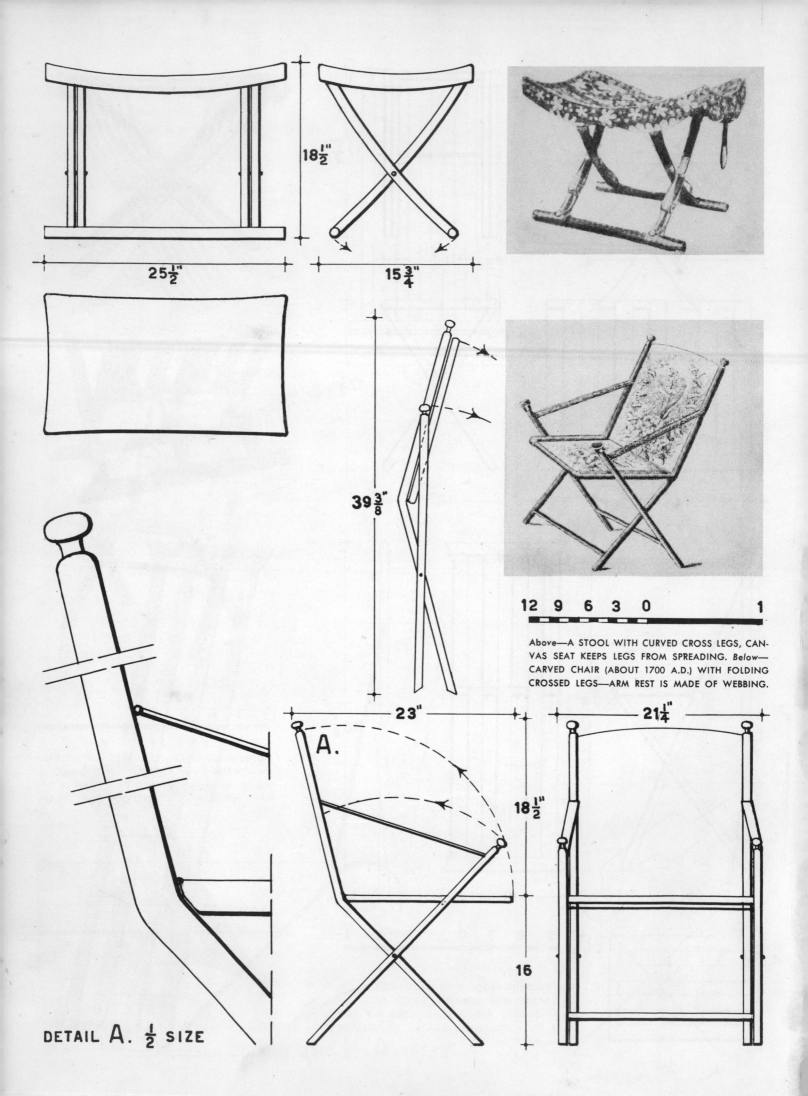

18½"

25½"

15¾"

39⅜"

12 9 6 3 0 1

Above—A STOOL WITH CURVED CROSS LEGS, CANVAS SEAT KEEPS LEGS FROM SPREADING. *Below*—CARVED CHAIR (ABOUT 1700 A.D.) WITH FOLDING CROSSED LEGS—ARM REST IS MADE OF WEBBING.

A.

23"

21¼"

18½"

16

DETAIL A. ½ SIZE

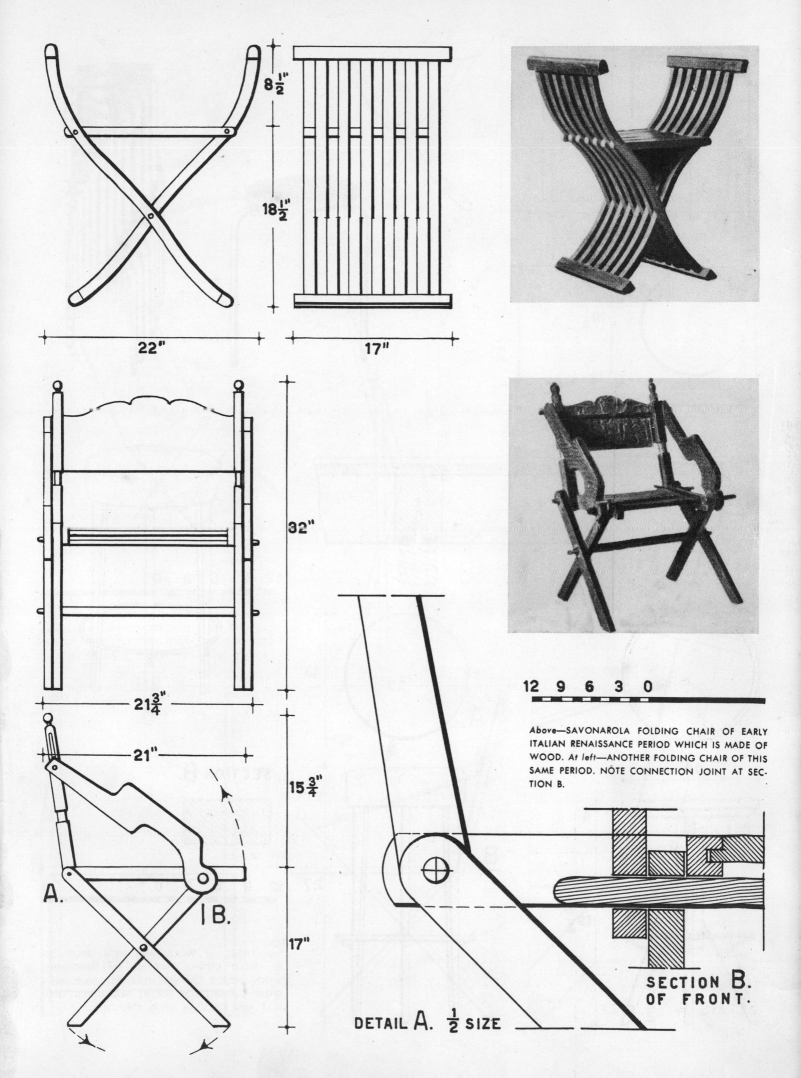

8½"

18½"

22"

17"

32"

21¾"

21"

15¾"

17"

A.

B.

DETAIL A. ½ SIZE

12 9 6 3 0

Above—SAVONAROLA FOLDING CHAIR OF EARLY ITALIAN RENAISSANCE PERIOD WHICH IS MADE OF WOOD. *At left*—ANOTHER FOLDING CHAIR OF THIS SAME PERIOD. NOTE CONNECTION JOINT AT SECTION B.

SECTION B. OF FRONT.

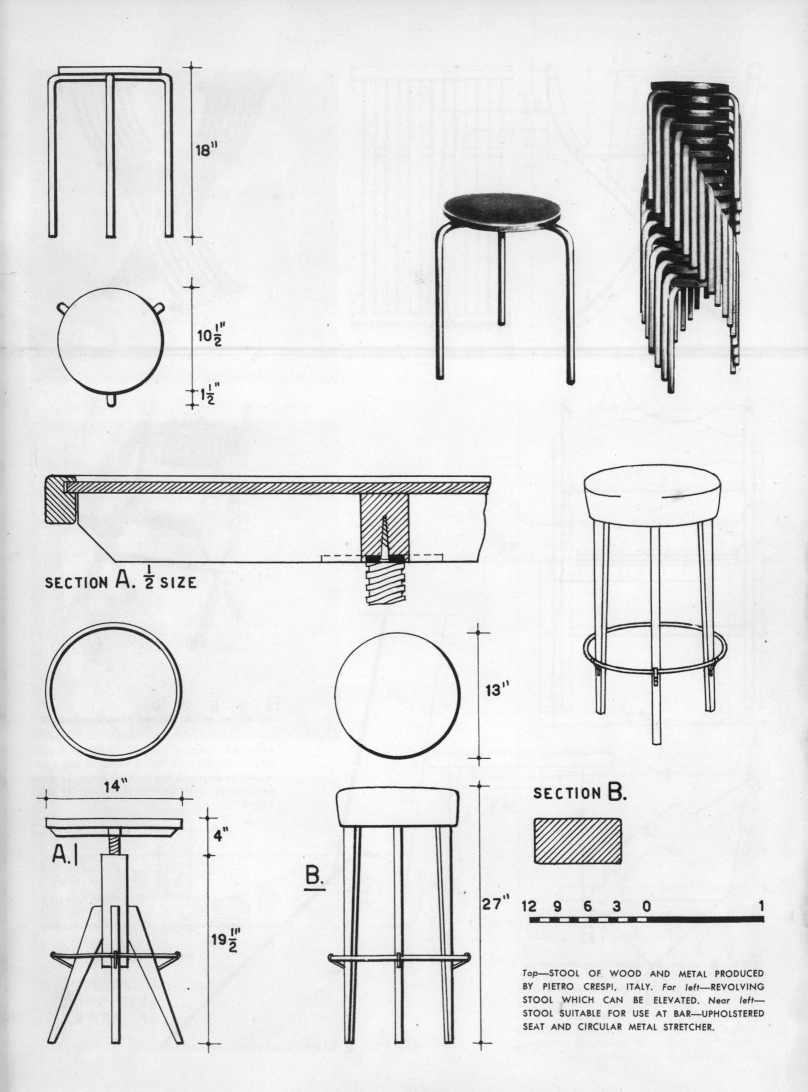

18"

10½"

1½"

SECTION A. ½ SIZE

14"

A.I

4"

19½"

13"

B.

SECTION B.

27"

12 9 6 3 0 1

Top—STOOL OF WOOD AND METAL PRODUCED BY PIETRO CRESPI, ITALY. *Far left*—REVOLVING STOOL WHICH CAN BE ELEVATED. *Near left*—STOOL SUITABLE FOR USE AT BAR—UPHOLSTERED SEAT AND CIRCULAR METAL STRETCHER.

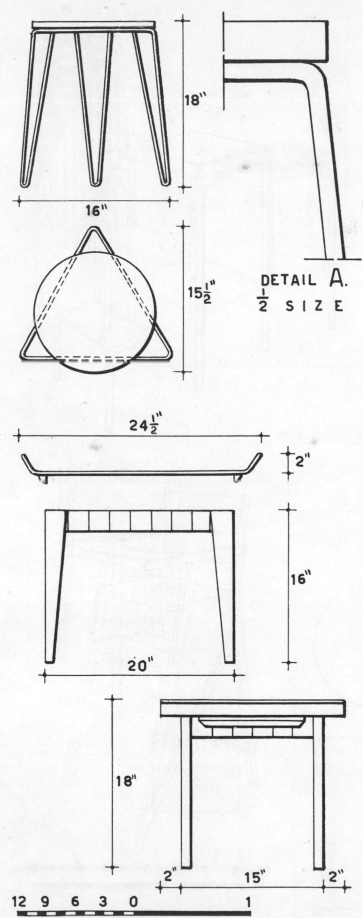

18"

16"

15½"

DETAIL A.
½ SIZE

24½"

2"

16"

20"

18"

2" 15" 2"

12 9 6 3 0   1

Top—STACKING STOOL IN METAL AND WOOD.
TOP HELD ON BY MEANS OF SCREWS THRU TUB-
ING. DESIGN BY FLORENCE S. KNOLL AND PRO-
DUCED BY KNOLL ASSOCIATES, INC. *Below*—BENCH
WITH REMOVABLE TRAY FOR USE AS STOOL OR
COFFEE TABLE. DESIGN BY SORENSEN AND JOHN-
SON, PRODUCED BY KNOLL ASSOCIATES, INC.

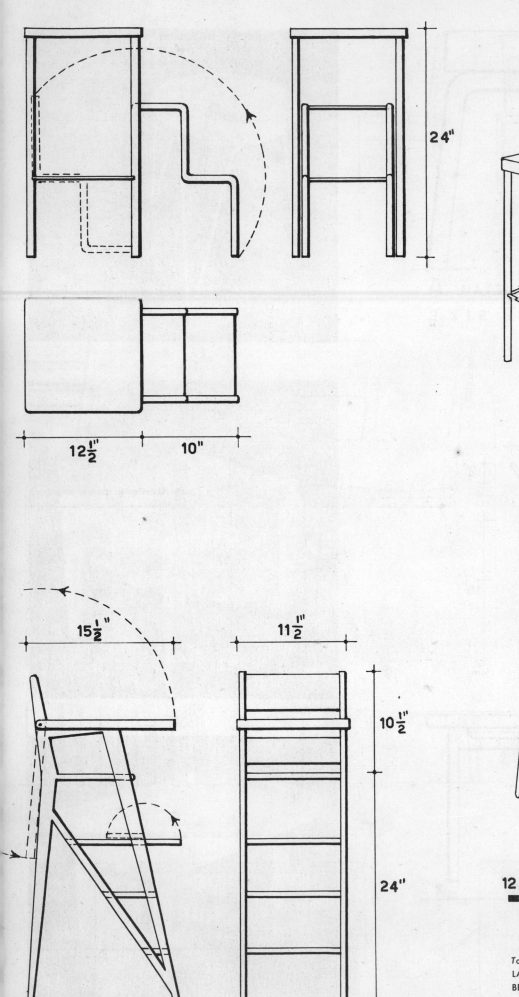

24"

12½"   10"

15½"   11½"

10½"

24"

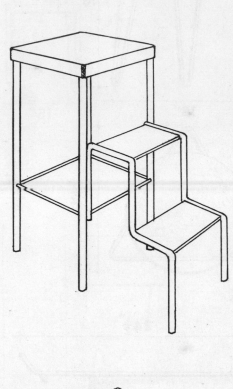

12 9 6 3 0   1

Top—STOOL WHICH CAN ALSO BE USED AS STEP-
LADDER. *Below*—CHILD'S HIGHCHAIR WHICH CAN
BE USED AS A STEPLADDER.

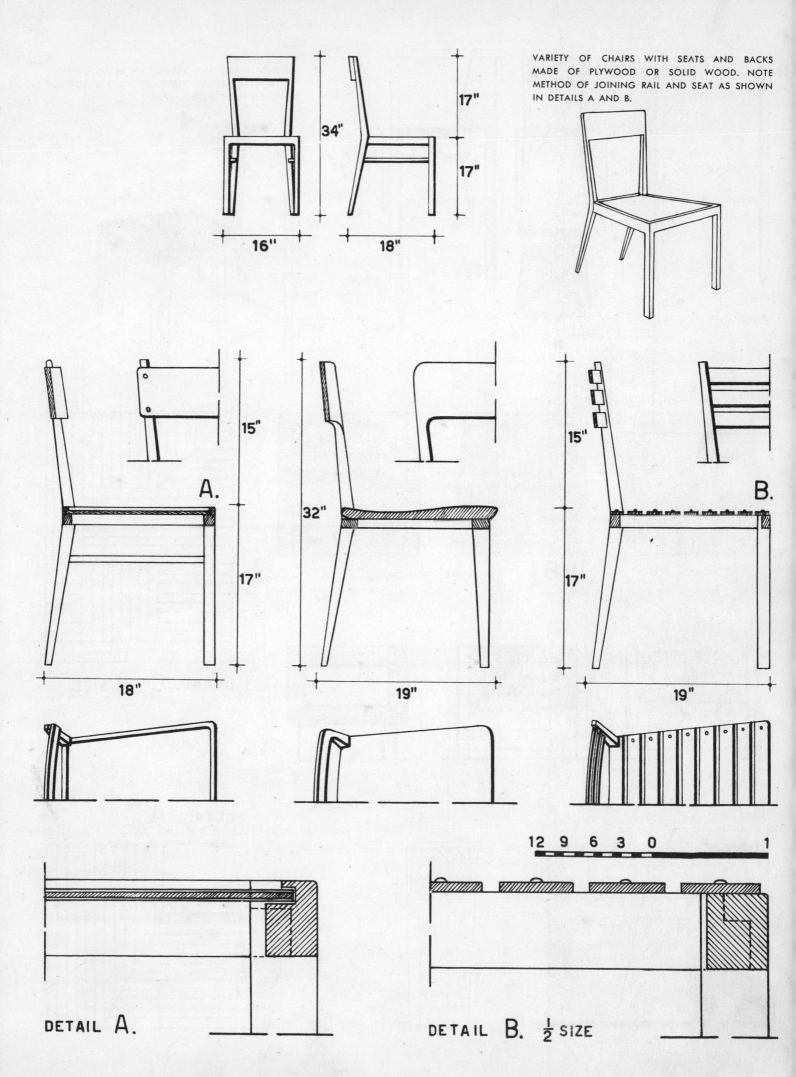

VARIETY OF CHAIRS WITH SEATS AND BACKS
MADE OF PLYWOOD OR SOLID WOOD. NOTE
METHOD OF JOINING RAIL AND SEAT AS SHOWN
IN DETAILS A AND B.

34"

17"

17"

16"

18"

15"

A.

32"

17"

15"

B.

17"

18"

19"

19"

12 9 6 3 0 1

DETAIL A.

DETAIL B. ½ SIZE

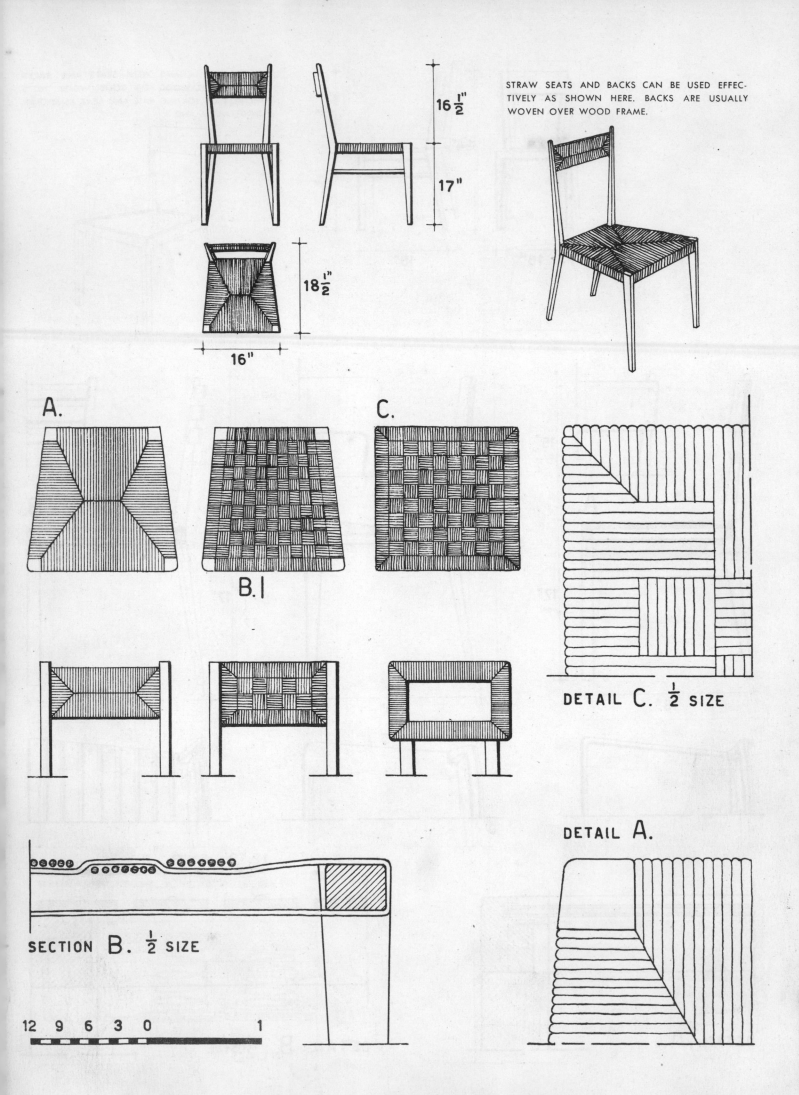

STRAW SEATS AND BACKS CAN BE USED EFFEC-
TIVELY AS SHOWN HERE. BACKS ARE USUALLY
WOVEN OVER WOOD FRAME.

16 1/2"

17"

18 1/2"

16"

A.

C.

B.I

DETAIL C. 1/2 SIZE

DETAIL A.

SECTION B. 1/2 SIZE

12 9 6 3 0   1

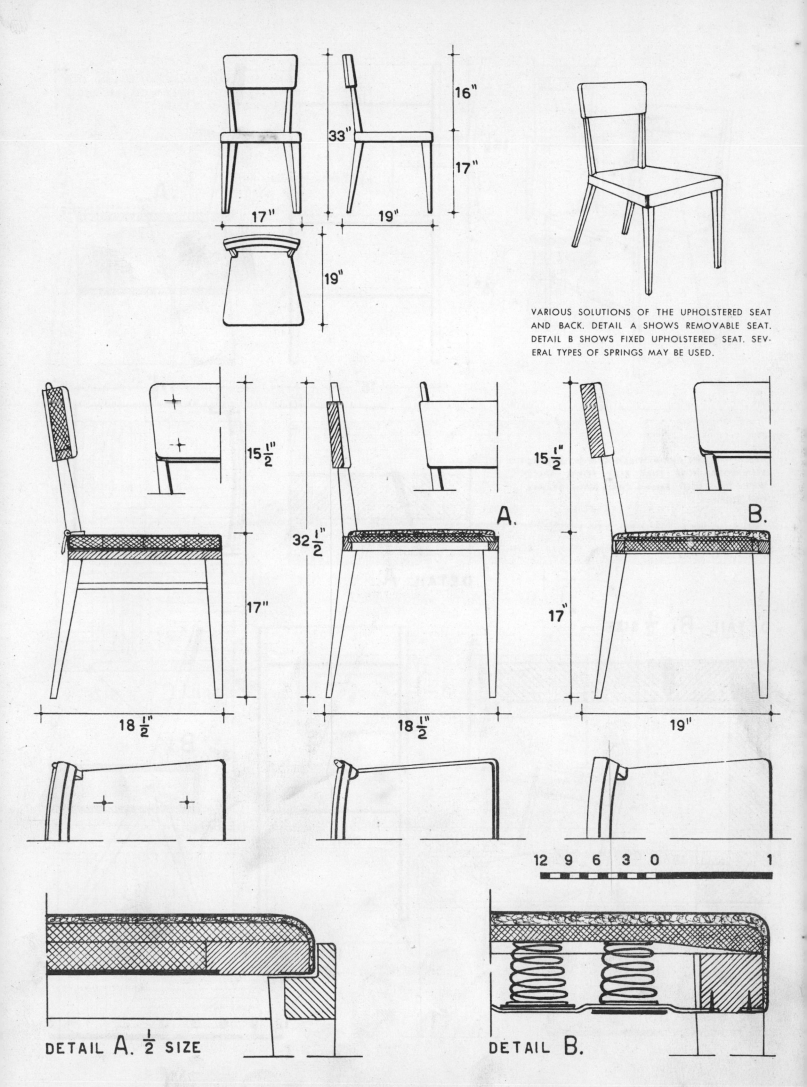

16"

33"

17"

17"

19"

19"

VARIOUS SOLUTIONS OF THE UPHOLSTERED SEAT AND BACK. DETAIL A SHOWS REMOVABLE SEAT. DETAIL B SHOWS FIXED UPHOLSTERED SEAT. SEVERAL TYPES OF SPRINGS MAY BE USED.

15 $\frac{1}{2}$"

15 $\frac{1}{2}$"

32 $\frac{1}{2}$"

17"

17"

A.

B.

18 $\frac{1}{2}$"

18 $\frac{1}{2}$"

19"

12 9 6 3 0   1

DETAIL A. $\frac{1}{2}$ SIZE

DETAIL B.

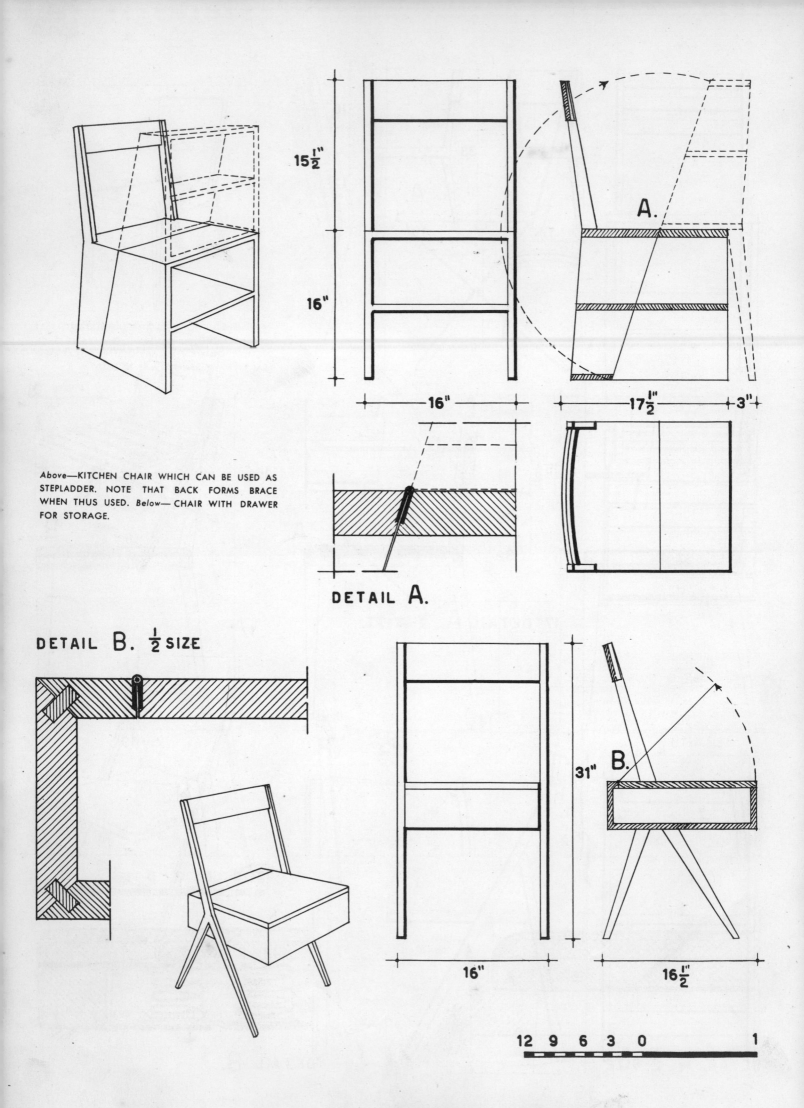

15 1/2"

16"

16"

17 1/2" 3"

Above—KITCHEN CHAIR WHICH CAN BE USED AS STEPLADDER. NOTE THAT BACK FORMS BRACE WHEN THUS USED. *Below*— CHAIR WITH DRAWER FOR STORAGE.

DETAIL A.

DETAIL B. 1/2 SIZE

A.

B.

31"

16"

16 1/2"

12 9 6 3 0   1

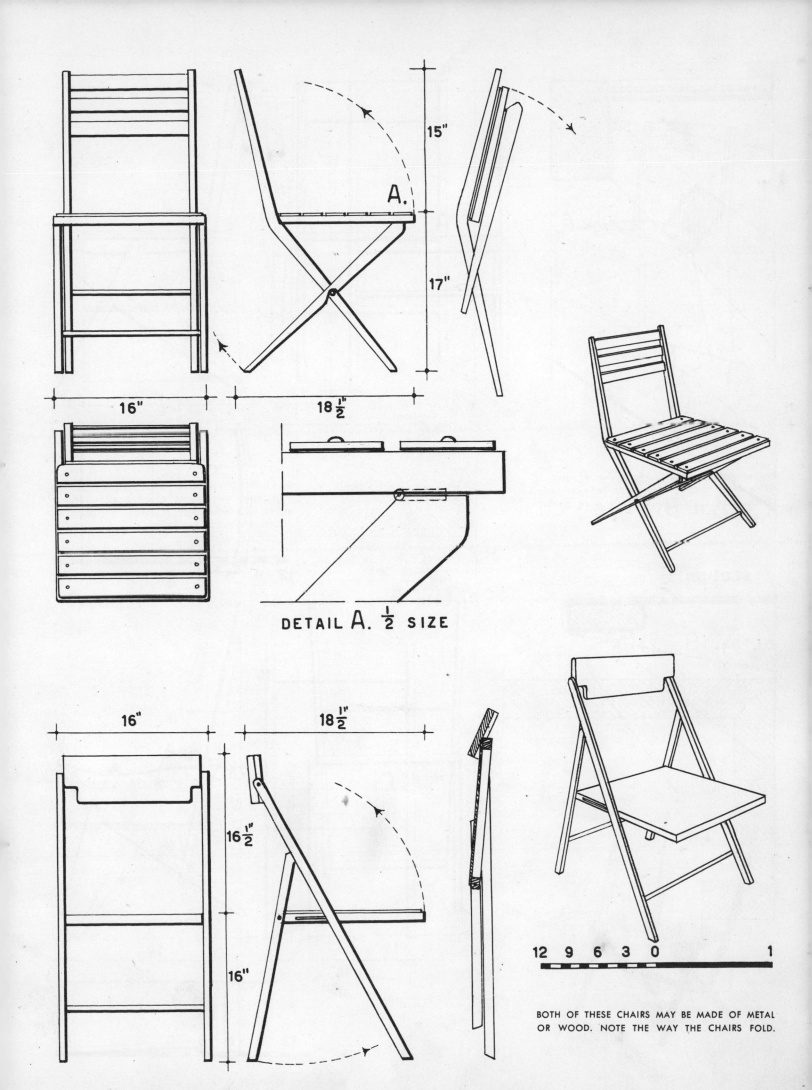

15"

17"

A.

16"

18 ½"

DETAIL A. ½ SIZE

16"

18 ½"

16 ½"

16"

12 9 6 3 0   1

BOTH OF THESE CHAIRS MAY BE MADE OF METAL
OR WOOD. NOTE THE WAY THE CHAIRS FOLD.

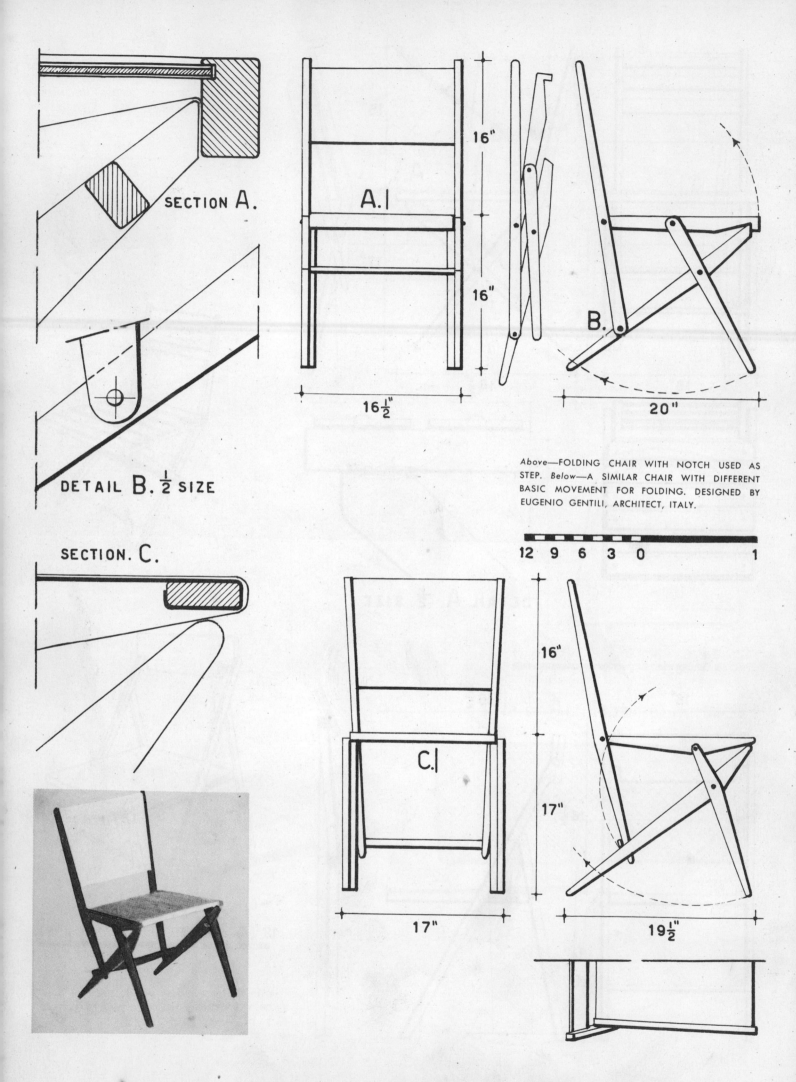

SECTION A.

DETAIL B. ½ SIZE

SECTION. C.

A.1

16"

16"

16½"

B.

20"

Above—FOLDING CHAIR WITH NOTCH USED AS STEP. *Below*—A SIMILAR CHAIR WITH DIFFERENT BASIC MOVEMENT FOR FOLDING. DESIGNED BY EUGENIO GENTILI, ARCHITECT, ITALY.

12 9 6 3 0   1

C.1

16"

17"

17"

19½"

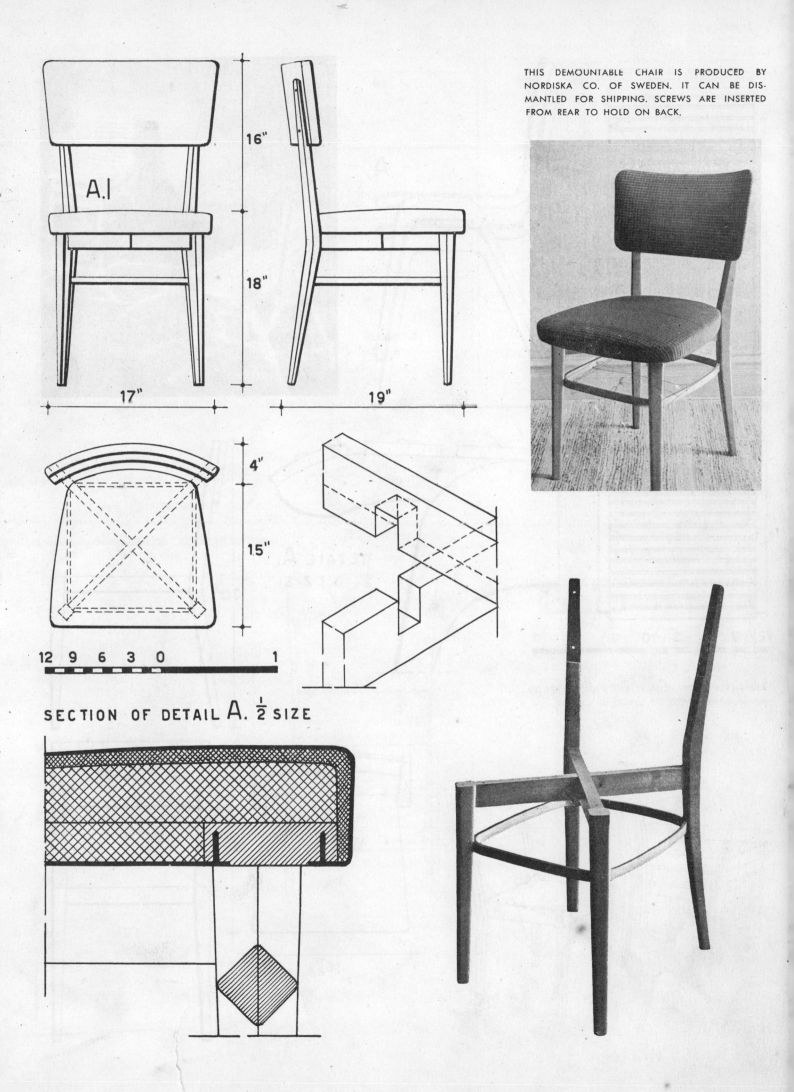

A.I

16"

18"

17"

19"

4"

15"

12 9 6 3 0   1

SECTION OF DETAIL A. ½ SIZE

THIS DEMOUNTABLE CHAIR IS PRODUCED BY NORDISKA CO. OF SWEDEN. IT CAN BE DISMANTLED FOR SHIPPING. SCREWS ARE INSERTED FROM REAR TO HOLD ON BACK.

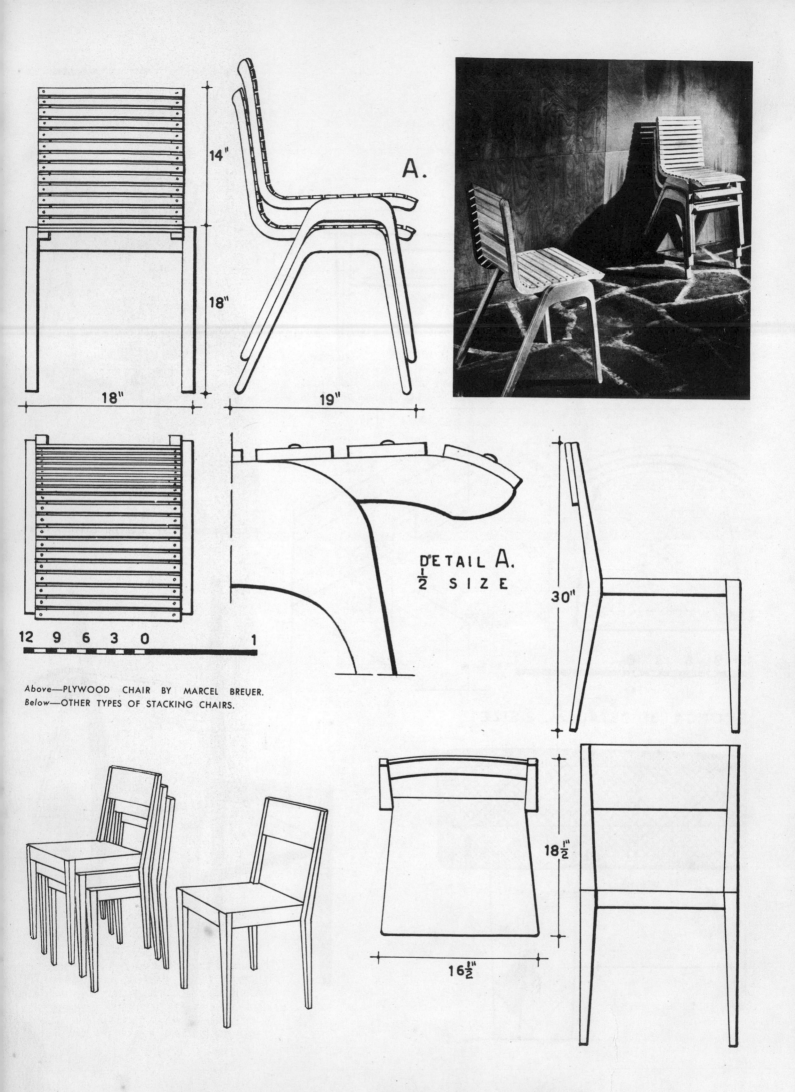

14"

18"

18"

19"

A.

12 9 6 3 0   1

DETAIL A.
½ SIZE

30"

18½"

16½"

Above—PLYWOOD CHAIR BY MARCEL BREUER.
Below—OTHER TYPES OF STACKING CHAIRS.

$11\frac{1}{4}''$

$28\frac{3}{4}''$

$17\frac{1}{2}''$

$22\frac{1}{4}''$

12 9 6 3 0   1

11"

$15\frac{3}{4}''$

25"

DESIGNED BY CHARLES EAMES AND PRODUCED BY
HERMAN MILLER, THESE TWO DESIGNS HAVE
FOUND WIDE ACCEPTANCE. SEAT AND BACK OF
BOTH DESIGNS ARE OF MOLDED PLYWOOD, LEGS
ARE WOOD OR METAL. THE SEAT AND BACK OF
BOTH REST ON SMALL RUBBER CUSHIONS.

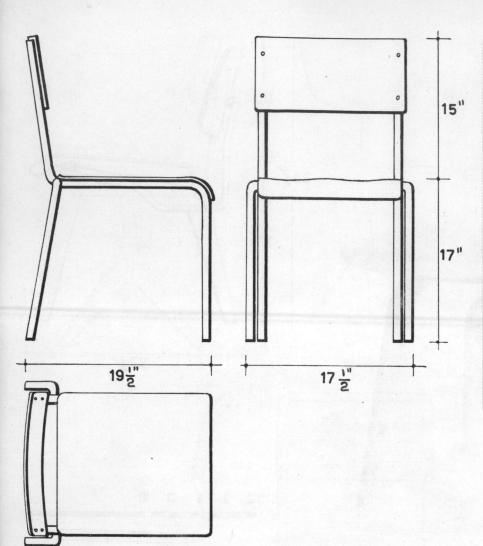

15"

17"

19 ½"

17 ½"

PLYWOOD BACK AND SEAT OVER METAL FRAME.
THESE STACKING CHAIRS ARE PRODUCED BY PIETRO
CRESPI CO., ITALY.

12 9 6 3 0   1

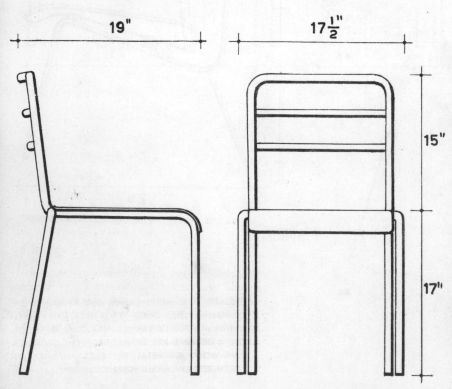

19"

17 ½"

15"

17"

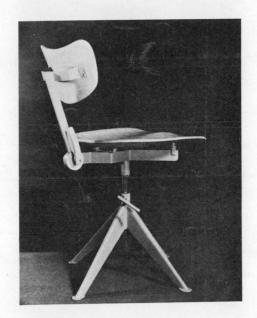

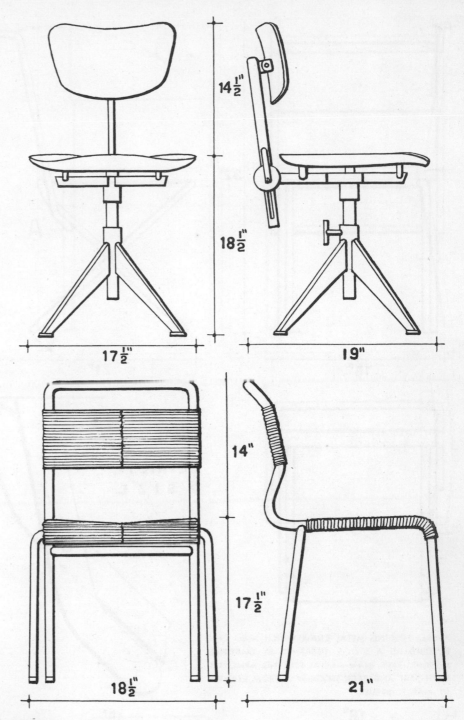

14$\frac{1}{2}$"

18$\frac{1}{2}$"

17$\frac{1}{2}$"

19"

14"

17$\frac{1}{2}$"

18$\frac{1}{2}$"

21"

12 9 6 3 0   1

Top—OFFICE TYPE CHAIR DESIGNED BY ODELBERG-
OLSON OF SWEDEN AND PRODUCED BY KNOLL
ASSOCIATES, INC. *Below*—METAL STACKING CHAIR
WITH NYLON CORD SEAT AND BACK. DESIGNED
BY ANDRE DUPRES OF FRANCE AND PRODUCED BY
KNOLL ASSOCIATES, INC.

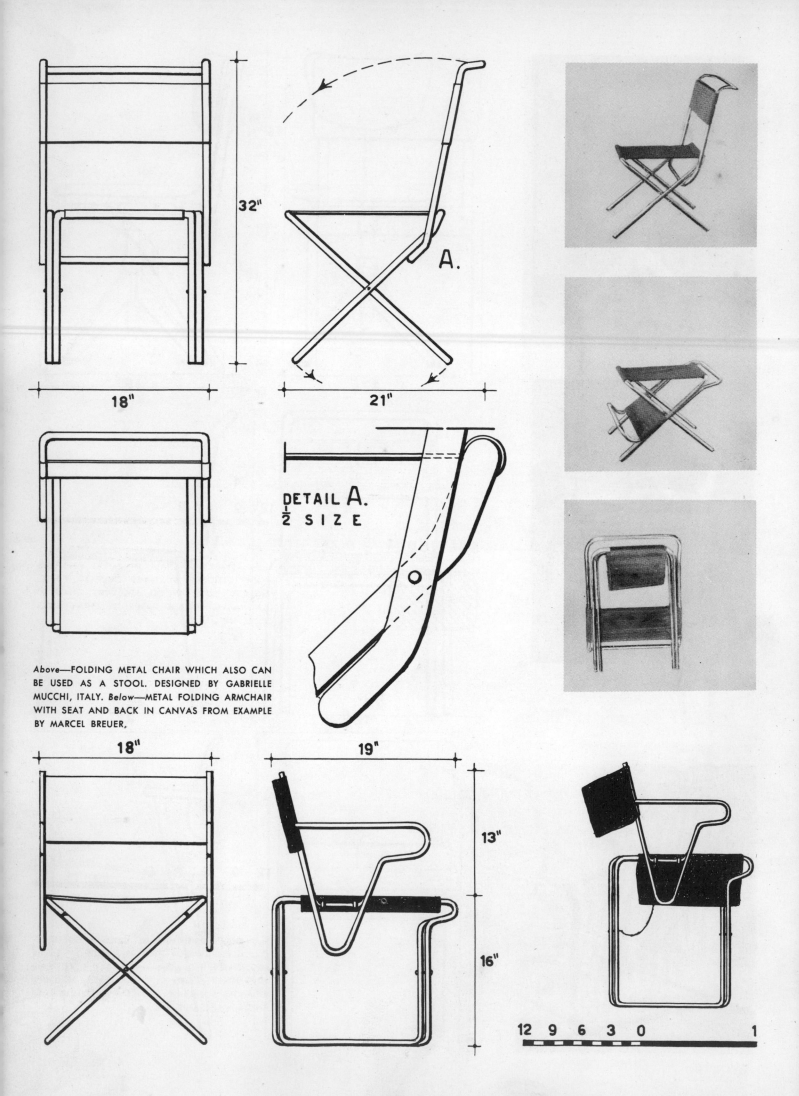

32"

18"

21"

A.

DETAIL A.
½ SIZE

Above—FOLDING METAL CHAIR WHICH ALSO CAN
BE USED AS A STOOL. DESIGNED BY GABRIELLE
MUCCHI, ITALY. Below—METAL FOLDING ARMCHAIR
WITH SEAT AND BACK IN CANVAS FROM EXAMPLE
BY MARCEL BREUER,

18"

19"

13"

16"

12 9 6 3 0   1

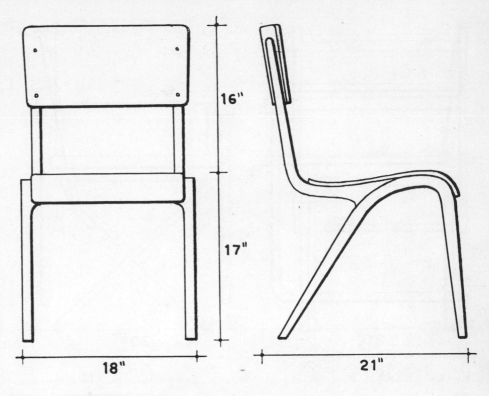

16"

17"

18"

21"

SECTION A. $\frac{1}{2}$ SIZE

12 9 6 3 0   1

Above—STACKING CHAIR IN METAL AND PLY-WOOD DESIGNED BY JAMES LEONARD, F.S.I.A., ENGLAND. *Below*—WOOD STACKING CHAIR BY TAPIOVAARA, FINLAND. COURTESY KNOLL ASSO-CIATES, INC.

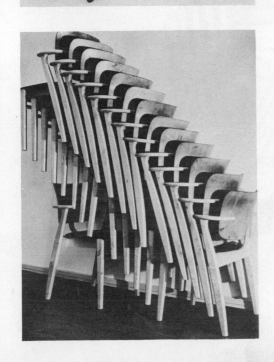

23"

22"

13"

18"

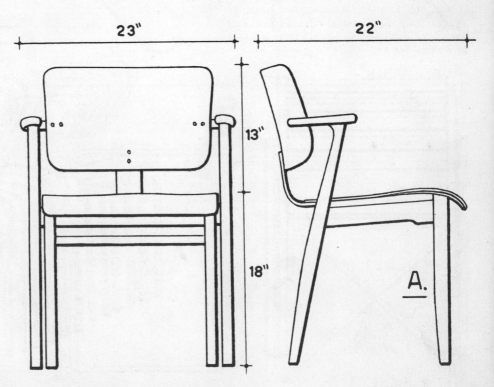

A.

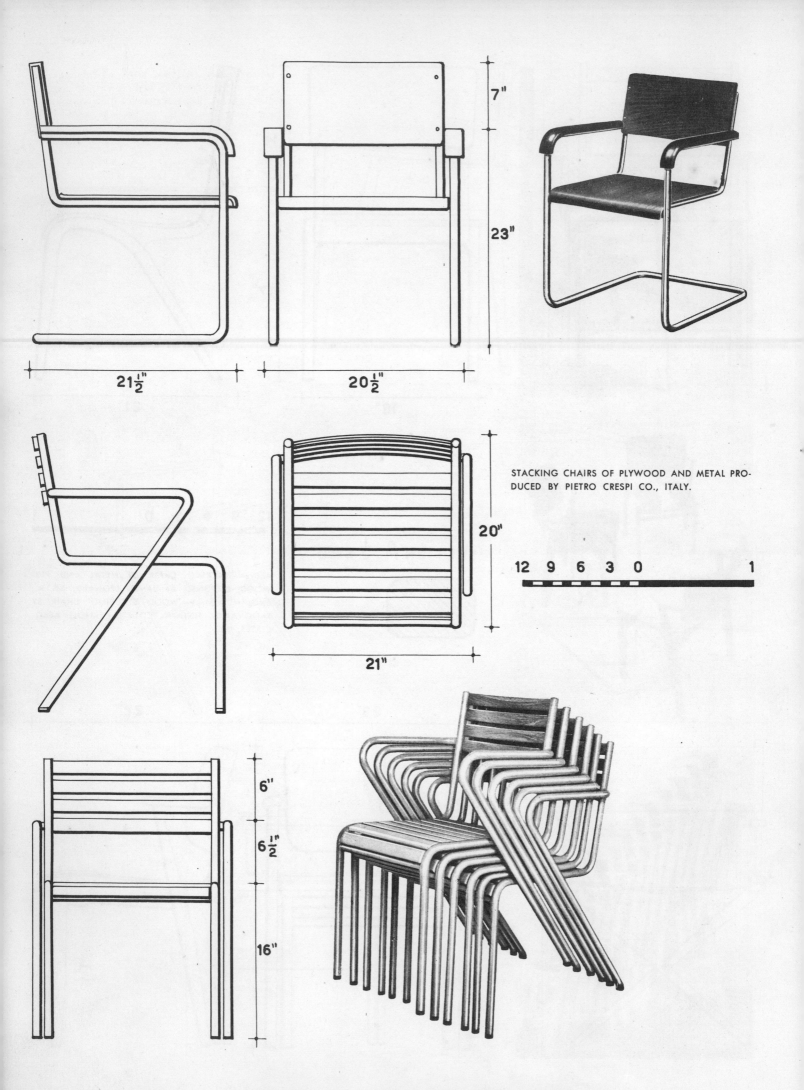

7"

23"

21½"

20½"

STACKING CHAIRS OF PLYWOOD AND METAL PRO-
DUCED BY PIETRO CRESPI CO., ITALY.

20"

12 9 6 3 0   1

21"

6"

6½"

16"

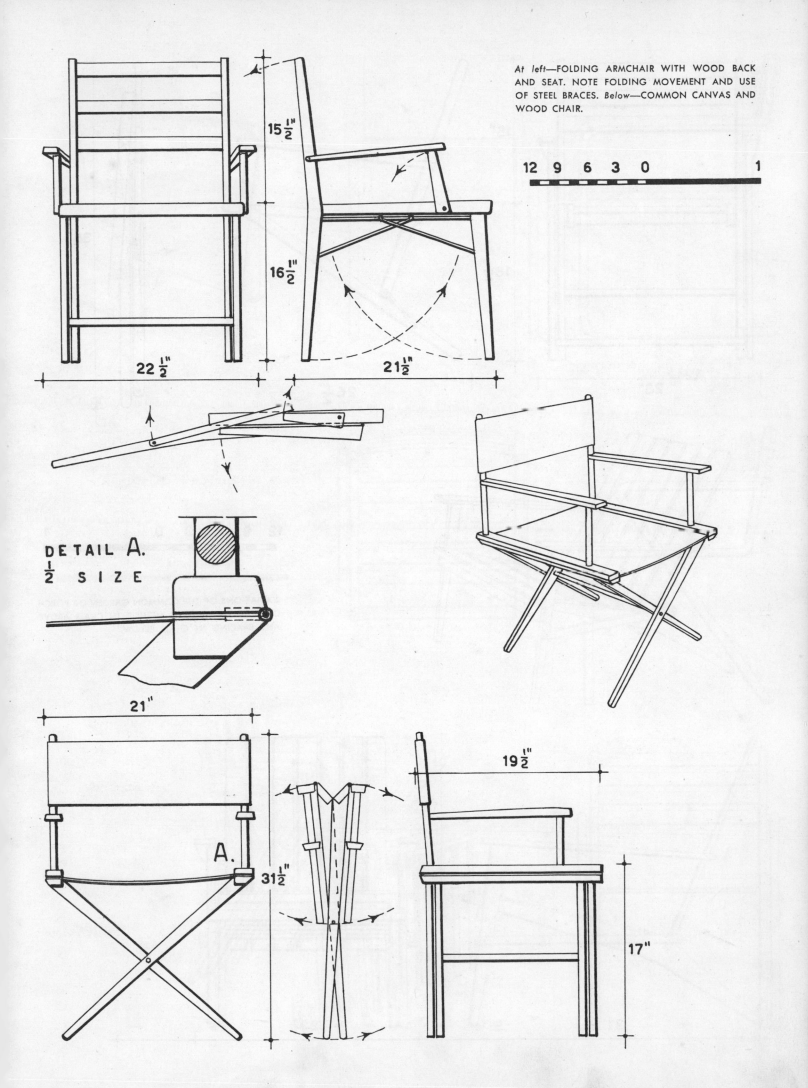

At left—FOLDING ARMCHAIR WITH WOOD BACK AND SEAT. NOTE FOLDING MOVEMENT AND USE OF STEEL BRACES. Below—COMMON CANVAS AND WOOD CHAIR.

15½"

16½"

22½"

21½"

12 9 6 3 0   1

DETAIL A.
½ SIZE

21"

A.

31½"

19½"

17"

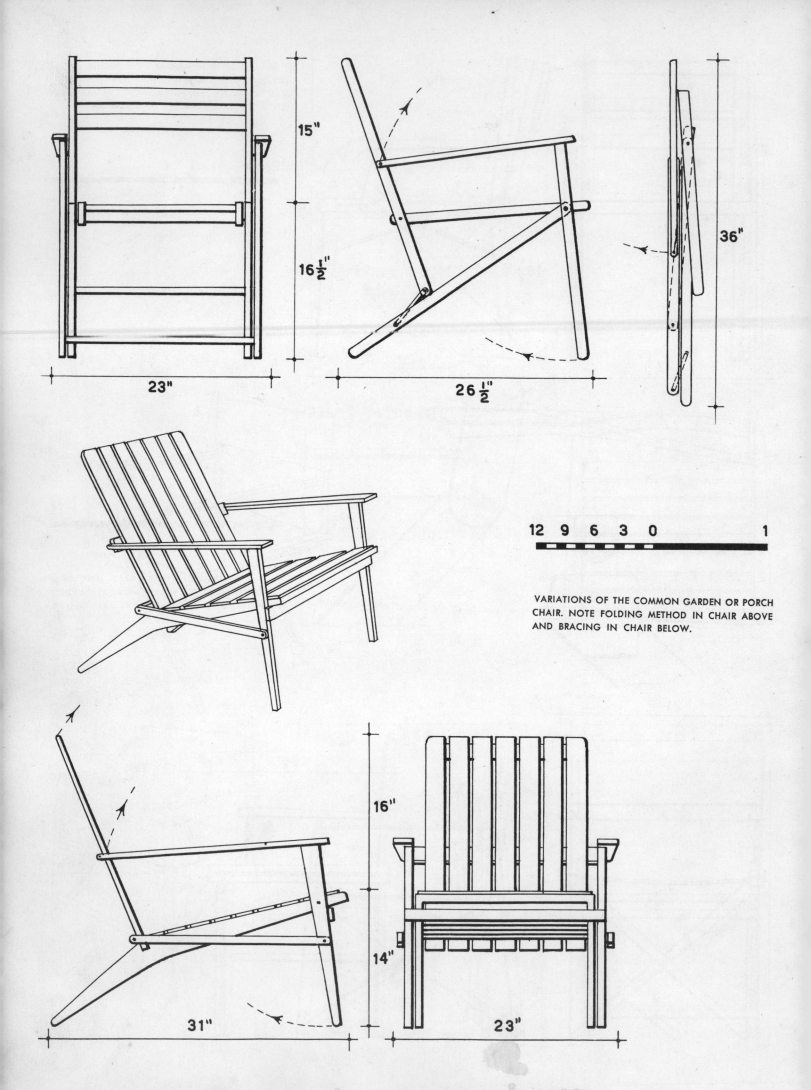

15"

16½"

23"

26½"

36"

12 9 6 3 0   1

VARIATIONS OF THE COMMON GARDEN OR PORCH
CHAIR. NOTE FOLDING METHOD IN CHAIR ABOVE
AND BRACING IN CHAIR BELOW.

16"

14"

31"

23"

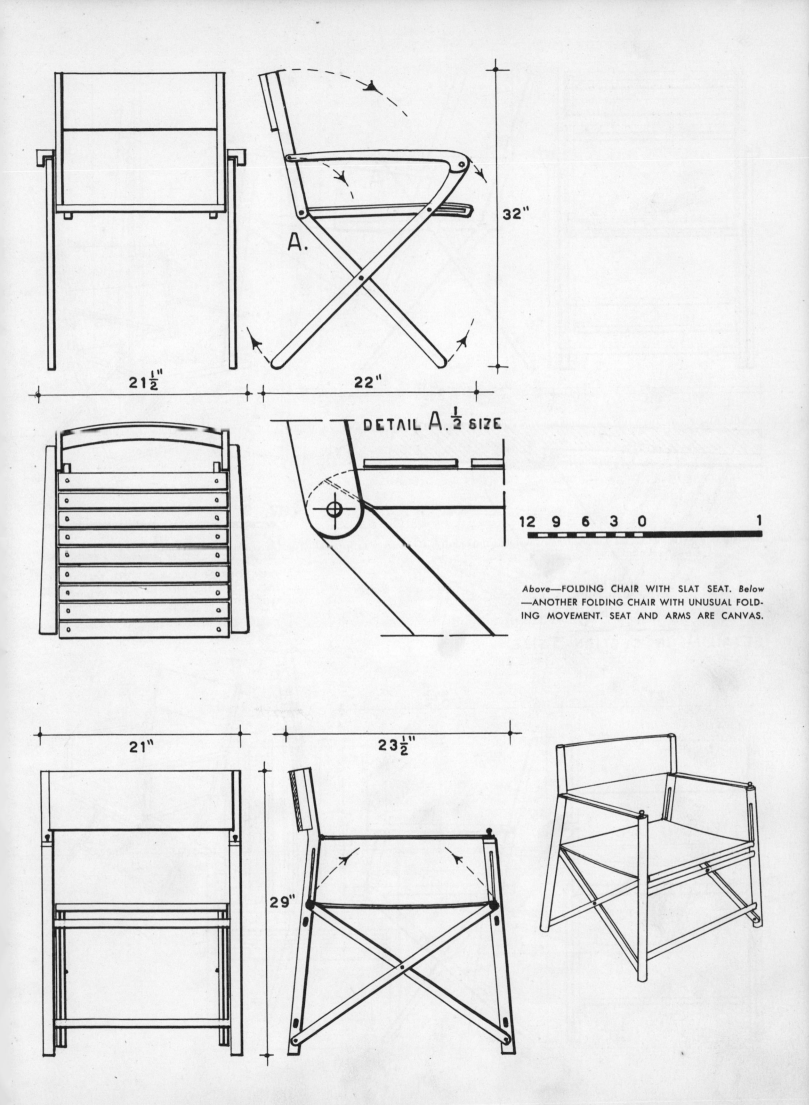

21½"

32"

22"

A.

DETAIL A. ½ SIZE

12 9 6 3 0   1

Above—FOLDING CHAIR WITH SLAT SEAT. *Below*—ANOTHER FOLDING CHAIR WITH UNUSUAL FOLDING MOVEMENT. SEAT AND ARMS ARE CANVAS.

21"

23½"

29"

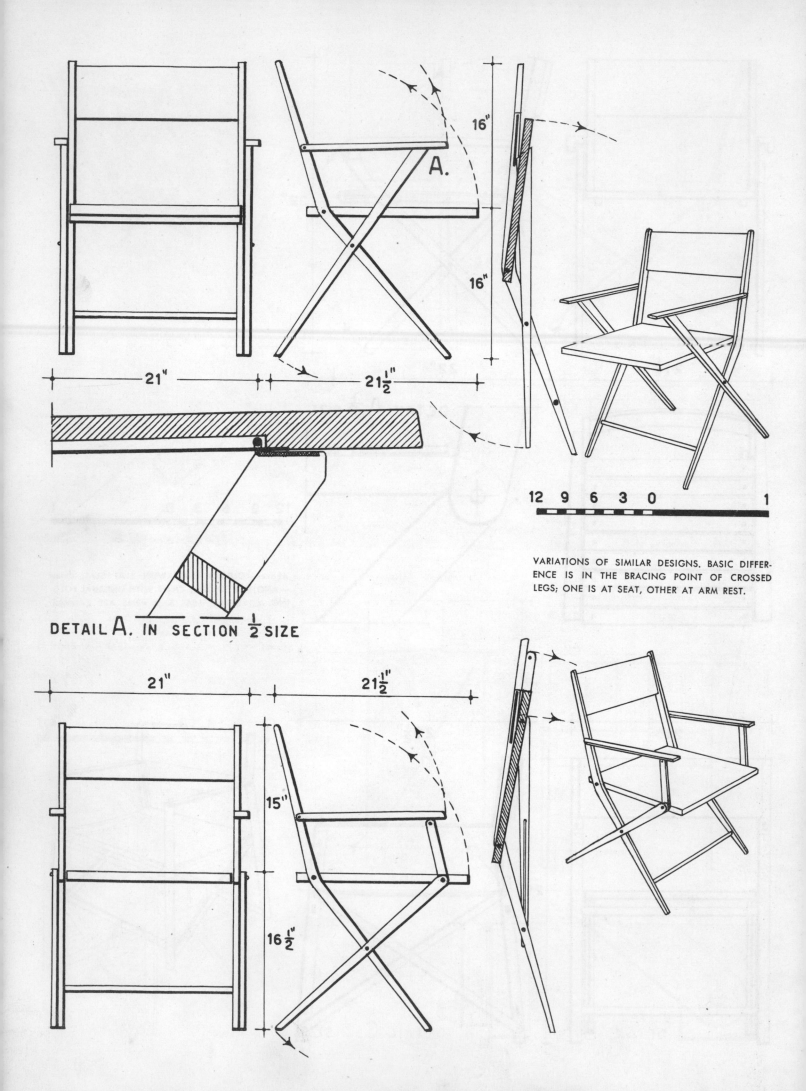

16"

16"

21"

21½"

A.

DETAIL A. IN SECTION ½ SIZE

12 9 6 3 0 1

VARIATIONS OF SIMILAR DESIGNS. BASIC DIFFER-
ENCE IS IN THE BRACING POINT OF CROSSED
LEGS; ONE IS AT SEAT, OTHER AT ARM REST.

21"

21½"

15"

16½"

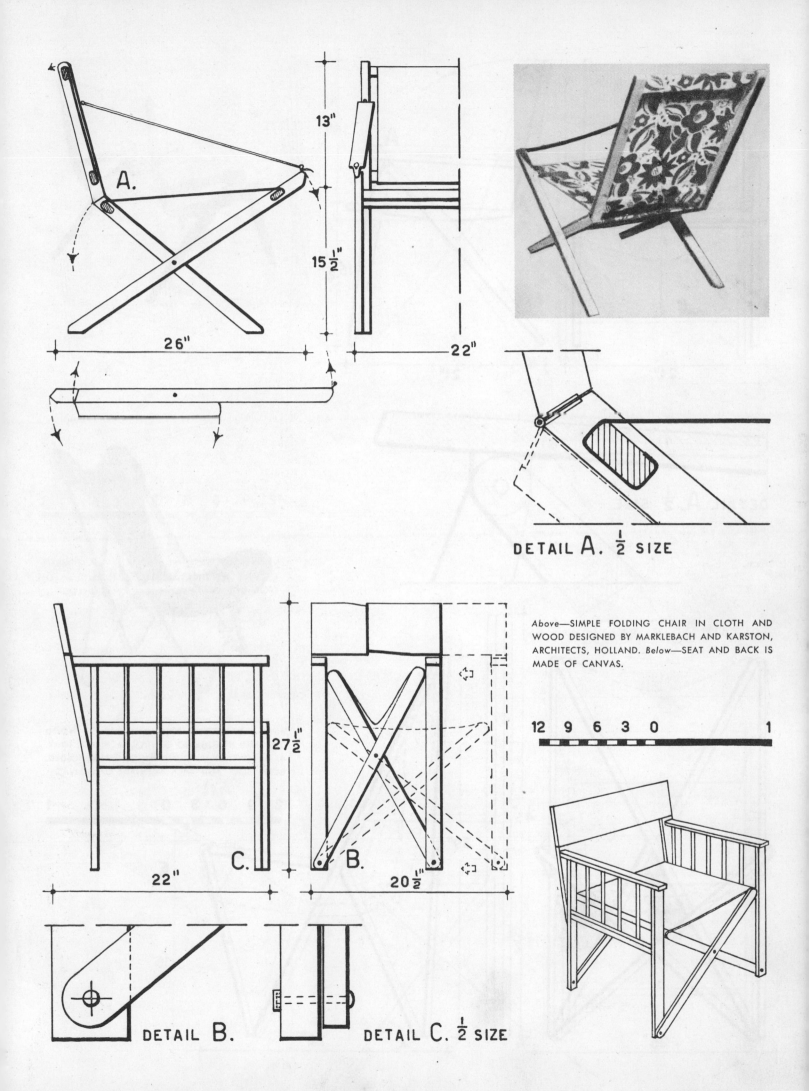

A.

13"

15 1/2"

26"

22"

DETAIL A. 1/2 SIZE

Above—SIMPLE FOLDING CHAIR IN CLOTH AND WOOD DESIGNED BY MARKLEBACH AND KARSTON, ARCHITECTS, HOLLAND. Below—SEAT AND BACK IS MADE OF CANVAS.

12 9 6 3 0 1

27 1/2"

C.

22"

B.

20 1/2"

DETAIL B.

DETAIL C. 1/2 SIZE

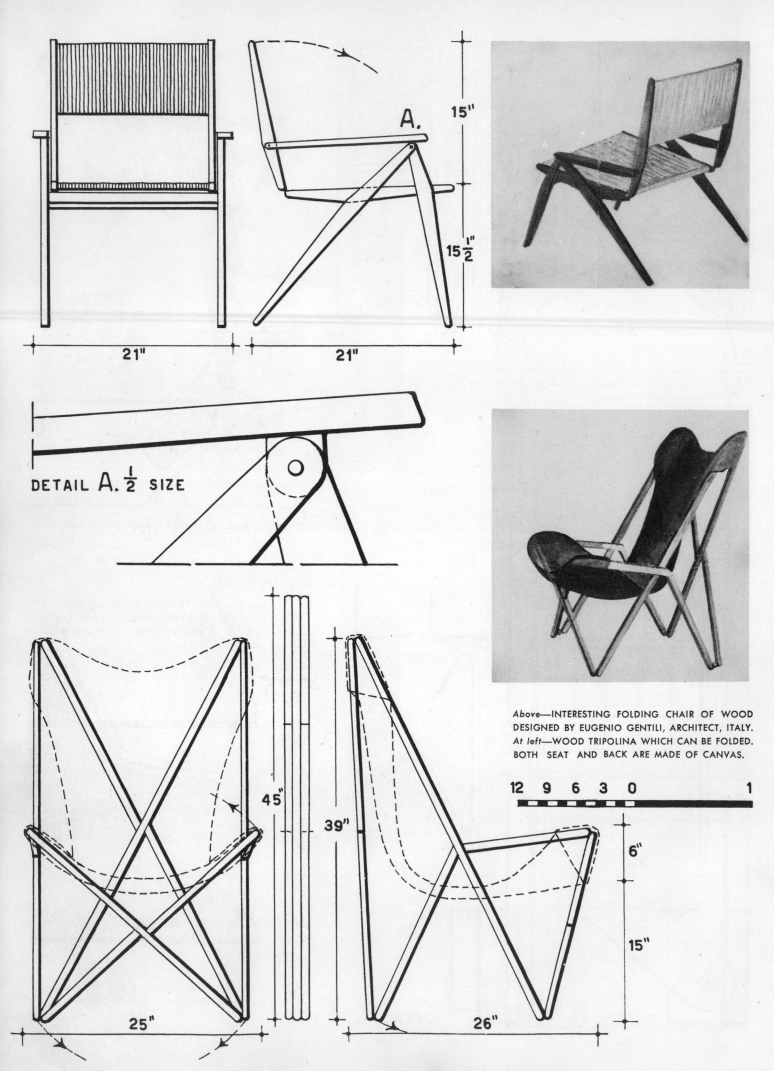

15"

15½"

21"

21"

DETAIL A. ½ SIZE

A.

45"

39"

25"

26"

6"

15"

Above—INTERESTING FOLDING CHAIR OF WOOD DESIGNED BY EUGENIO GENTILI, ARCHITECT, ITALY. *At left*—WOOD TRIPOLINA WHICH CAN BE FOLDED. BOTH SEAT AND BACK ARE MADE OF CANVAS.

12 9 6 3 0   1

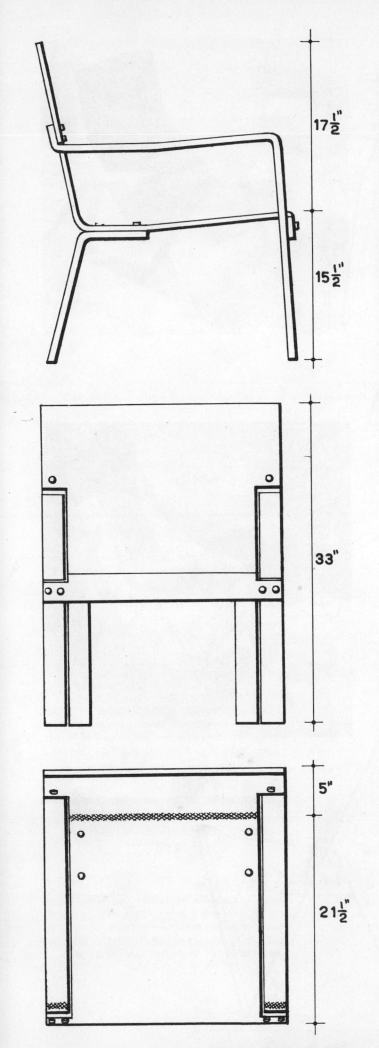

17 1/2"

15 1/2"

33"

5"

21 1/2"

12 9 6 3 0   1

DEMOUNTABLE PLYWOOD ARMCHAIR. IT WAS DE-
SIGNED BY VITTORIANO VIGANO; ITALY.

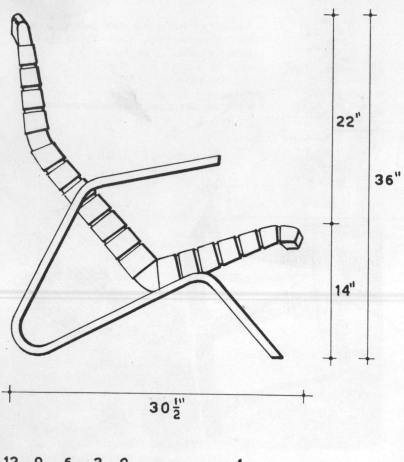

22"

36"

14"

30½"

12 9 6 3 0   1

34"

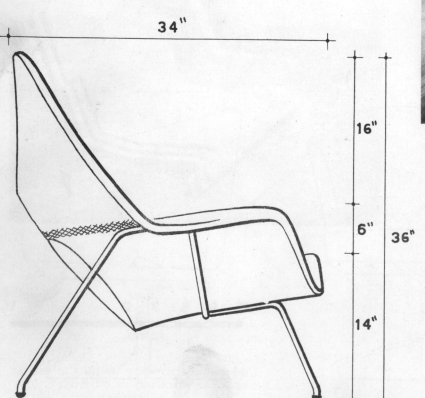

16"

6"   36"

14"

Above—ARMCHAIR WITH BENT LAMINATED WOOD
FRAME. COVERING IS WOVEN STRIPS OF CLOTH.
Below—FORMED PLASTIC ARMCHAIR WITH STEEL
LEGS. BOTH CHAIRS DESIGNED BY EERO SAARINEN
AND PRODUCED BY KNOLL ASSOCIATES, INC.

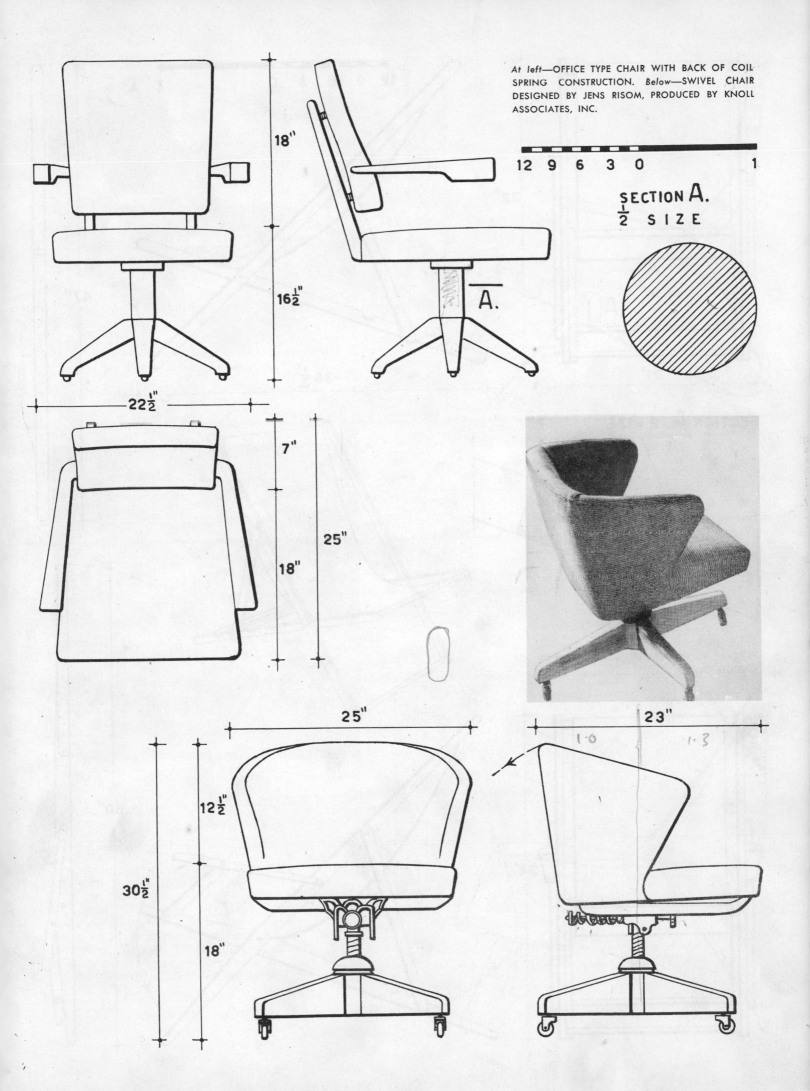

18"

16½"

22½"

SECTION A.
½ SIZE

At left—OFFICE TYPE CHAIR WITH BACK OF COIL SPRING CONSTRUCTION. Below—SWIVEL CHAIR DESIGNED BY JENS RISOM, PRODUCED BY KNOLL ASSOCIATES, INC.

12 9 6 3 0   1

A.

7"

25"

18"

25"

23"

12½"

30½"

18"

29

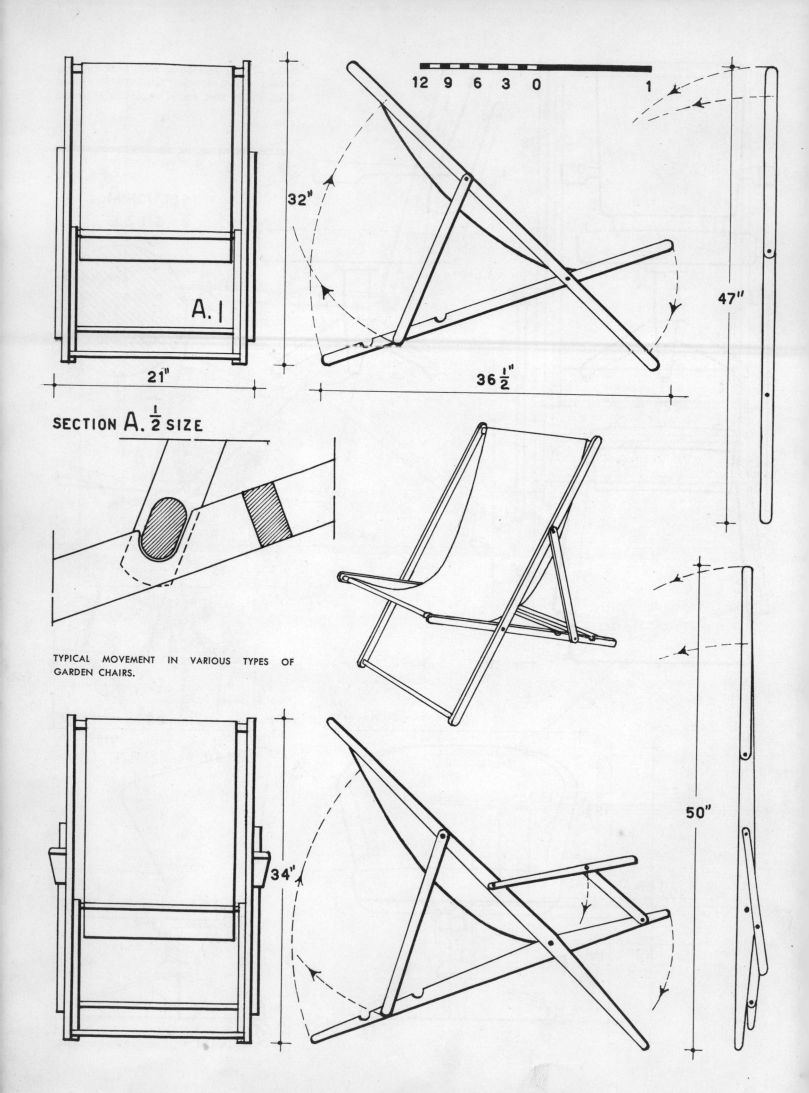

A. I

32"

21"

12 9 6 3 0   1

36 ½"

47"

SECTION A. ½ SIZE

TYPICAL MOVEMENT IN VARIOUS TYPES OF
GARDEN CHAIRS.

34"

50"

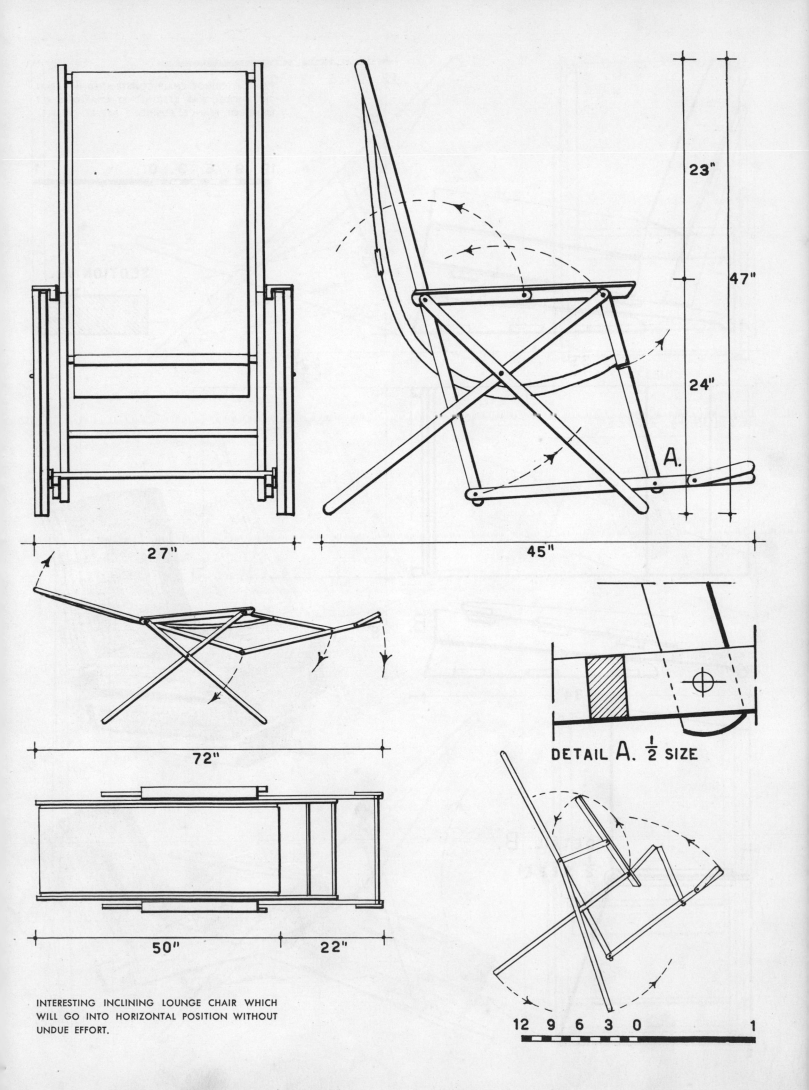

27"

23"

47"

24"

A.

45"

72"

DETAIL A. ½ SIZE

50"   22"

INTERESTING INCLINING LOUNGE CHAIR WHICH
WILL GO INTO HORIZONTAL POSITION WITHOUT
UNDUE EFFORT.

12 9 6 3 0   1

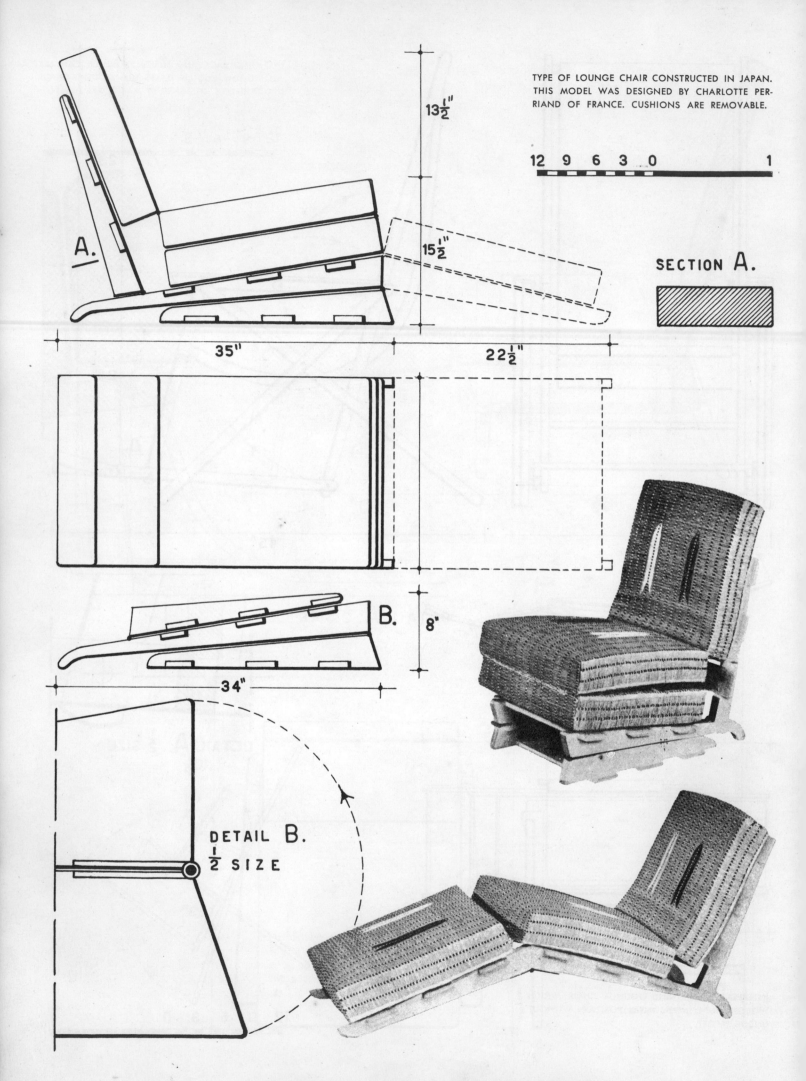

13½"

TYPE OF LOUNGE CHAIR CONSTRUCTED IN JAPAN.
THIS MODEL WAS DESIGNED BY CHARLOTTE PER-
RIAND OF FRANCE. CUSHIONS ARE REMOVABLE.

12 9 6 3 0   1

A.

15½"

SECTION A.

35"   22½"

B.   8'

34"

DETAIL B.
½ SIZE

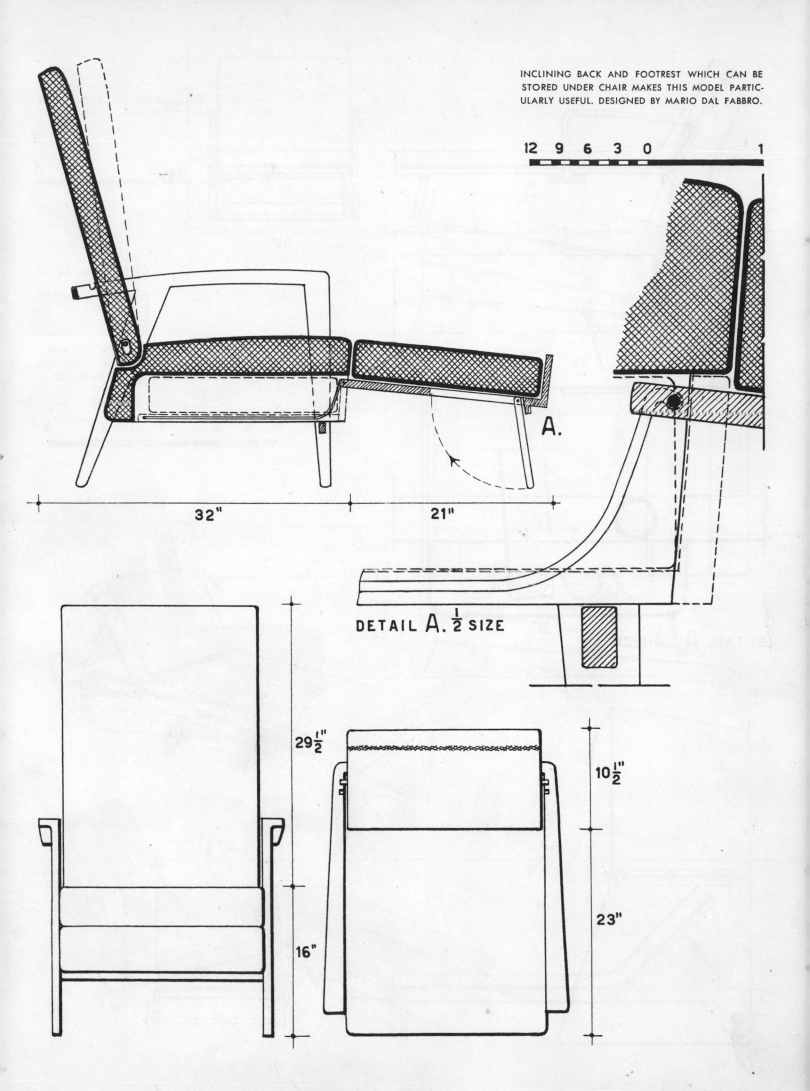

INCLINING BACK AND FOOTREST WHICH CAN BE
STORED UNDER CHAIR MAKES THIS MODEL PARTIC-
ULARLY USEFUL. DESIGNED BY MARIO DAL FABBRO.

12 9 6 3 0   1

A.

32"   21"

DETAIL A. $\frac{1}{2}$ SIZE

$29\frac{1}{2}$"

$10\frac{1}{2}$"

23"

16"

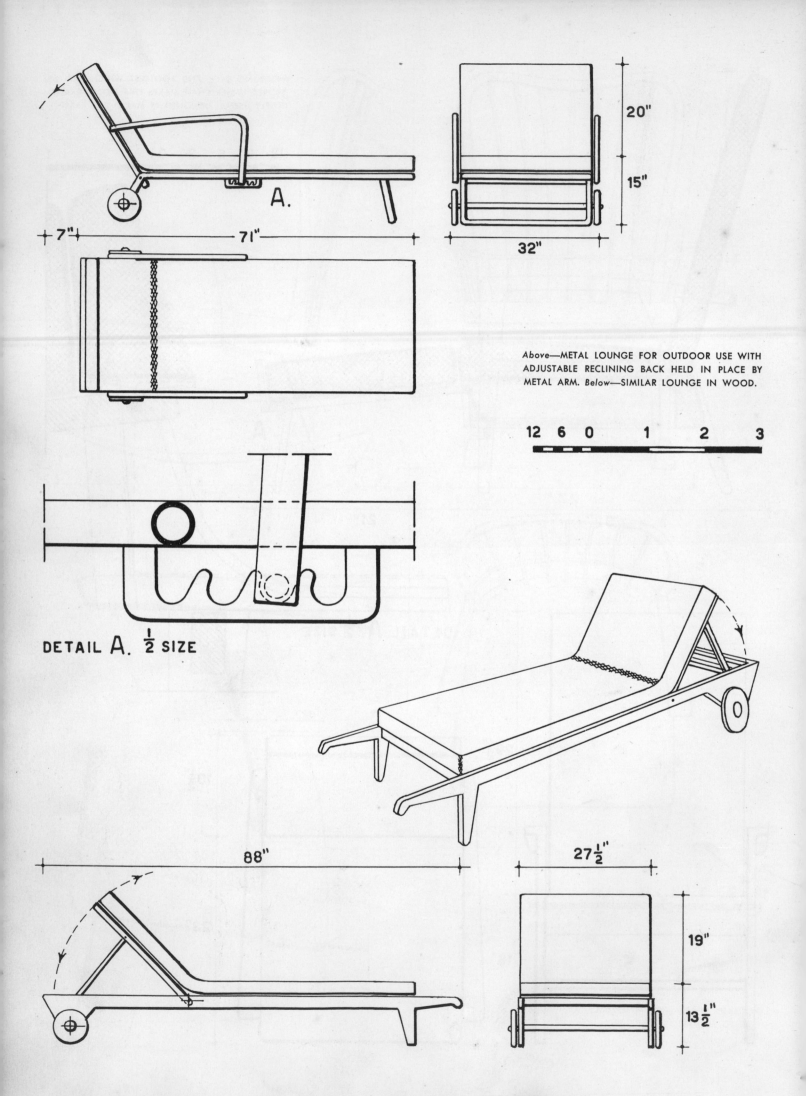

A.

7" 71"

20"

15"

32"

DETAIL A. ½ SIZE

Above—METAL LOUNGE FOR OUTDOOR USE WITH
ADJUSTABLE RECLINING BACK HELD IN PLACE BY
METAL ARM. *Below*—SIMILAR LOUNGE IN WOOD.

12 6 0   1   2   3

88"

27½"

19"

13½"

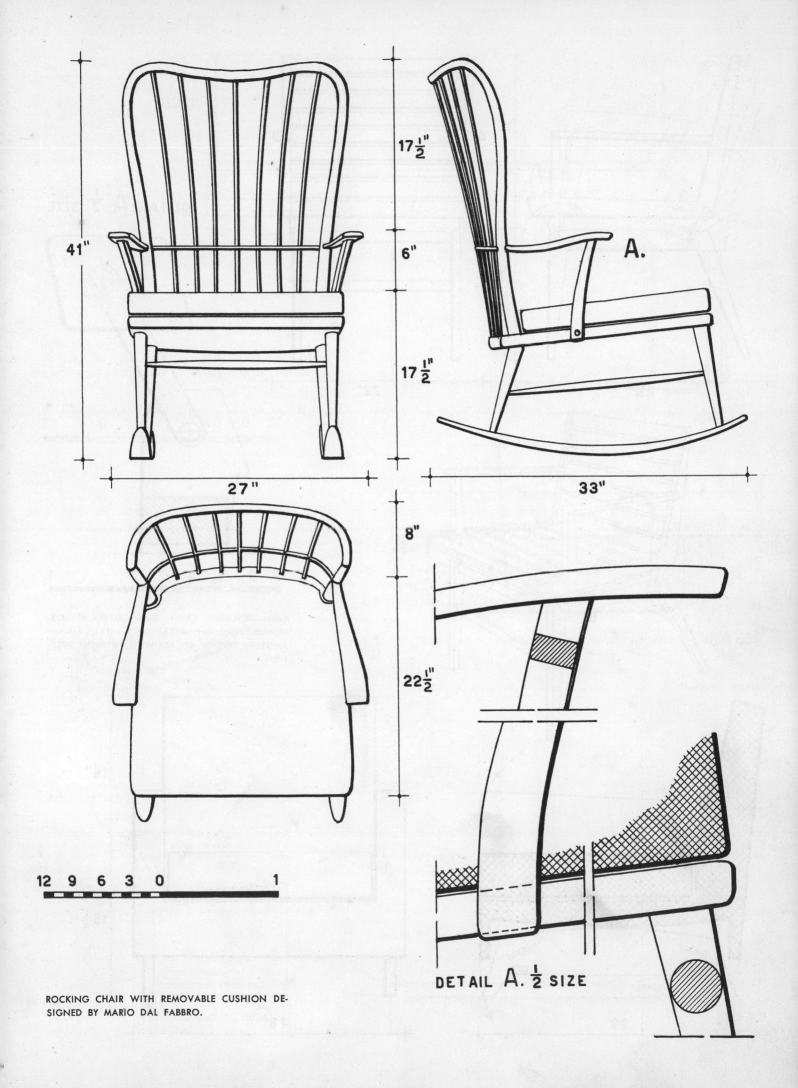

41"

17 1/2"

6"

17 1/2"

A.

27"

33"

8"

22 1/2"

12 9 6 3 0 1

DETAIL A. 1/2 SIZE

ROCKING CHAIR WITH REMOVABLE CUSHION DE-
SIGNED BY MARIO DAL FABBRO.

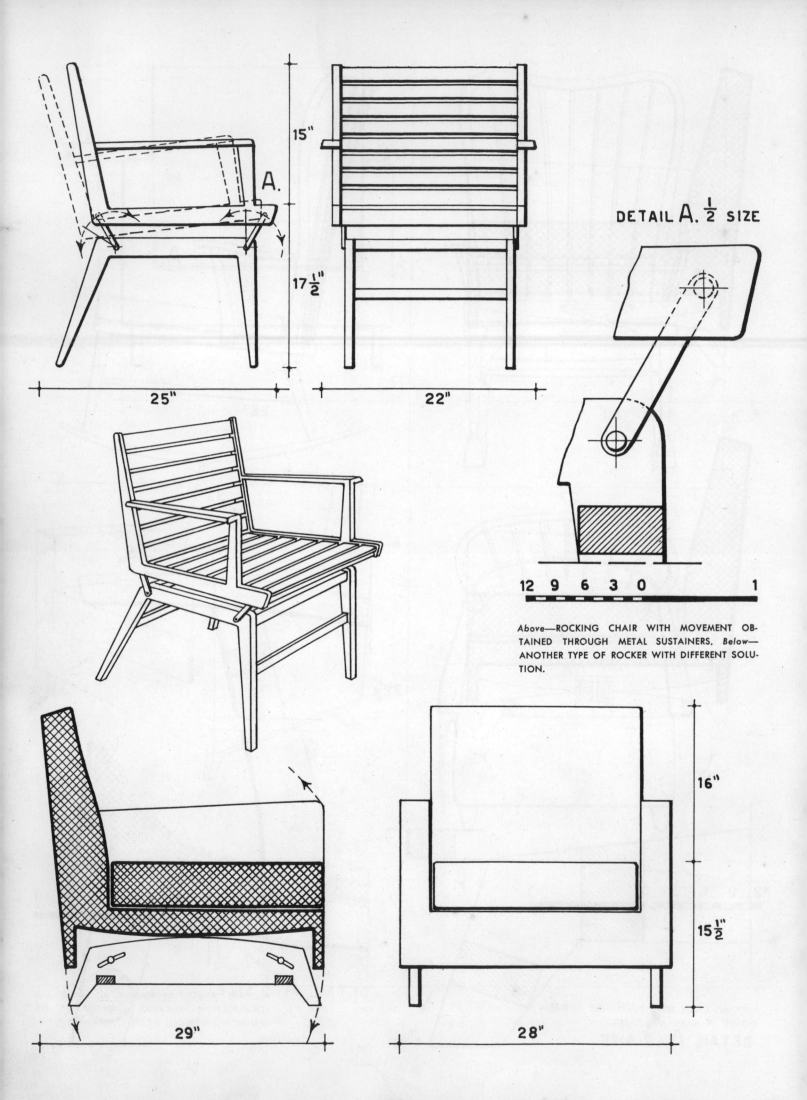

15"

17 1/2"

25"

22"

A.

DETAIL A. 1/2 SIZE

12 9 6 3 0   1

Above—ROCKING CHAIR WITH MOVEMENT OB-
TAINED THROUGH METAL SUSTAINERS. *Below*—
ANOTHER TYPE OF ROCKER WITH DIFFERENT SOLU-
TION.

16"

15 1/2"

29"

28"

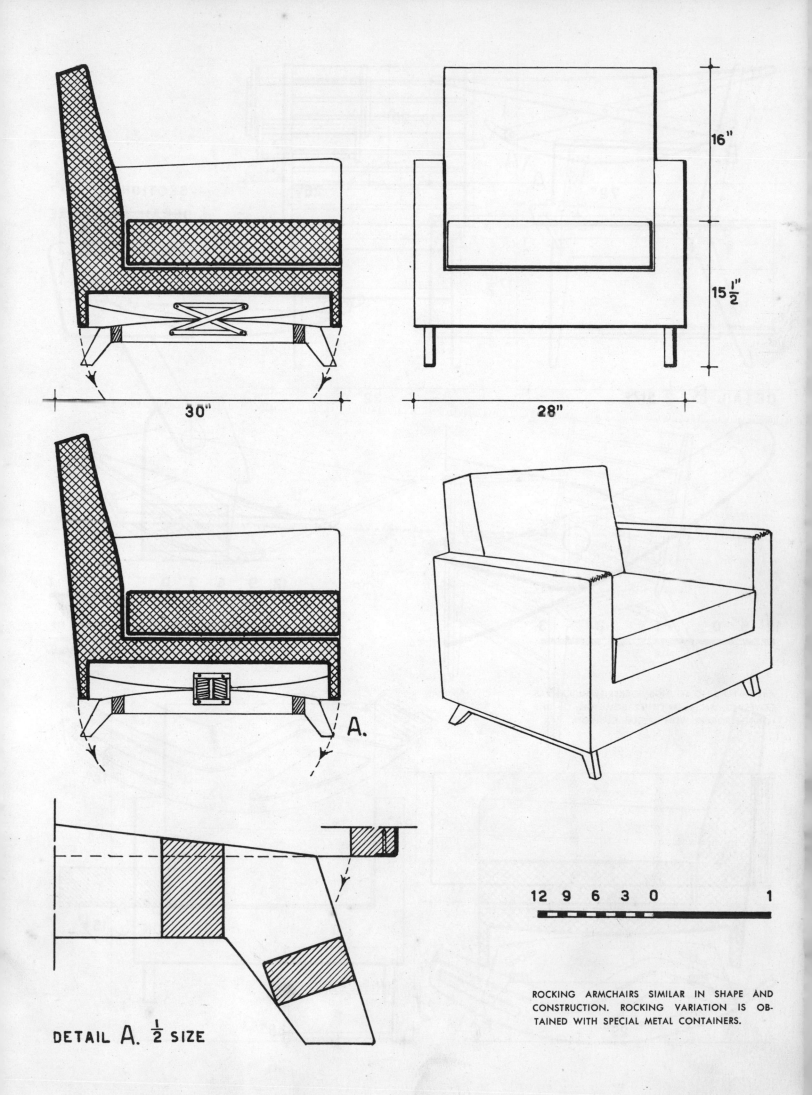

16"

15 ½"

30"

28"

A.

DETAIL A. ½ SIZE

12 9 6 3 0   1

ROCKING ARMCHAIRS SIMILAR IN SHAPE AND
CONSTRUCTION. ROCKING VARIATION IS OB-
TAINED WITH SPECIAL METAL CONTAINERS.

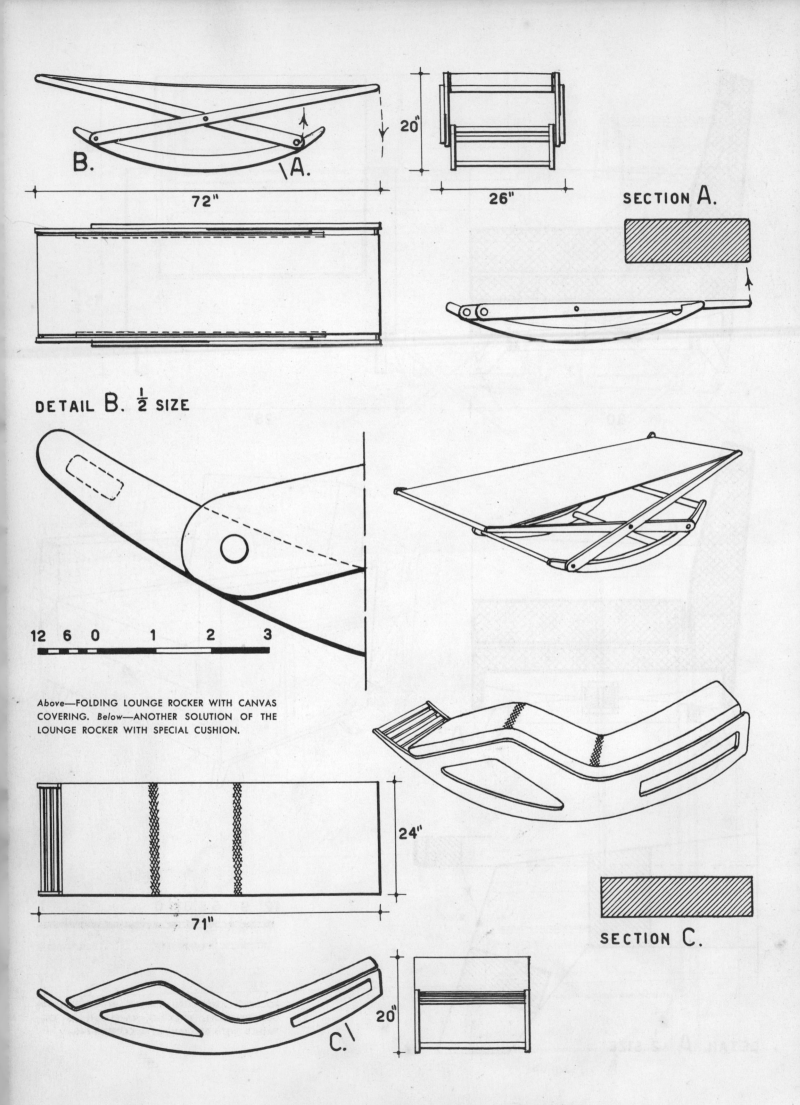

B.　　　　　　　　　　　　　\A.

20"

72"　　　　　　　26"

SECTION A.

DETAIL B. ½ SIZE

12 6 0 1 2 3

Above—FOLDING LOUNGE ROCKER WITH CANVAS COVERING. *Below*—ANOTHER SOLUTION OF THE LOUNGE ROCKER WITH SPECIAL CUSHION.

SECTION C.

24"

71"

C.\

20"

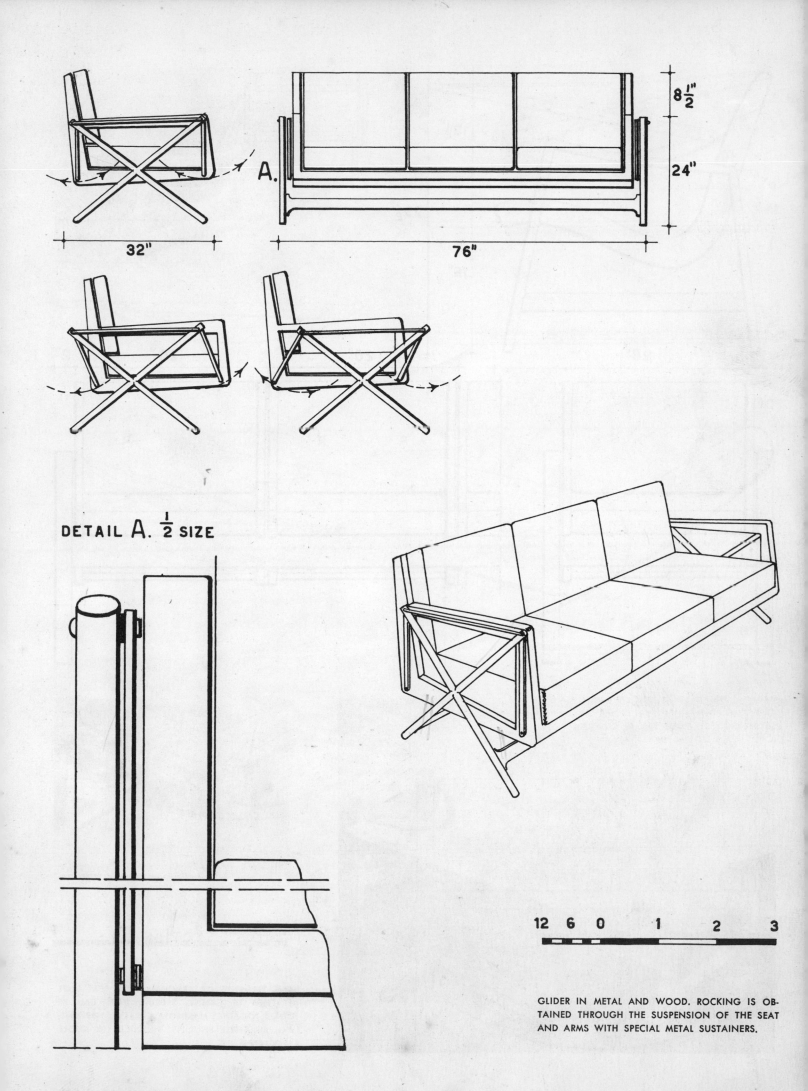

8 1/2"

24"

32"

76"

A.

DETAIL A. 1/2 SIZE

12 6 0 1 2 3

GLIDER IN METAL AND WOOD. ROCKING IS OB-
TAINED THROUGH THE SUSPENSION OF THE SEAT
AND ARMS WITH SPECIAL METAL SUSTAINERS.

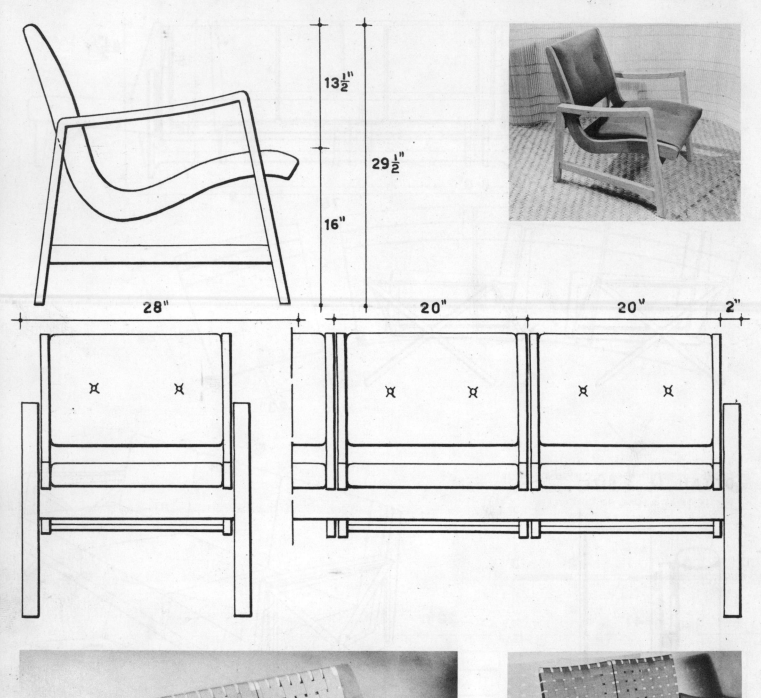

13½"

29½"

16"

28"   20"   20"   2"

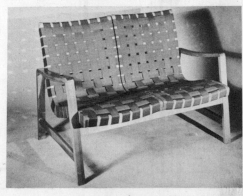

12 9 6 3 0   1

BASIC ELEMENTS OF ARMCHAIR WITH SEAT UNIT
ATTACHED TO CRADLE. SPECIAL UNITS CAN BE
JOINED TOGETHER MAKING A CAPACITY FOR ONE,
TWO, OR THREE PERSONS. PRODUCED BY KNOLL
ASSOCIATES, INC.

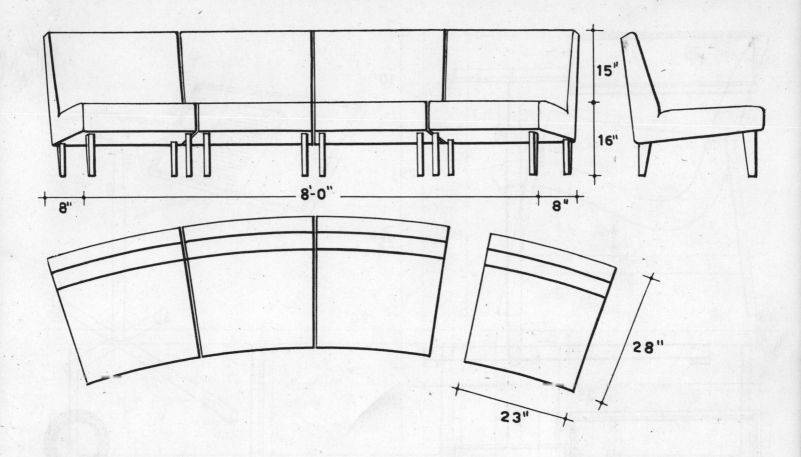

15"

16"

8'-0"

8"

8"

28"

23"

Above—CHAIR WHICH CAN BE USED SINGULARLY OR WITH OTHERS TO FORM A CURVED DIVAN OR SOFA. *Below*—SIMILAR CHAIRS TO BE USED INDIVIDUALLY OR AS A SOFA, NO CURVATURE.

12 6 0 1 2 3

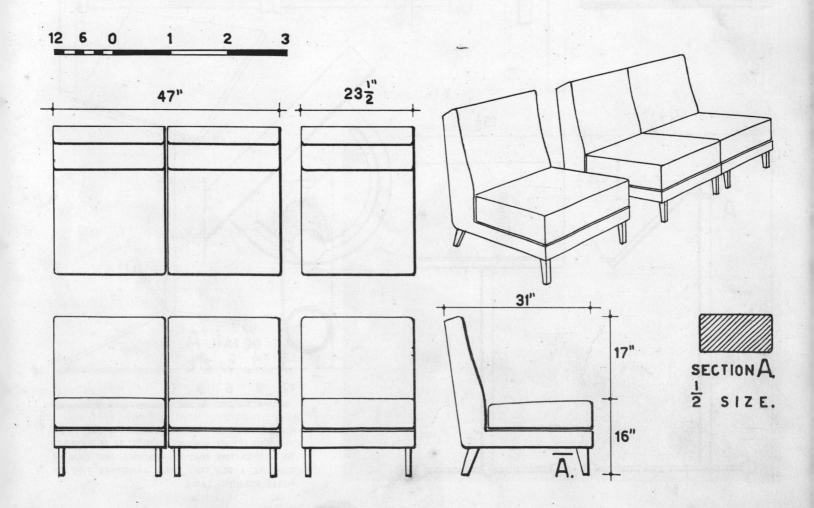

47"

23½"

31"

17"

16"

SECTION A
½ SIZE.

Ā.

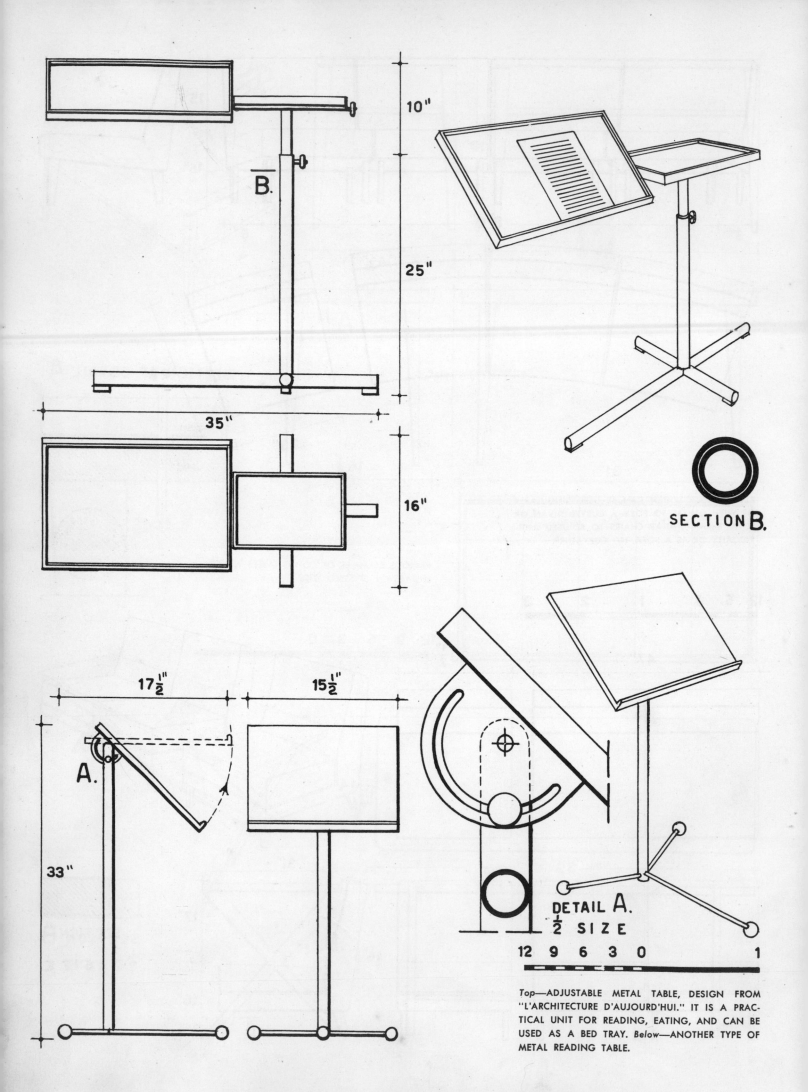

10"

$\overline{B.}$

25"

35"

16"

$17\frac{1}{2}"$ $15\frac{1}{2}"$

A.

33"

SECTION B.

DETAIL A.
$\frac{1}{2}$ SIZE

12 9 6 3 0   1

Top—ADJUSTABLE METAL TABLE, DESIGN FROM "L'ARCHITECTURE D'AUJOURD'HUI." IT IS A PRACTICAL UNIT FOR READING, EATING, AND CAN BE USED AS A BED TRAY. *Below*—ANOTHER TYPE OF METAL READING TABLE.

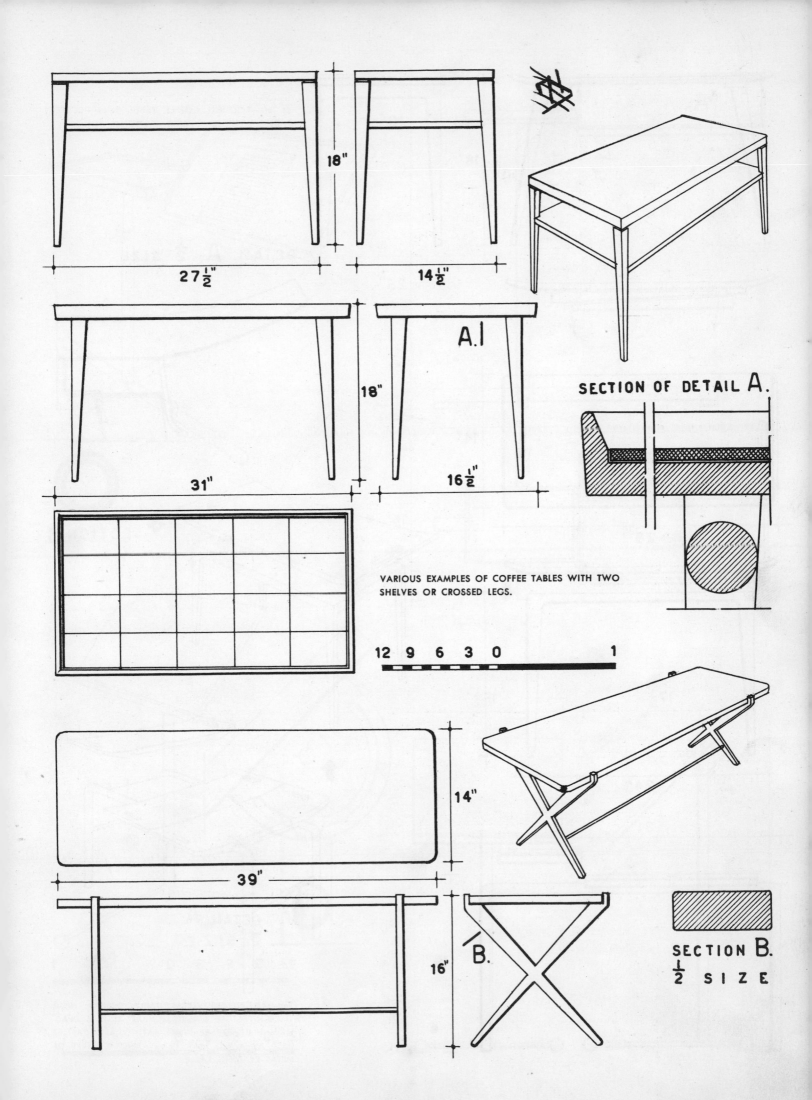

18"

27½"

14½"

A.1

18"

31"

16½"

SECTION OF DETAIL A.

VARIOUS EXAMPLES OF COFFEE TABLES WITH TWO
SHELVES OR CROSSED LEGS.

12 9 6 3 0   1

14"

39"

16"

B.

SECTION B.
½ SIZE

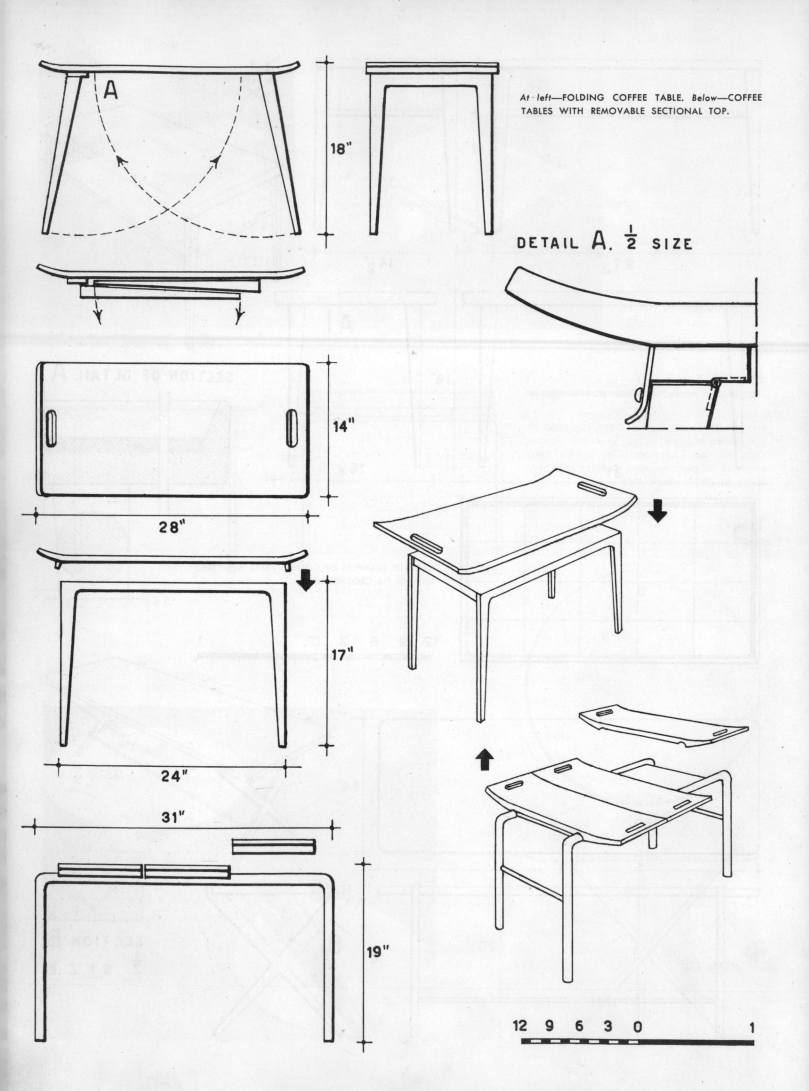

18"

*At left—*FOLDING COFFEE TABLE. *Below—*COFFEE TABLES WITH REMOVABLE SECTIONAL TOP.

DETAIL A. $\frac{1}{2}$ SIZE

14"

28"

17"

24"

31"

19"

12 9 6 3 0   1

12 9 6 3 0 1

At right—STACKING COFFEE TABLE, DESIGNED BY ABEL SORENSEN, PRODUCED BY KNOLL ASSOCIATES, INC. *Below*—DEMOUNTABLE COFFEE TABLE DESIGNED BY HANS BELLMAN, SWITZERLAND, PRODUCED BY KNOLL ASSOCIATES, INC.

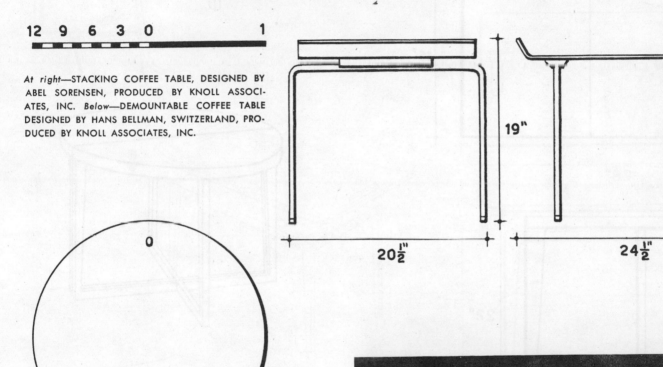

19"

20½"

24½"

0

24"

20"

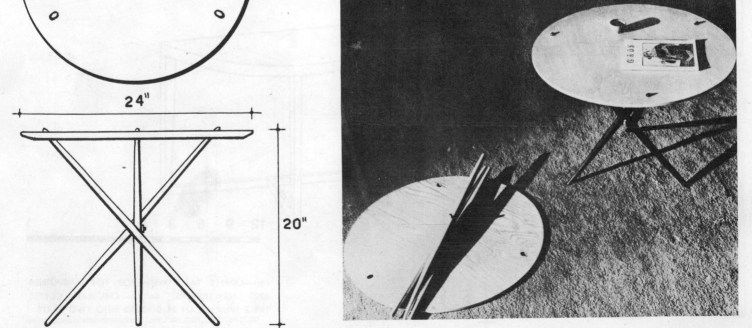

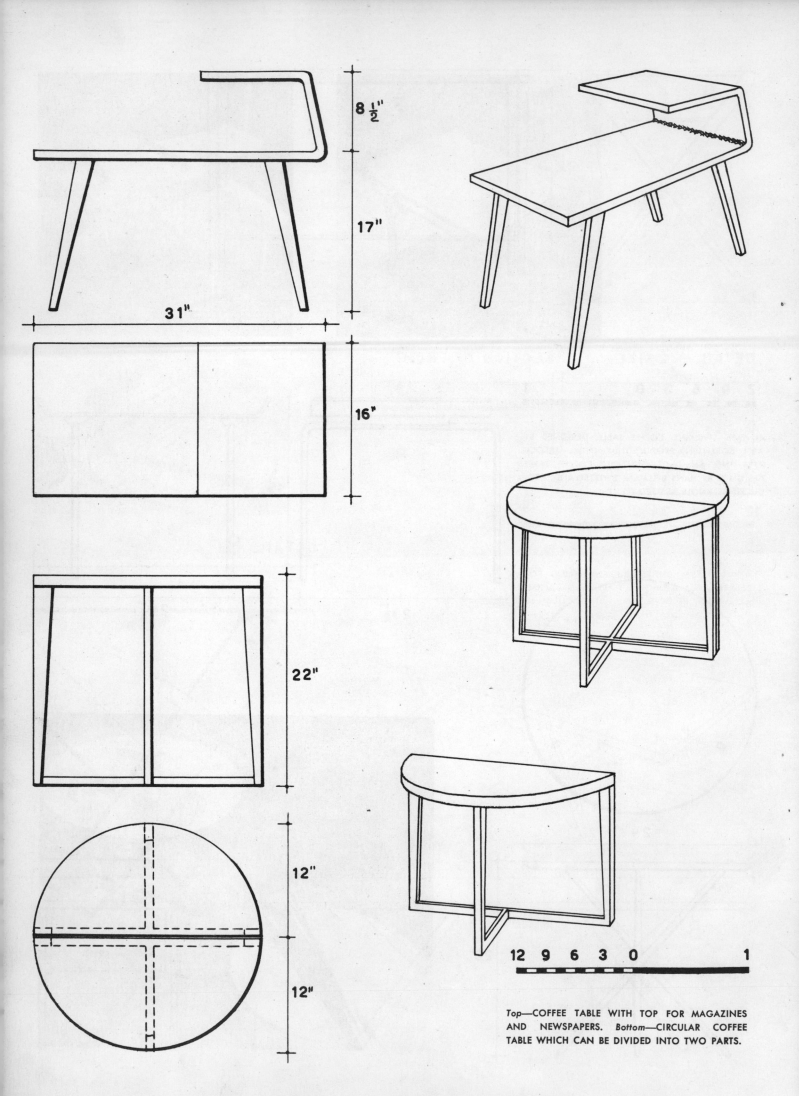

8 ½"

17"

31"

16"

22"

12"

12"

12 9 6 3 0   1

Top—COFFEE TABLE WITH TOP FOR MAGAZINES
AND NEWSPAPERS. *Bottom*—CIRCULAR COFFEE
TABLE WHICH CAN BE DIVIDED INTO TWO PARTS.

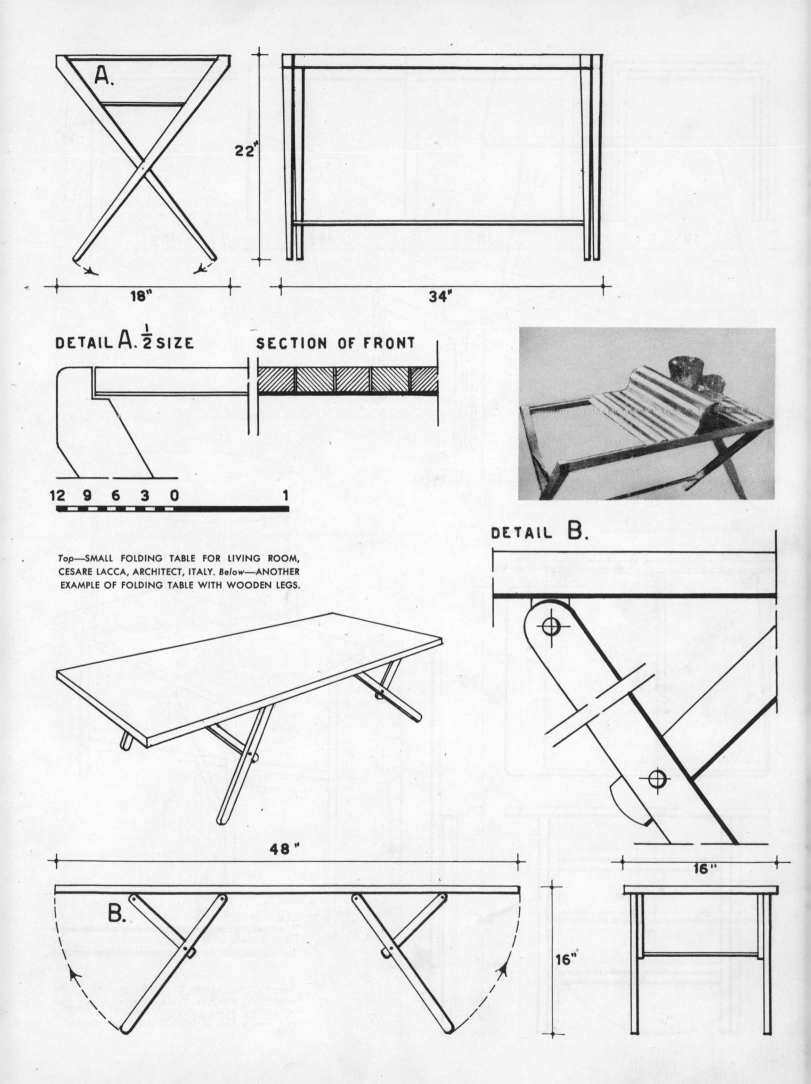

A.

22"

18"

34"

DETAIL A. $\frac{1}{2}$ SIZE

SECTION OF FRONT

12 9 6 3 0   1

Top—SMALL FOLDING TABLE FOR LIVING ROOM,
CESARE LACCA, ARCHITECT, ITALY. *Below*—ANOTHER
EXAMPLE OF FOLDING TABLE WITH WOODEN LEGS.

DETAIL **B.**

B.

48"

16"

16"

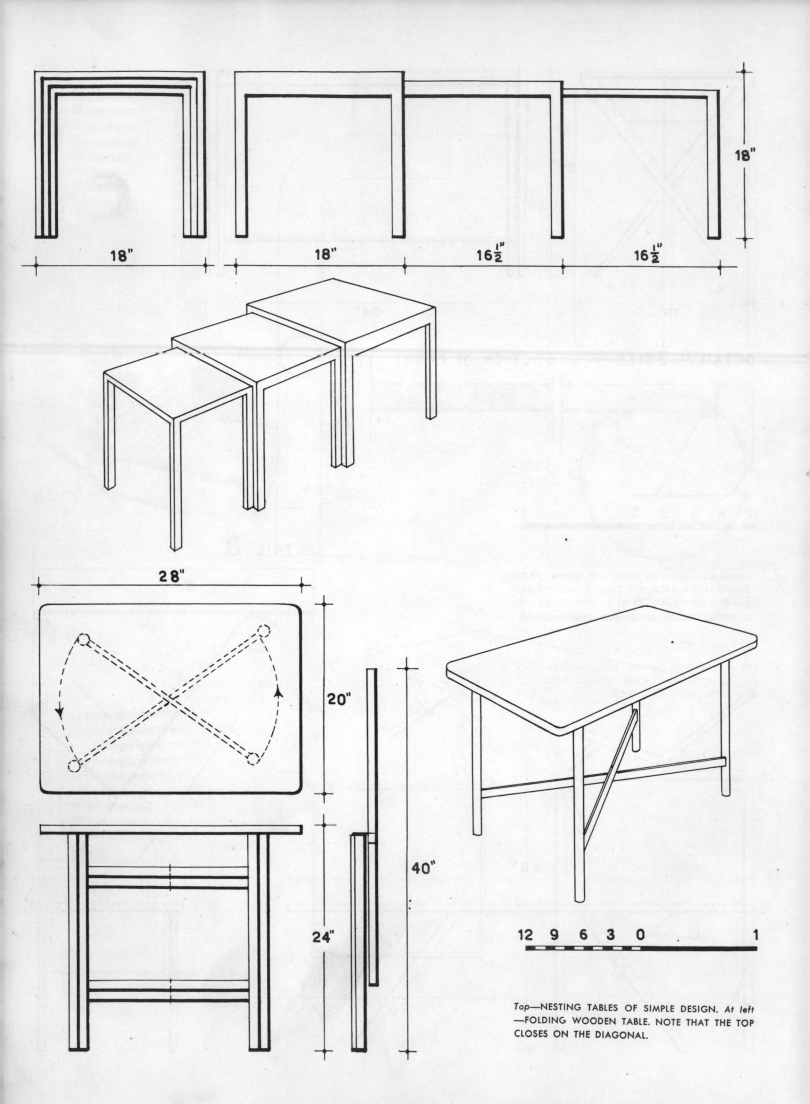

18"

18"

18"

16½"

16½"

28"

20"

40"

24"

12 9 6 3 0   1

Top—NESTING TABLES OF SIMPLE DESIGN. *At left*—FOLDING WOODEN TABLE. NOTE THAT THE TOP CLOSES ON THE DIAGONAL.

A.

29"

SECTION OF
DETAIL A. $\frac{1}{2}$ SIZE

20"

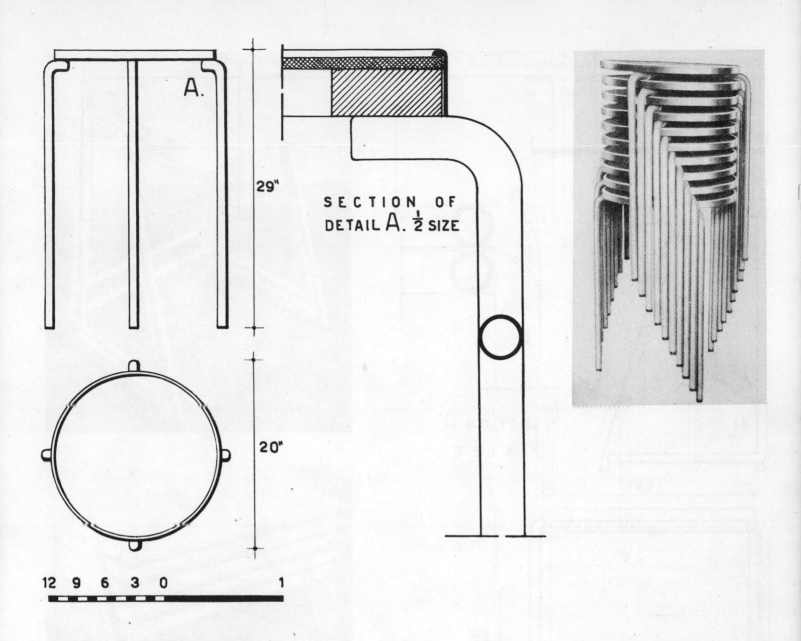

12 9 6 3 0   1

METAL STACKING TABLES BOTH ROUND AND
SQUARE, COMMONLY USED IN BARS. PRODUCED
BY PIETRO CRESPI CO., ITALY.

29"

20"

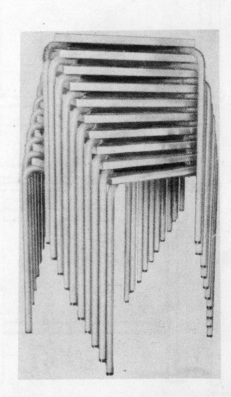

WOOD AND METAL STACKING TABLES, PARTICU-
LARLY USEFUL IN SCHOOLS. DESIGNED BY JAMES
LEONARD, F.S.I.A., ENGLAND. INTRODUCED IN THE
U.S.A. BY KNOLL ASSOCIATES, INC.

12 9 6 3 0 1

18"

A.

SECTION A.
½ SIZE

22"

29"

36"

18"

22"

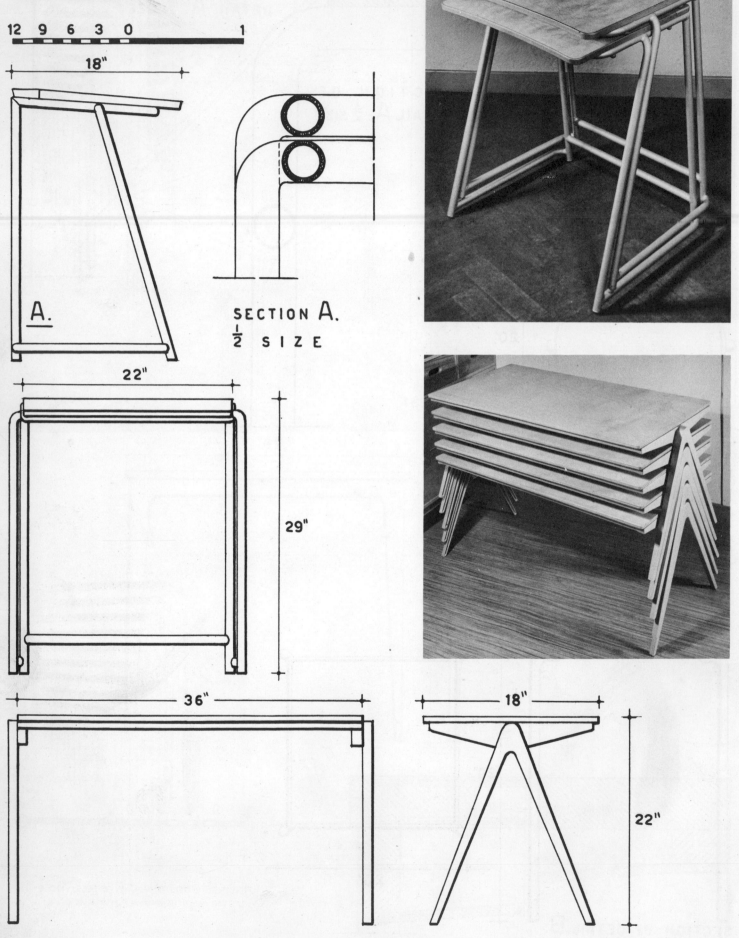

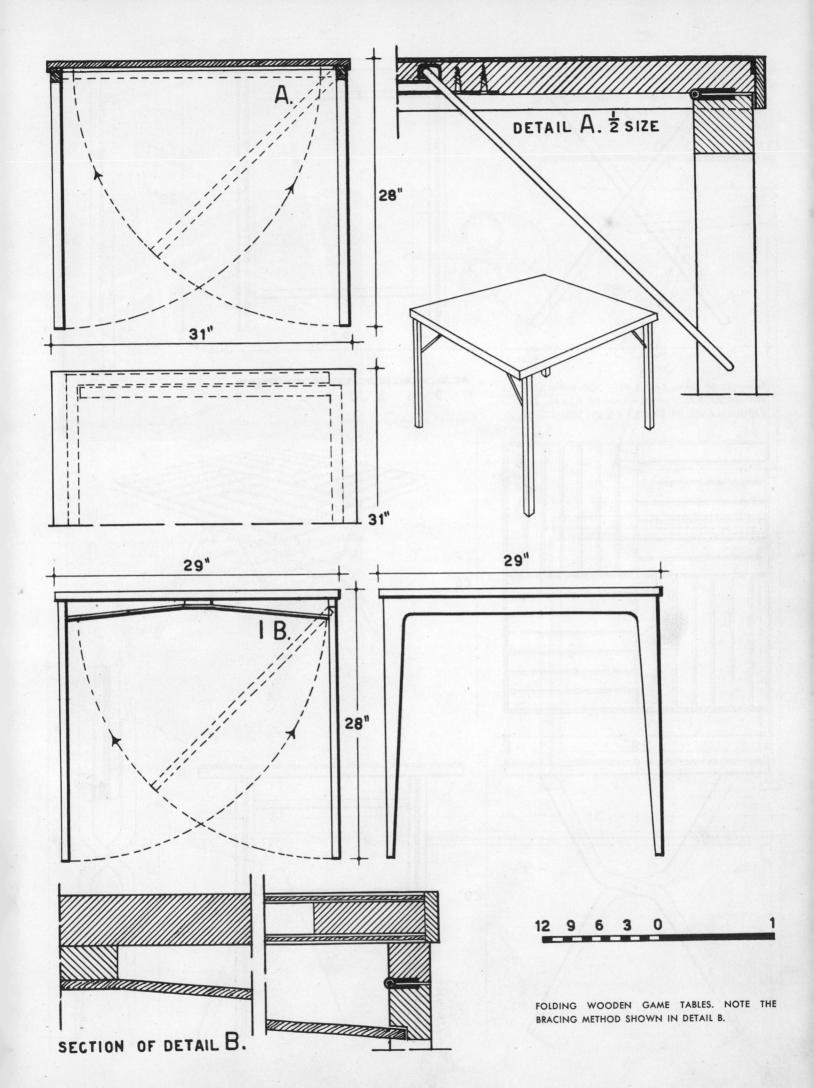

A.

DETAIL A. ½ SIZE

28"

31"

31"

29"

I B.

29"

28"

12 9 6 3 0 1

SECTION OF DETAIL B.

FOLDING WOODEN GAME TABLES. NOTE THE
BRACING METHOD SHOWN IN DETAIL B.

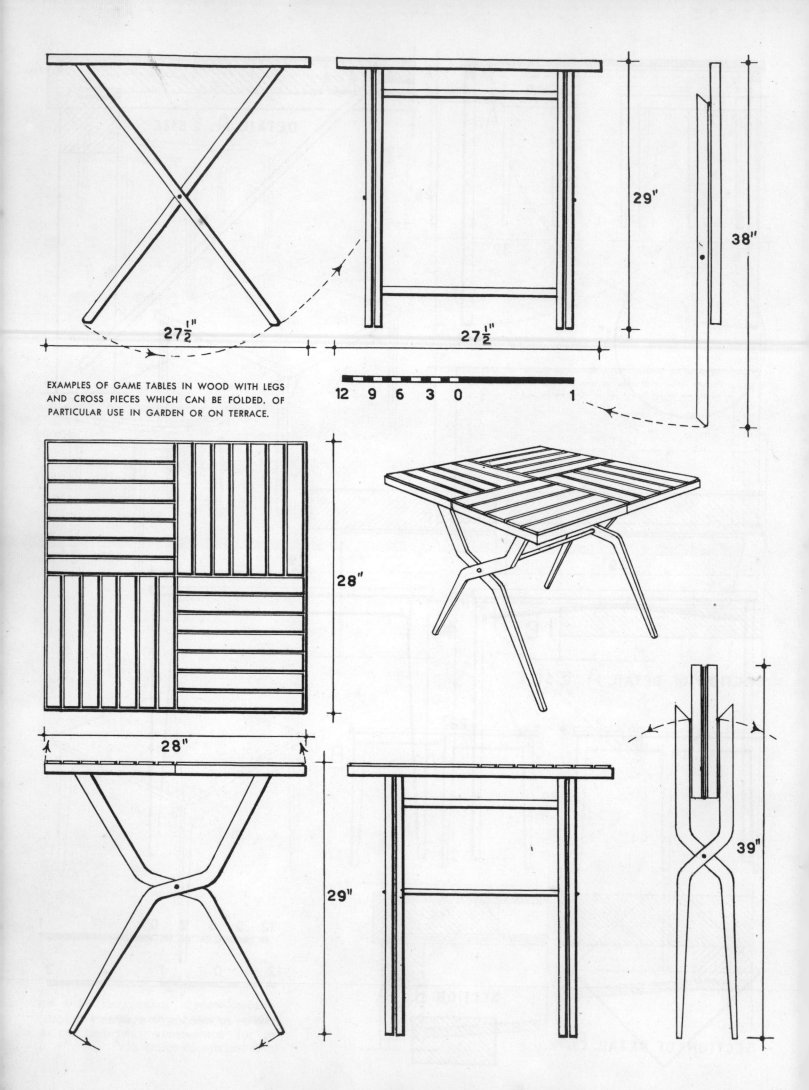

EXAMPLES OF GAME TABLES IN WOOD WITH LEGS AND CROSS PIECES WHICH CAN BE FOLDED. OF PARTICULAR USE IN GARDEN OR ON TERRACE.

27½"

29"

38"

12 9 6 3 0   1

28"

28"

29"

39"

52

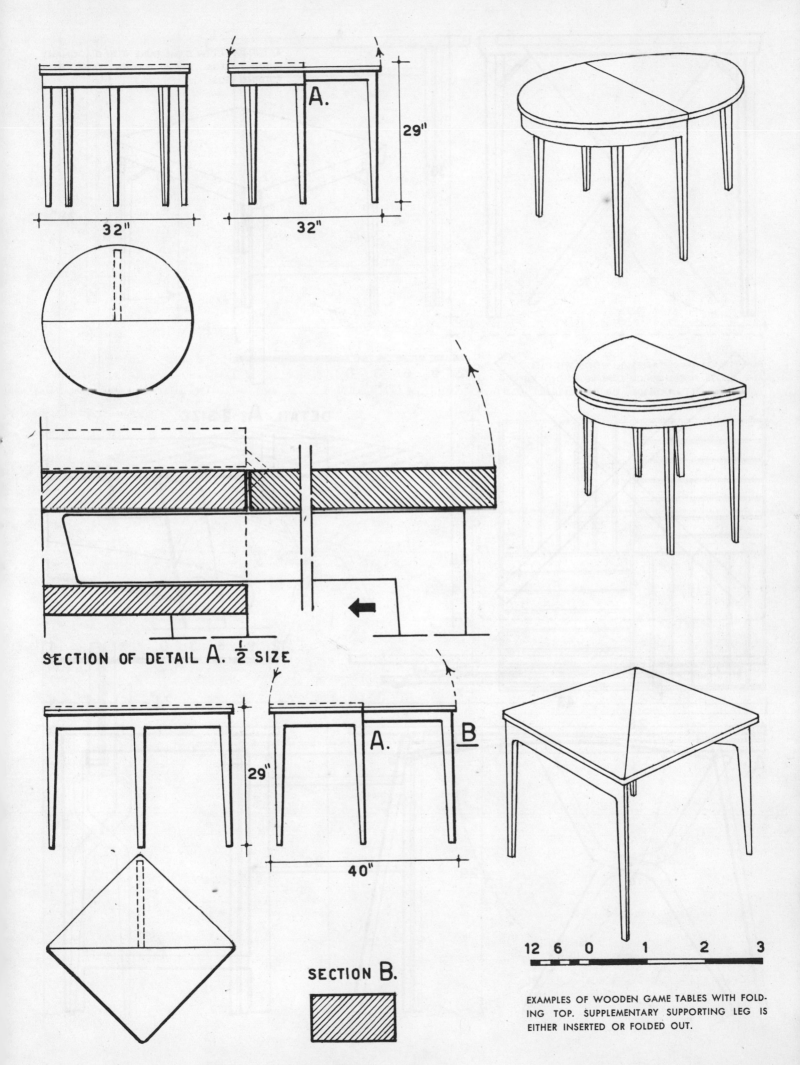

29"

32"

32"

A.

SECTION OF DETAIL A. ½ SIZE

29"

A.

B

40"

SECTION B.

12 6 0 1 2 3

EXAMPLES OF WOODEN GAME TABLES WITH FOLD-
ING TOP. SUPPLEMENTARY SUPPORTING LEG IS
EITHER INSERTED OR FOLDED OUT.

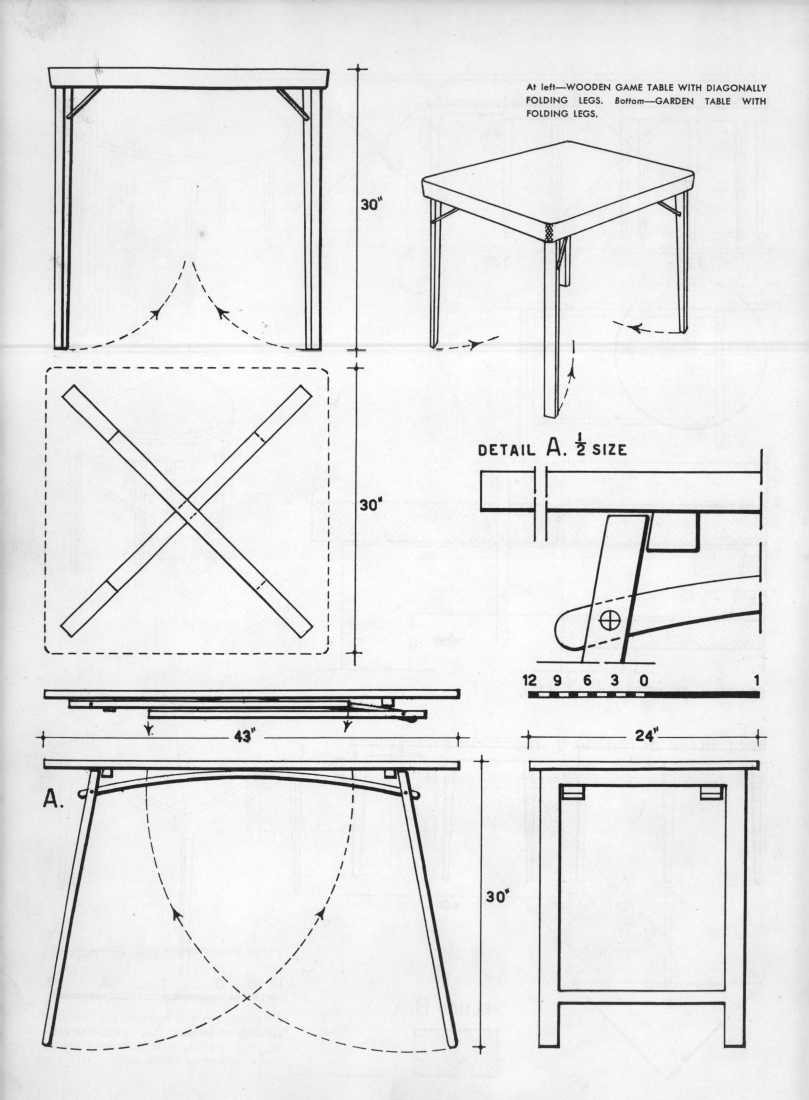

At left—WOODEN GAME TABLE WITH DIAGONALLY FOLDING LEGS. *Bottom*—GARDEN TABLE WITH FOLDING LEGS.

30"

30"

DETAIL A. ½ SIZE

12 9 6 3 0   1

A.

43"

30"

24"

30"

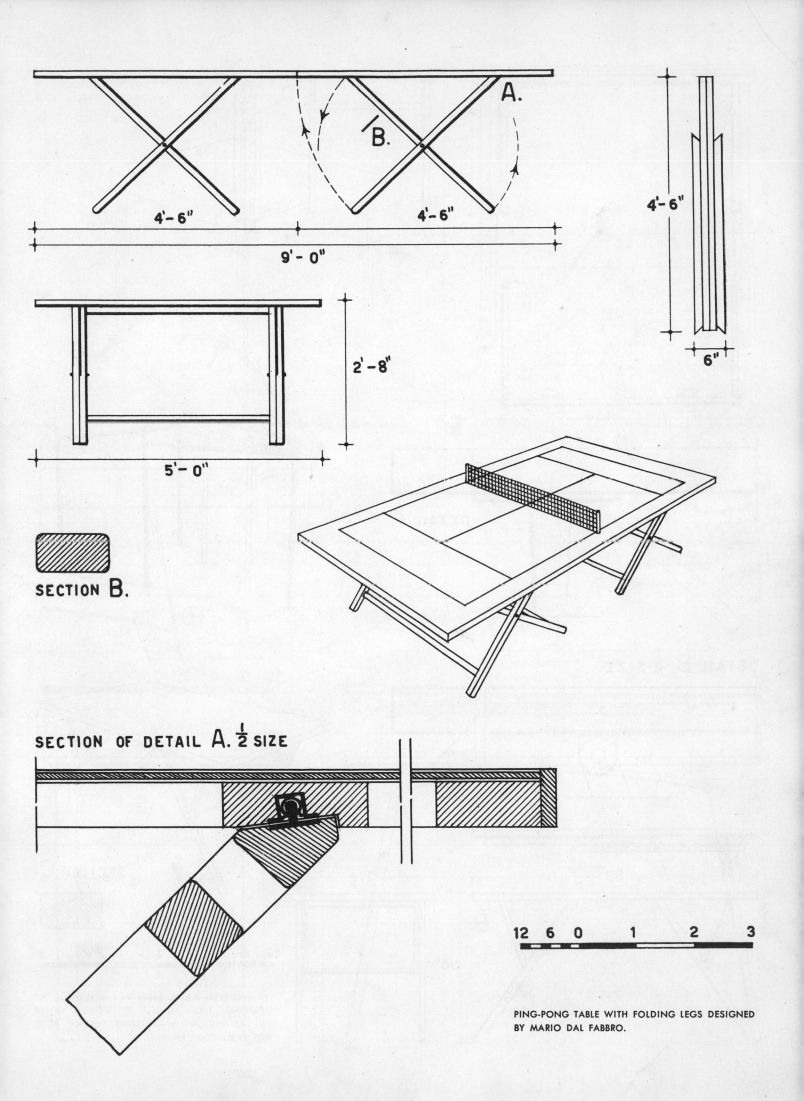

A.

B.

4'- 6"

4'- 6"

9'- 0"

4'- 6"

6"

2'- 8"

5'- 0"

SECTION **B.**

SECTION OF DETAIL **A.** ½ SIZE

12 6 0 1 2 3

PING-PONG TABLE WITH FOLDING LEGS DESIGNED
BY MARIO DAL FABBRO.

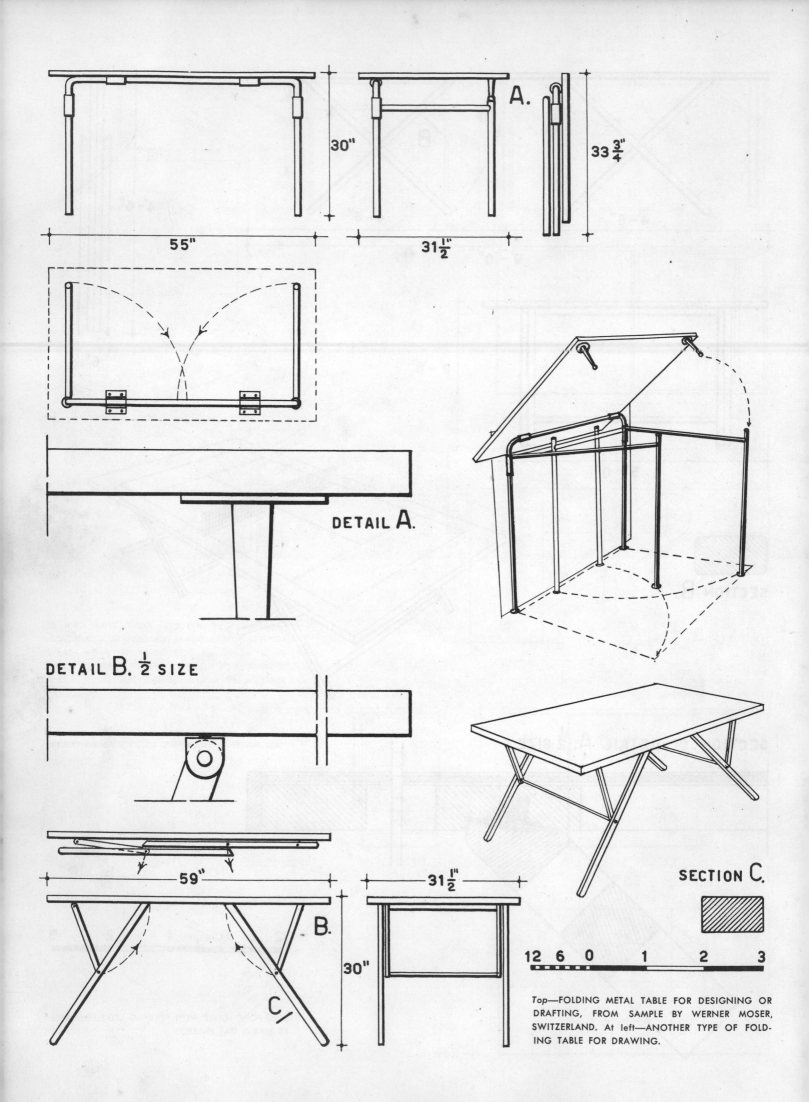

30"

55"

31 1/2"

A.

33 3/4"

DETAIL A.

DETAIL B. 1/2 SIZE

59"

31 1/2"

B.

30"

C.

SECTION C.

12 6 0 1 2 3

Top—FOLDING METAL TABLE FOR DESIGNING OR DRAFTING, FROM SAMPLE BY WERNER MOSER, SWITZERLAND. At left—ANOTHER TYPE OF FOLDING TABLE FOR DRAWING.

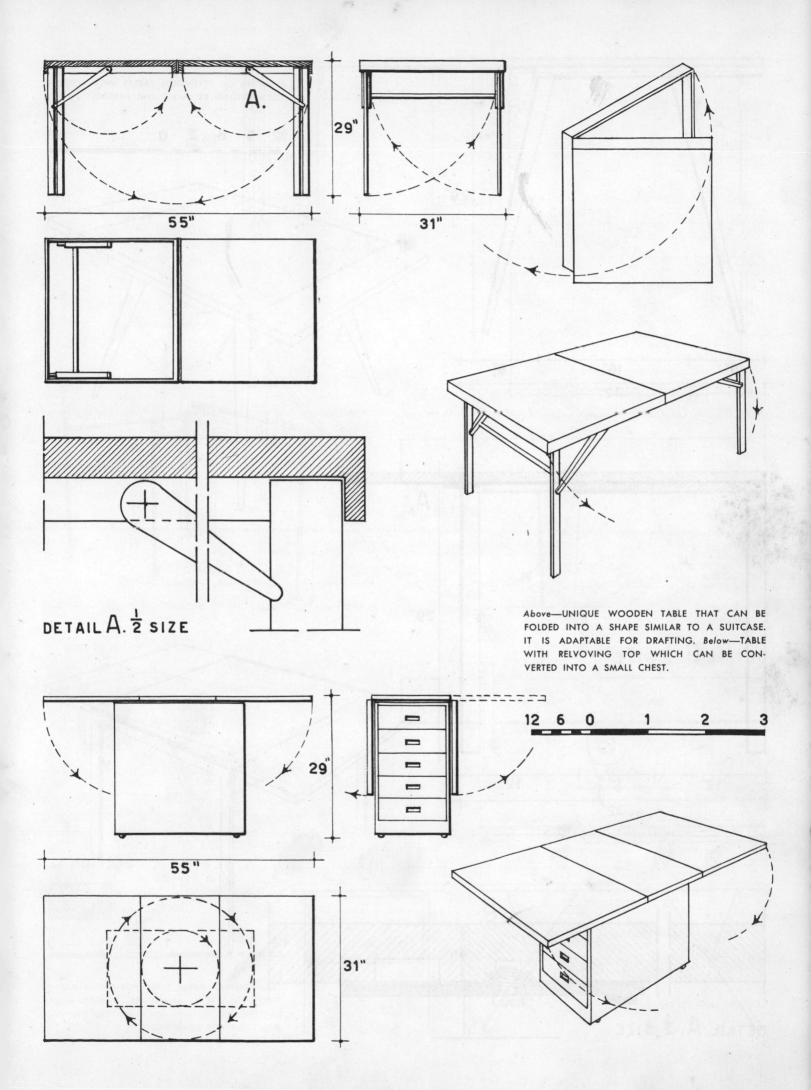

A.

29"

55"

31"

DETAIL A. $\frac{1}{2}$ SIZE

29"

55"

31"

Above—UNIQUE WOODEN TABLE THAT CAN BE
FOLDED INTO A SHAPE SIMILAR TO A SUITCASE.
IT IS ADAPTABLE FOR DRAFTING. *Below*—TABLE
WITH RELVOVING TOP WHICH CAN BE CON-
VERTED INTO A SMALL CHEST.

12 6 0   1   2   3

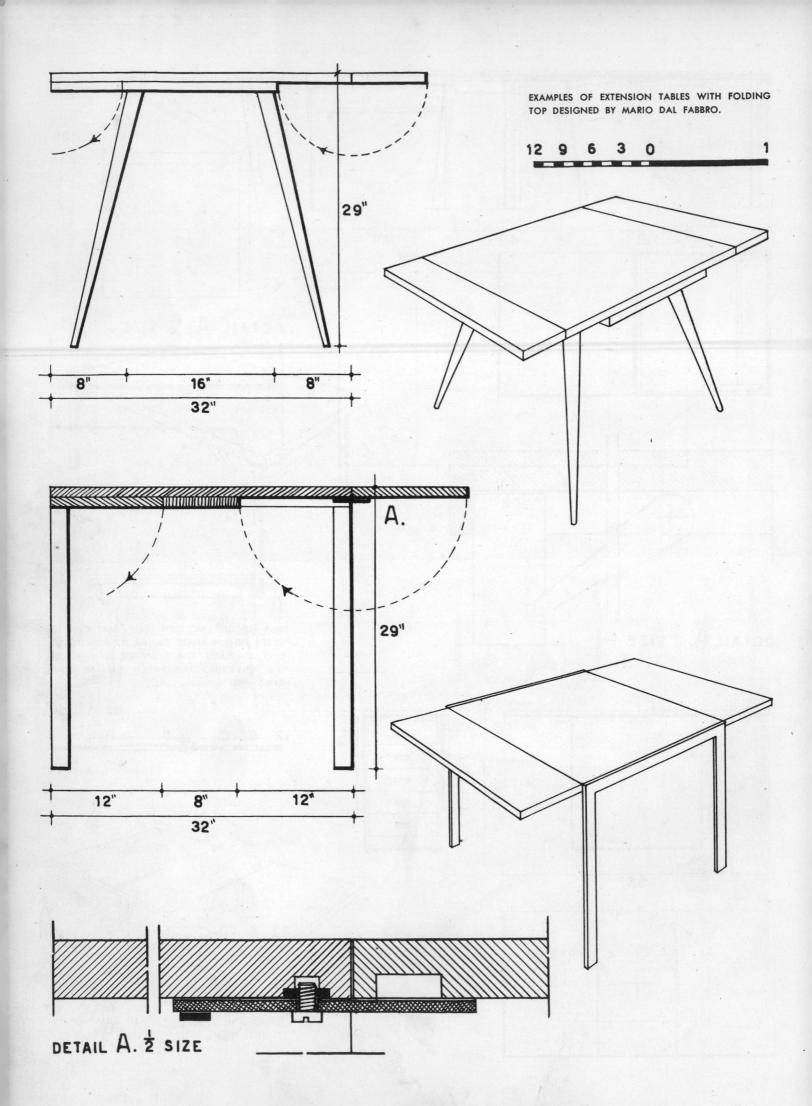

EXAMPLES OF EXTENSION TABLES WITH FOLDING
TOP DESIGNED BY MARIO DAL FABBRO.

29"

8" 16" 8"
32"

A.

29"

12" 8" 12"
32"

DETAIL A. ½ SIZE

12 9 6 3 0   1

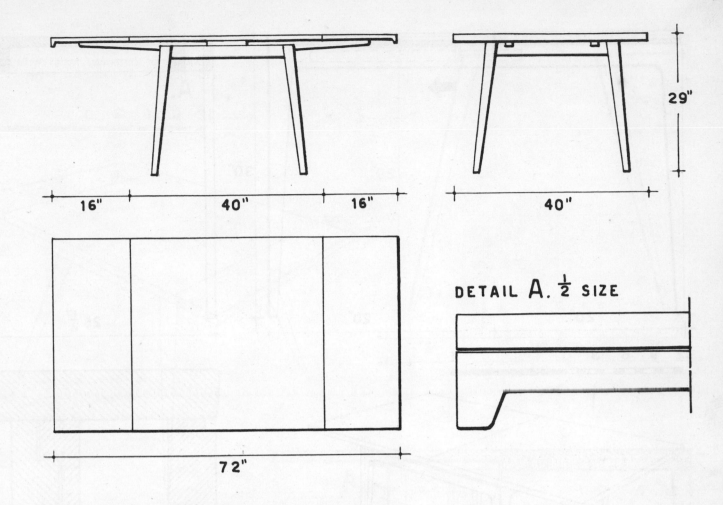

16" 40" 16"

72"

DETAIL A. ½ SIZE

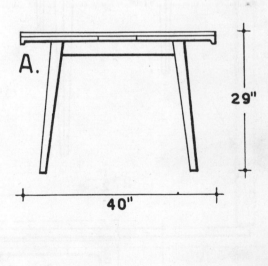

29"

40"

A.

29"

40"

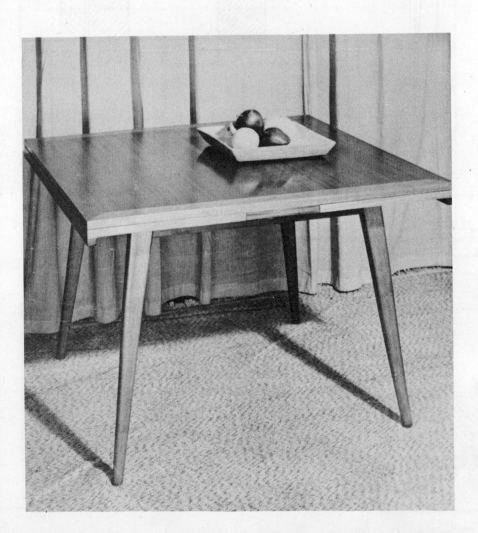

12 6 0 1 2 3

EXTENSION TABLE IN WOOD PRACTICAL FOR
GAMES AND DINING. DESIGNED AND PRODUCED
BY JENS RISOM, INC.

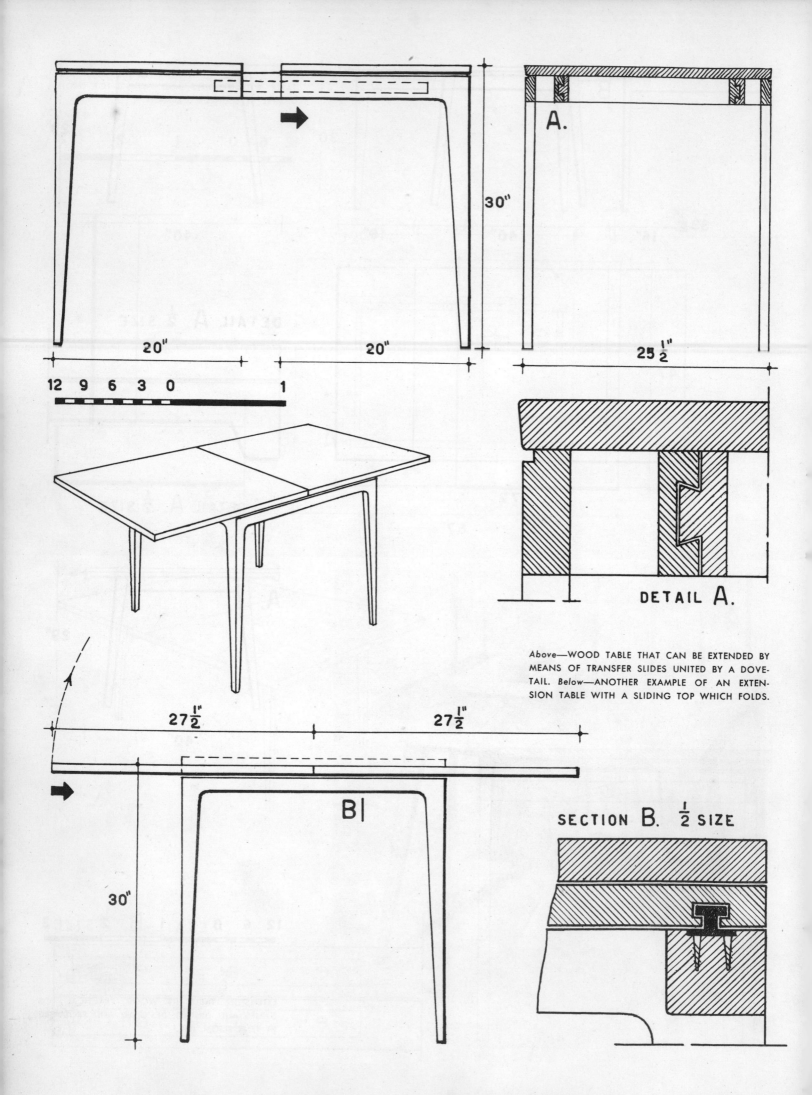

30"

20" 20"

12 9 6 3 0 1

25 ½"

A.

DETAIL A.

Above—WOOD TABLE THAT CAN BE EXTENDED BY MEANS OF TRANSFER SLIDES UNITED BY A DOVETAIL. *Below*—ANOTHER EXAMPLE OF AN EXTENSION TABLE WITH A SLIDING TOP WHICH FOLDS.

27 ½" 27 ½"

B|

30"

SECTION B. ½ SIZE

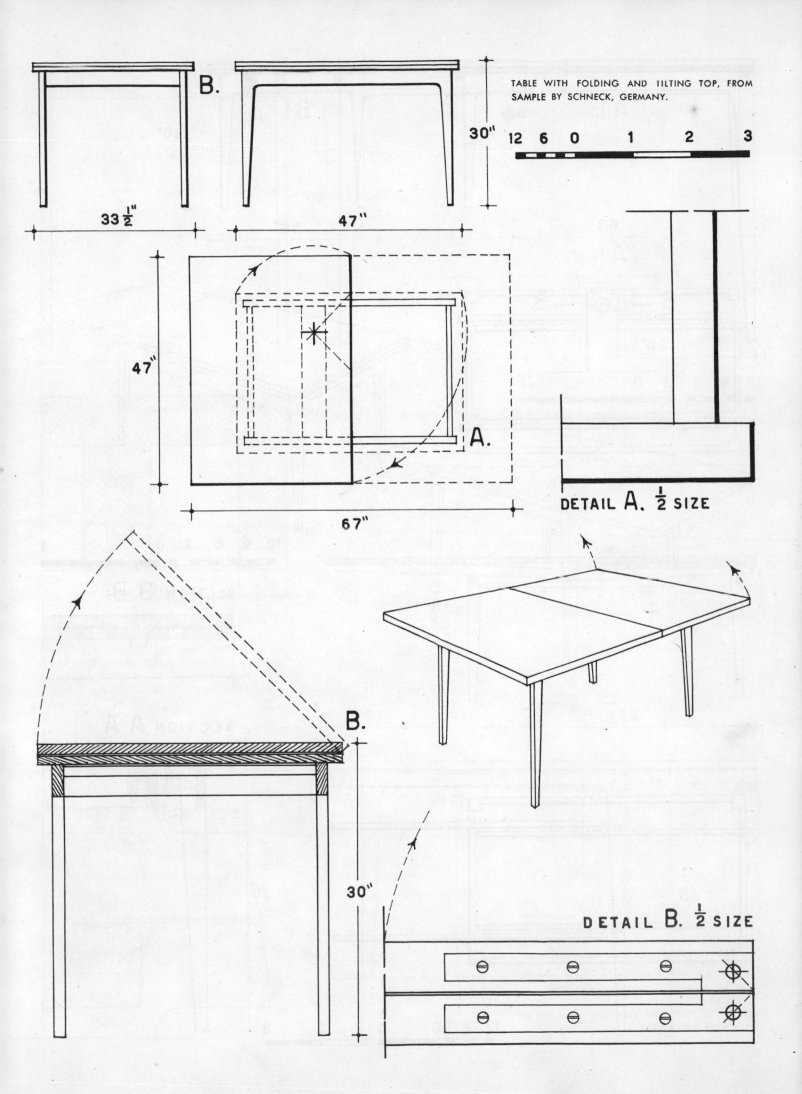

B.

TABLE WITH FOLDING AND TILTING TOP, FROM SAMPLE BY SCHNECK, GERMANY.

30"

33 1/2"

47"

47"

67"

A.

12 6 0 1 2 3

DETAIL A. 1/2 SIZE

B.

30"

DETAIL B. 1/2 SIZE

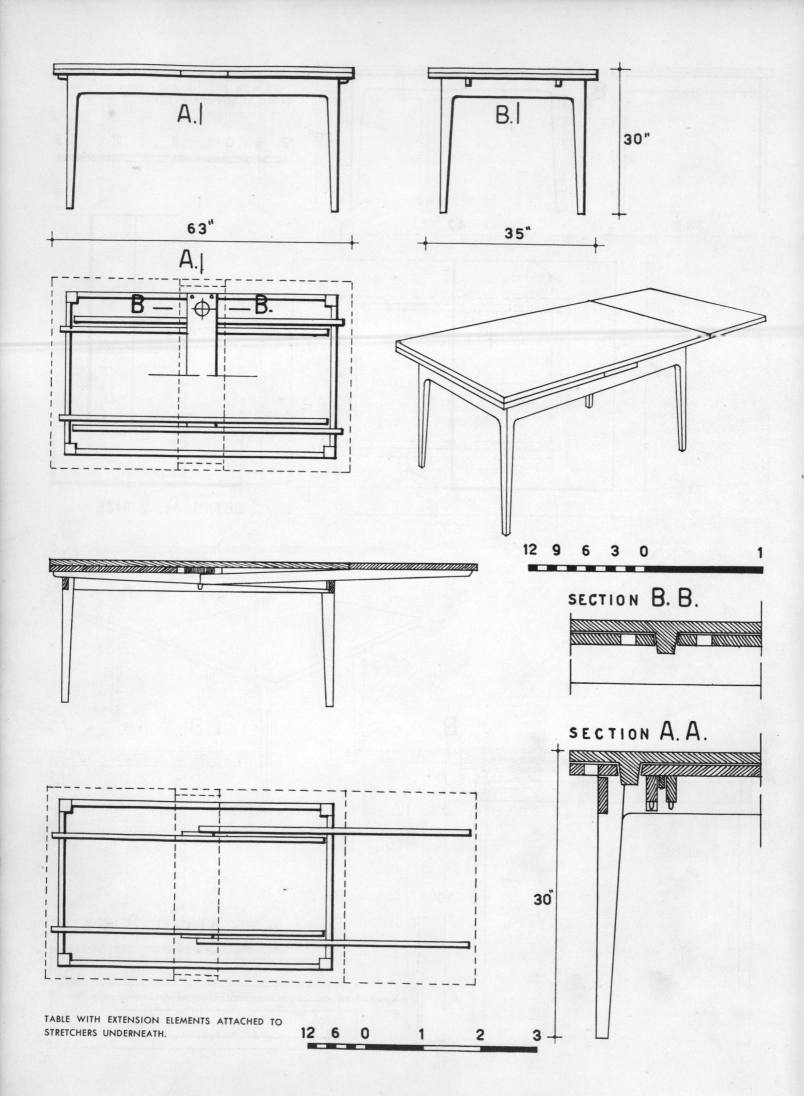

A.I

B.I

30"

63"

A.I

B — B.

35"

SECTION B. B.

SECTION A. A.

12 9 6 3 0   1

30"

TABLE WITH EXTENSION ELEMENTS ATTACHED TO
STRETCHERS UNDERNEATH.

12 6 0   1   2   3

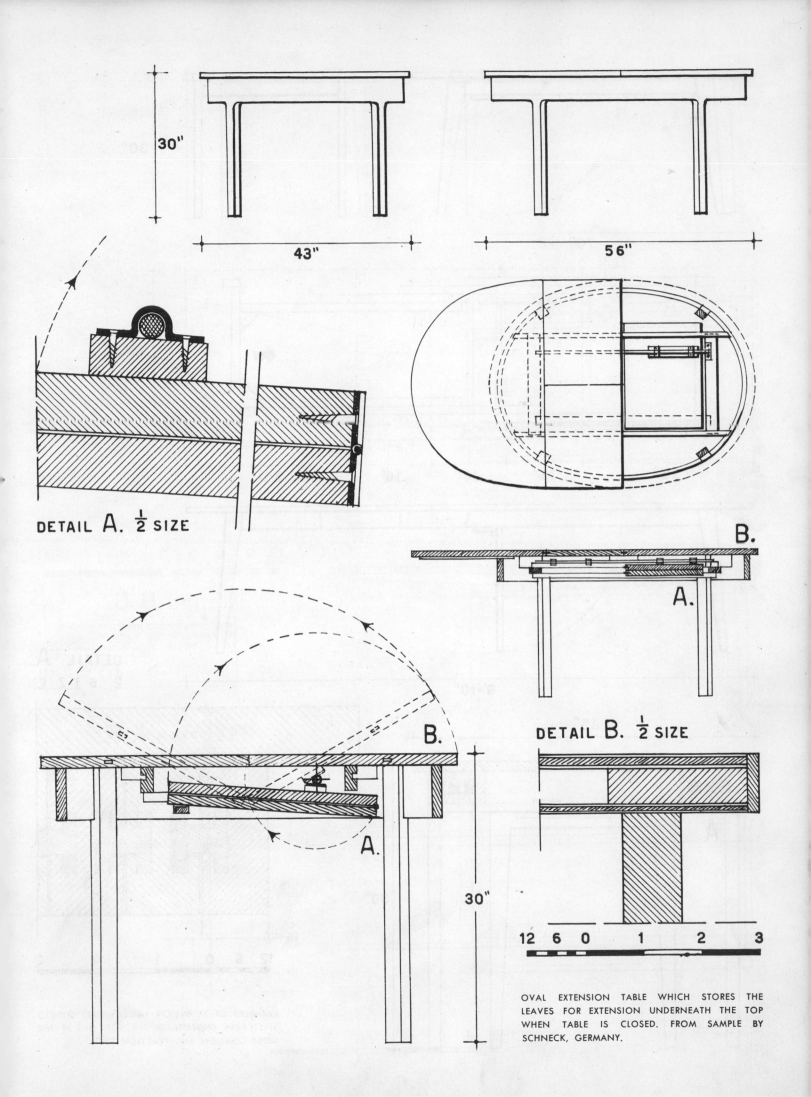

30"

43"

56"

DETAIL A. ½ SIZE

B.

A.

DETAIL B. ½ SIZE

B.

A.

30"

| 12 | 6 | 0 | 1 | 2 | 3 |

OVAL EXTENSION TABLE WHICH STORES THE
LEAVES FOR EXTENSION UNDERNEATH THE TOP
WHEN TABLE IS CLOSED. FROM SAMPLE BY
SCHNECK, GERMANY.

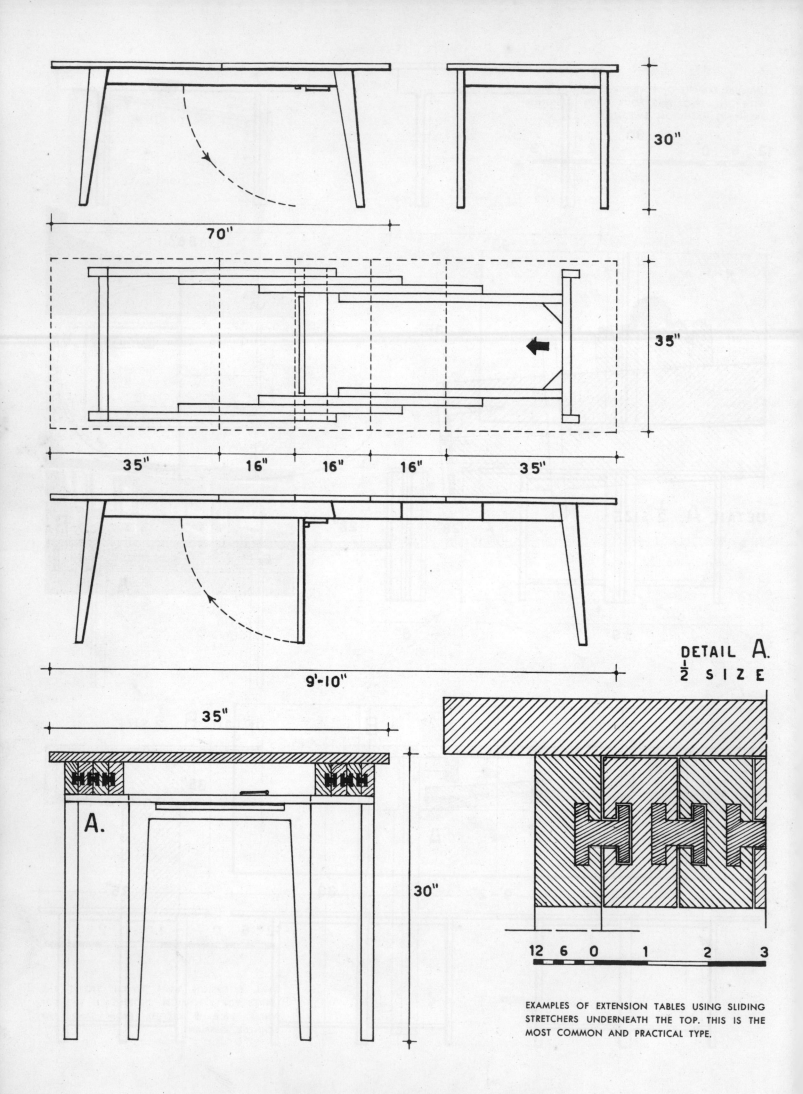

30"

70"

35"

35" 16" 16" 16" 35"

9'-10"

35"

A.

30"

DETAIL A.
½ SIZE

12 6 0 1 2 3

EXAMPLES OF EXTENSION TABLES USING SLIDING
STRETCHERS UNDERNEATH THE TOP. THIS IS THE
MOST COMMON AND PRACTICAL TYPE.

UNUSUAL EXAMPLE OF FOLDING EXTENSION TABLE
WITH ONE, TWO, AND FOUR UNITS, DESIGNED
BY BRUNO MATHSSON, SWEDEN.

12 6 0   1   2   3

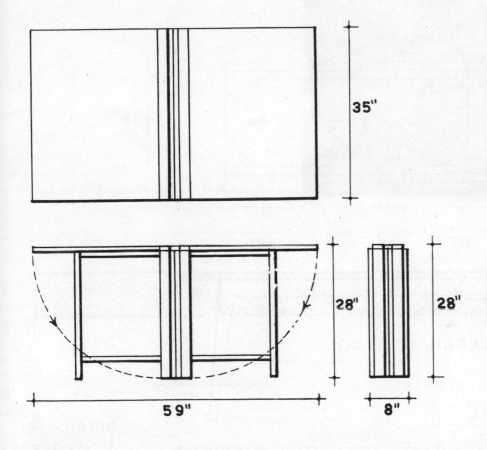

35"

28"

28"

59"

8"

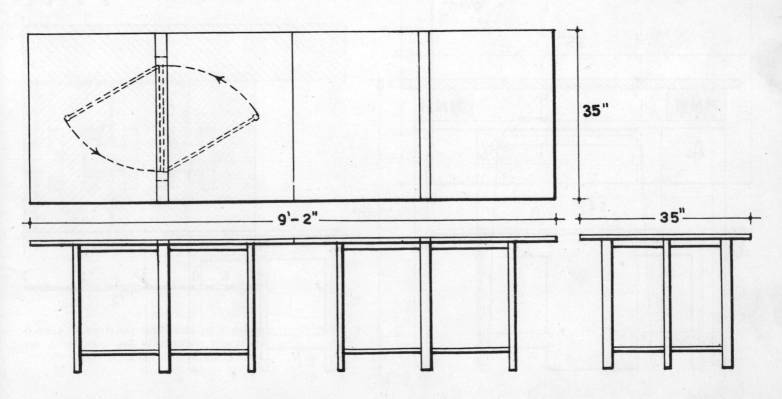

35"

9'-2"

35"

SOLID WOOD FOLDING TABLE DESIGNED BY
GEORGE NELSON, PRODUCED BY HERMAN MILLER,
INC. NOTE HINGES.

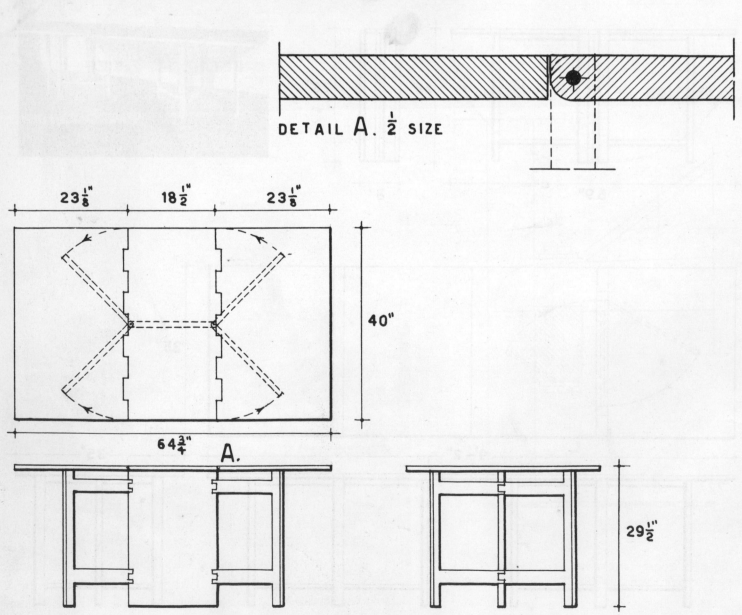

DETAIL A. ½ SIZE

23⅛" 18½" 23⅛"

40"

64¾" A.

29½"

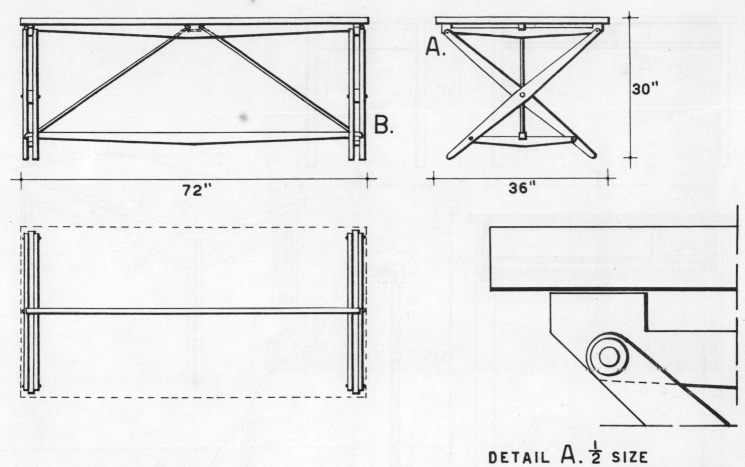

B.

72"

A.

30"

36"

SECTION OF DETAIL B.

DETAIL A. ½ SIZE

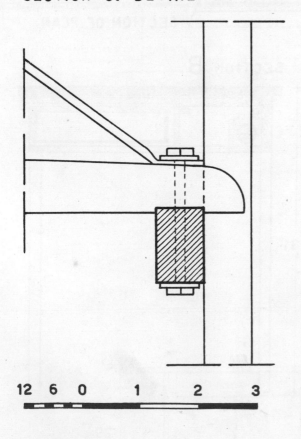

12 6 0   1   2   3

CROSS LEGGED TABLE USING METAL BRACES DE-
SIGNED BY FRANCO ALBINI, ITALY.

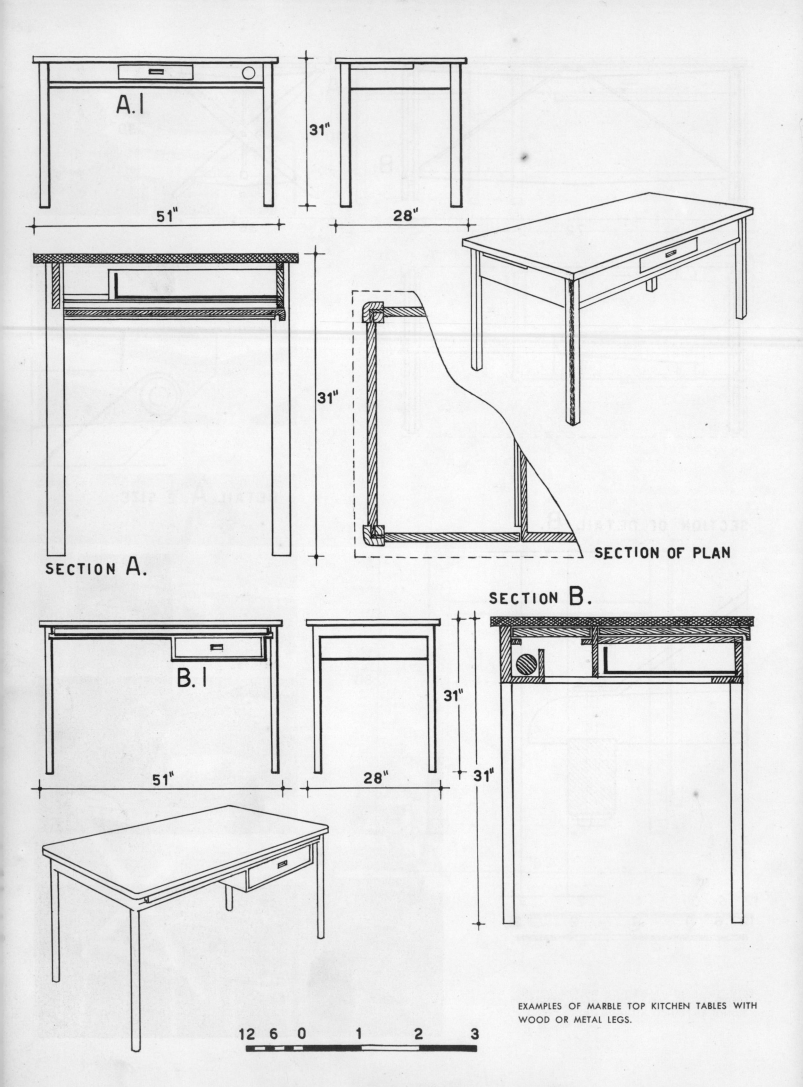

A.I

31"

51"

28"

31"

SECTION A.

SECTION OF PLAN

SECTION B.

B.I

31"

31"

51"

28"

EXAMPLES OF MARBLE TOP KITCHEN TABLES WITH WOOD OR METAL LEGS.

12 6 0   1   2   3

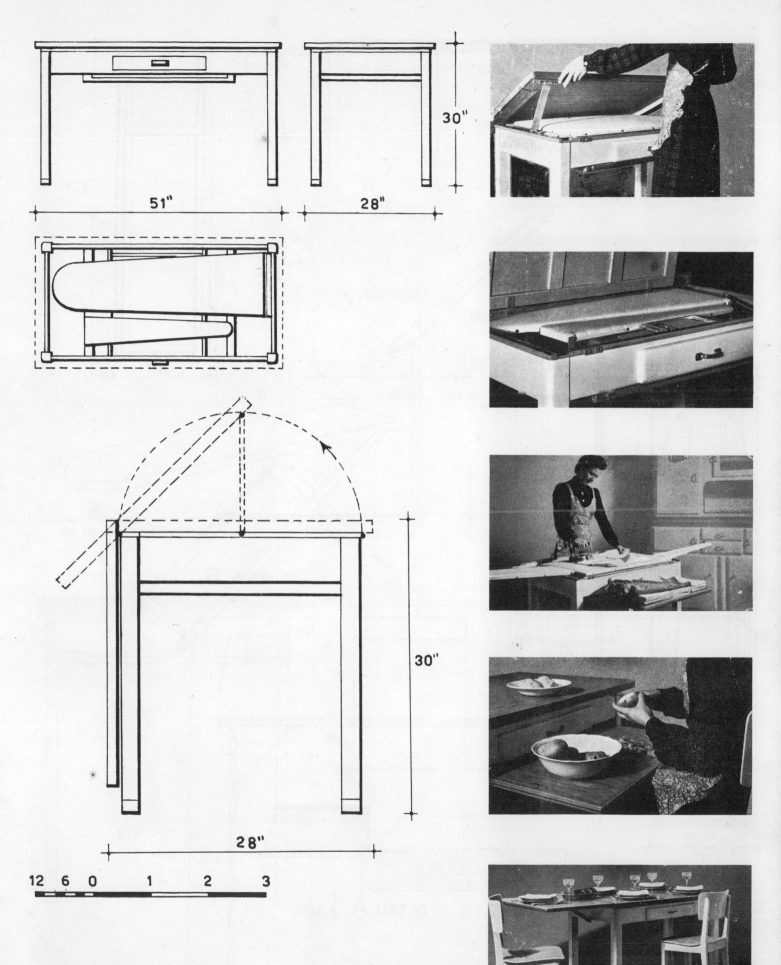

51" 28"

30"

30"

28"

12 6 0 1 2 3

PATENTED KITCHEN TABLE WITH BUILT-IN IRONING
BOARD DESIGNED BY EHDIS, SWITZERLAND.

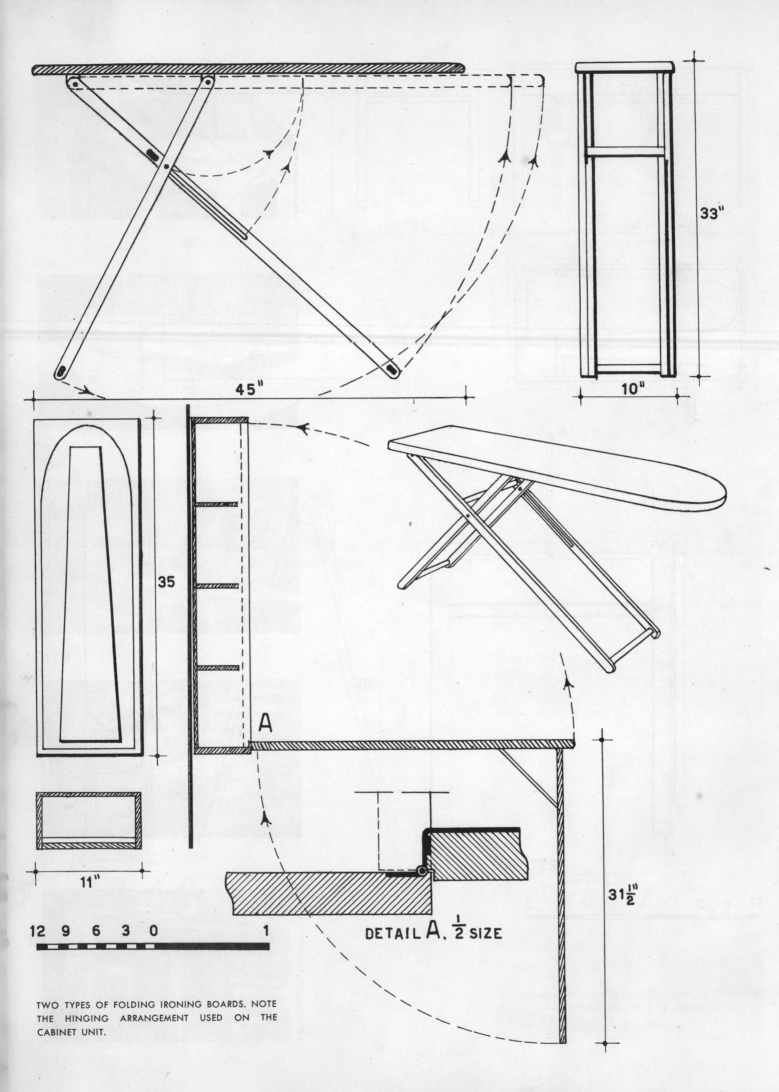

45"

33"

10"

35

11"

31 1/2"

12 9 6 3 0   1

DETAIL A. 1/2 SIZE

A

TWO TYPES OF FOLDING IRONING BOARDS. NOTE
THE HINGING ARRANGEMENT USED ON THE
CABINET UNIT.

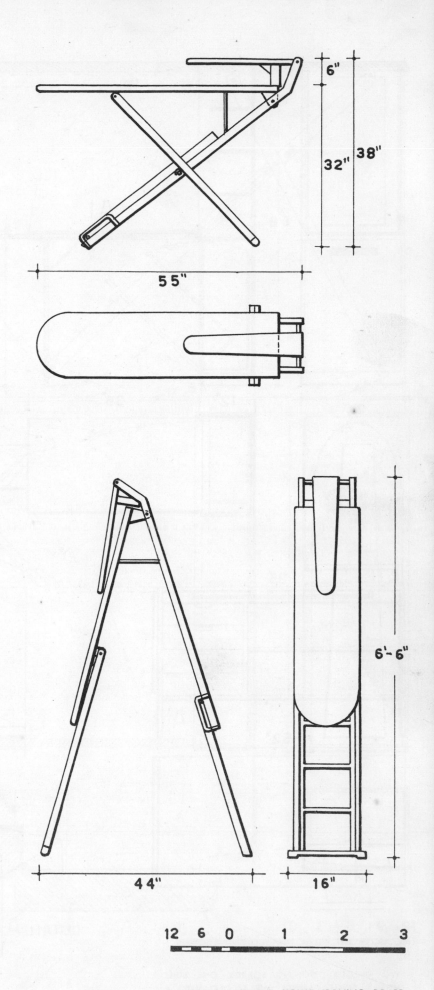

AN IDEAL APARTMENT HOUSE IRONING BOARD WHICH CAN ALSO BE USED AS A STEPLADDER, DESIGNED BY MARIO DAL FABBRO.

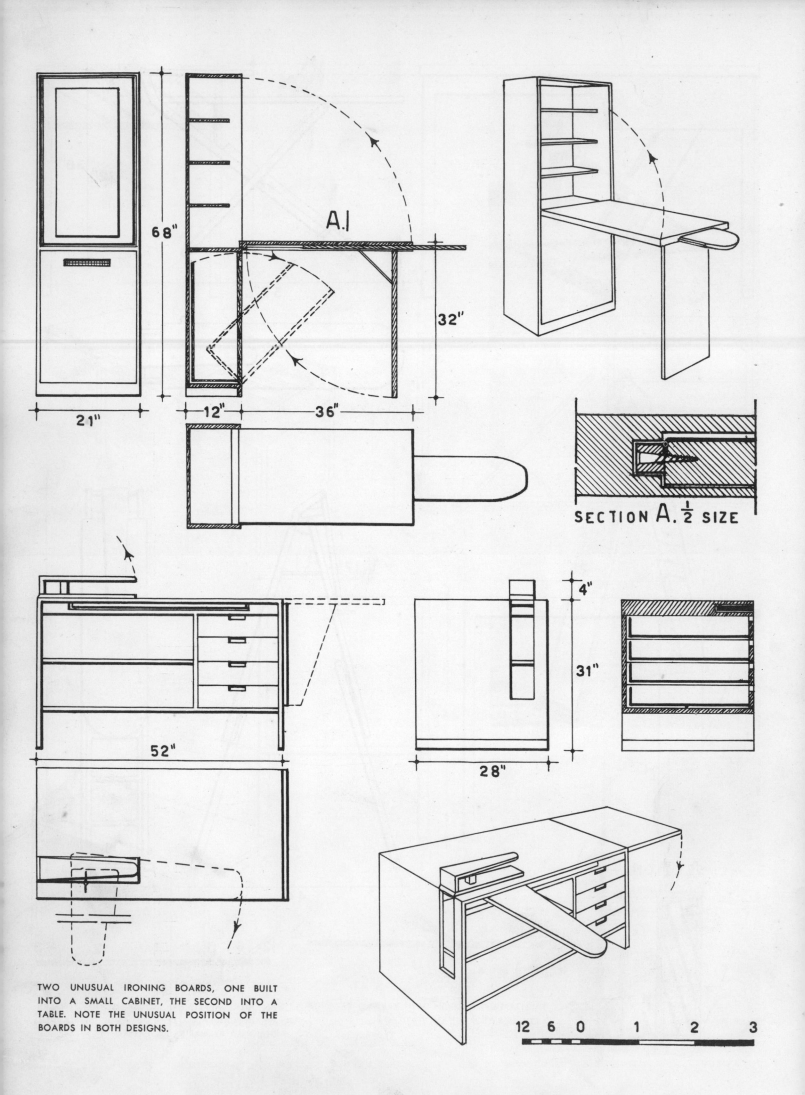

A.I

68"

32"

21"

12"

36"

SECTION A. ½ SIZE

4"

31"

52"

28"

TWO UNUSUAL IRONING BOARDS, ONE BUILT
INTO A SMALL CABINET, THE SECOND INTO A
TABLE. NOTE THE UNUSUAL POSITION OF THE
BOARDS IN BOTH DESIGNS.

12 6 0 1 2 3

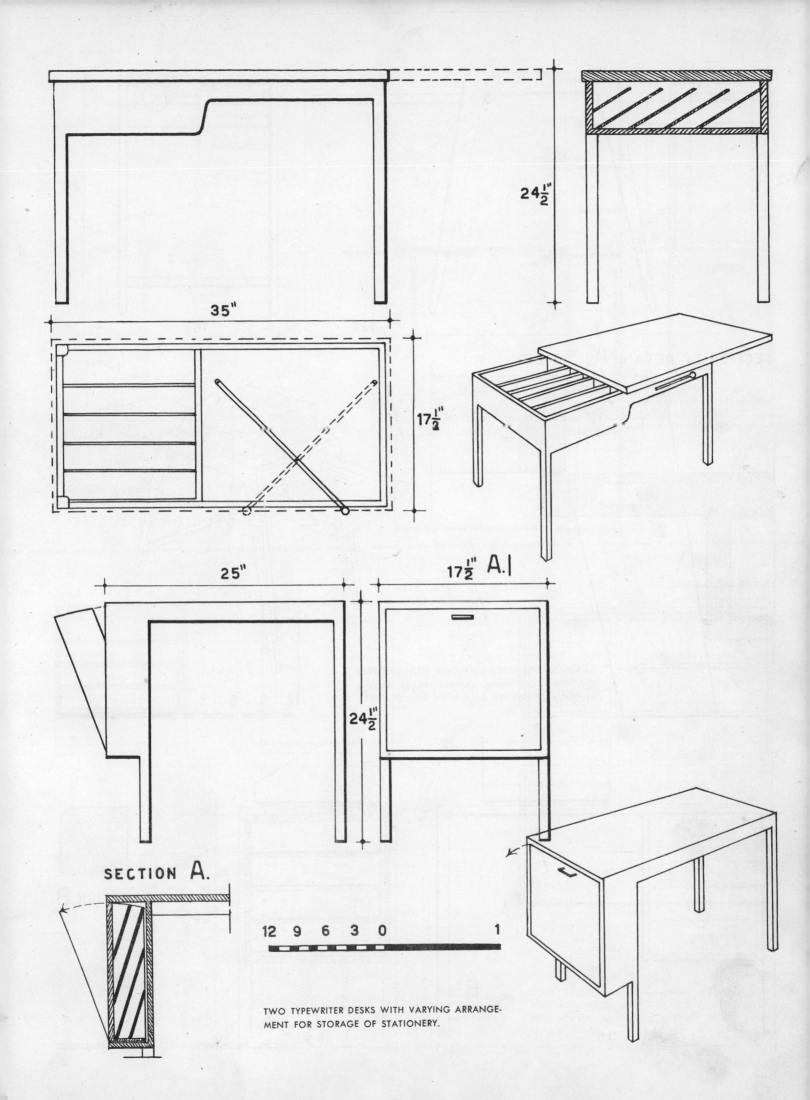

35"

24½"

17½"

A.1

25"

17½"

24½"

SECTION A.

12 9 6 3 0   1

TWO TYPEWRITER DESKS WITH VARYING ARRANGE-
MENT FOR STORAGE OF STATIONERY.

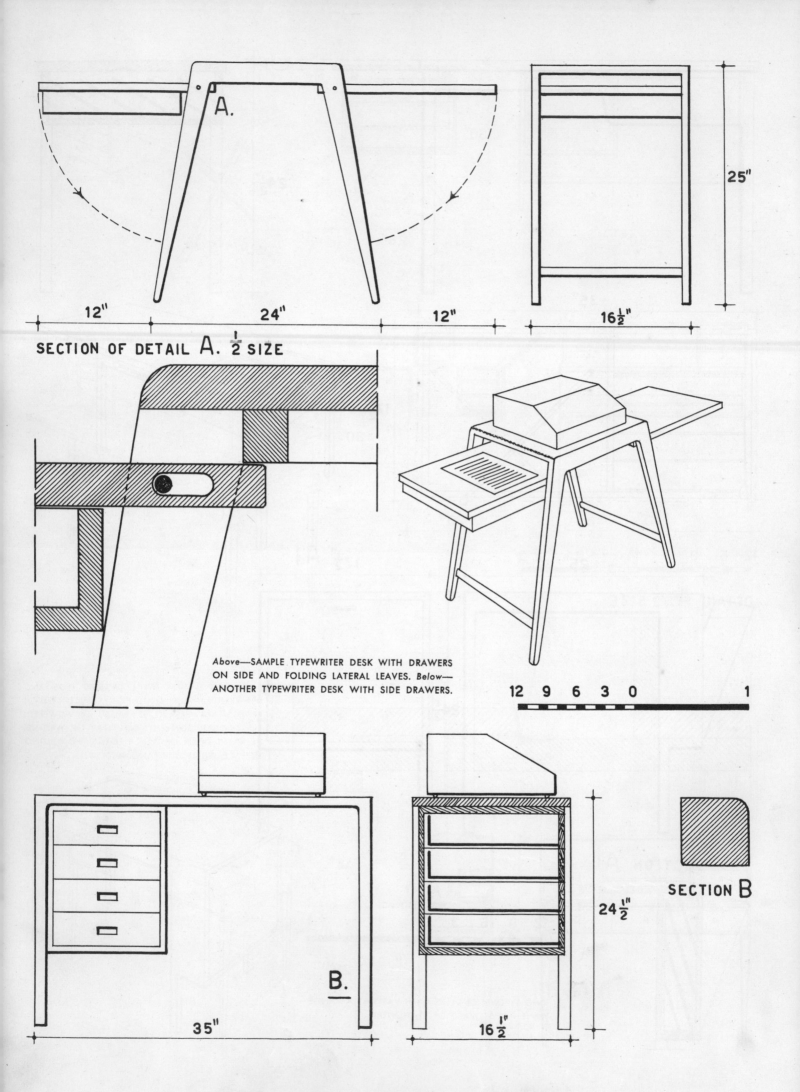

A.

25"

12"   24"   12"   16½"

SECTION OF DETAIL A. ½ SIZE

Above—SAMPLE TYPEWRITER DESK WITH DRAWERS
ON SIDE AND FOLDING LATERAL LEAVES. *Below*—
ANOTHER TYPEWRITER DESK WITH SIDE DRAWERS.

12 9 6 3 0   1

B.

SECTION B

35"   16½"   24½"

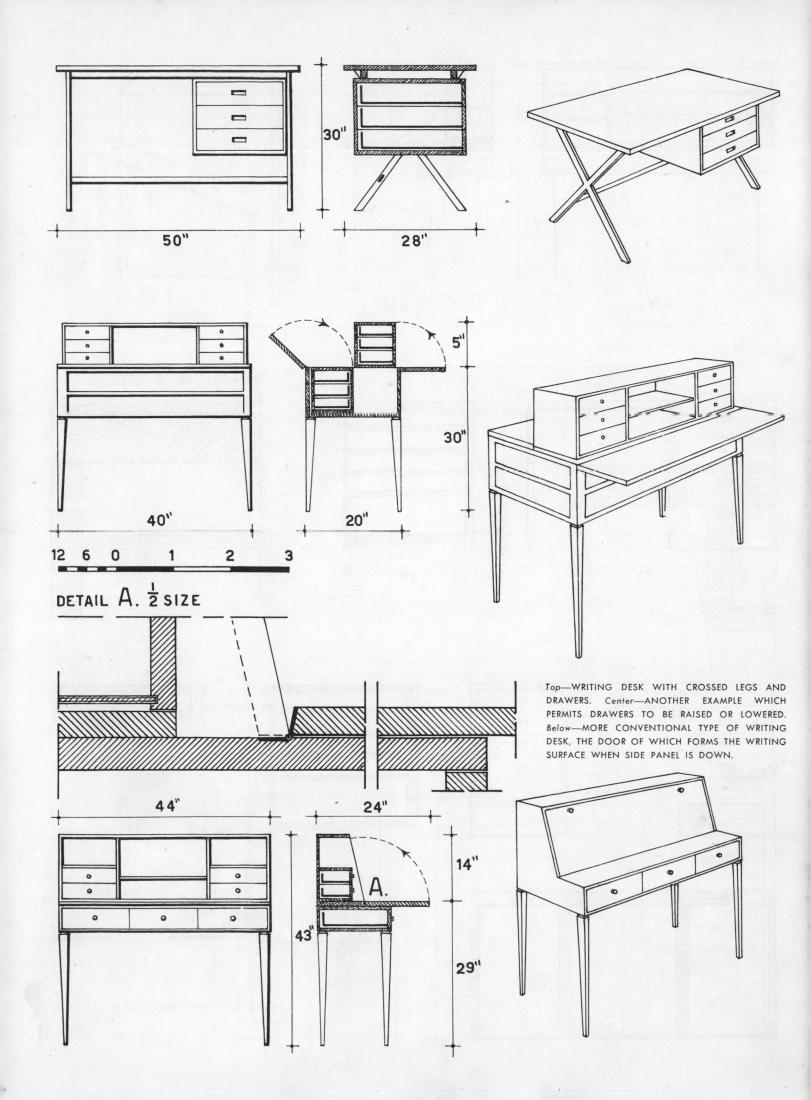

50"

30"

28"

40"

5"

30"

20"

12 6 0 1 2 3

DETAIL A. ½ SIZE

44"

24"

14"

43"

29"

Top—WRITING DESK WITH CROSSED LEGS AND DRAWERS. *Center*—ANOTHER EXAMPLE WHICH PERMITS DRAWERS TO BE RAISED OR LOWERED. *Below*—MORE CONVENTIONAL TYPE OF WRITING DESK, THE DOOR OF WHICH FORMS THE WRITING SURFACE WHEN SIDE PANEL IS DOWN.

A.

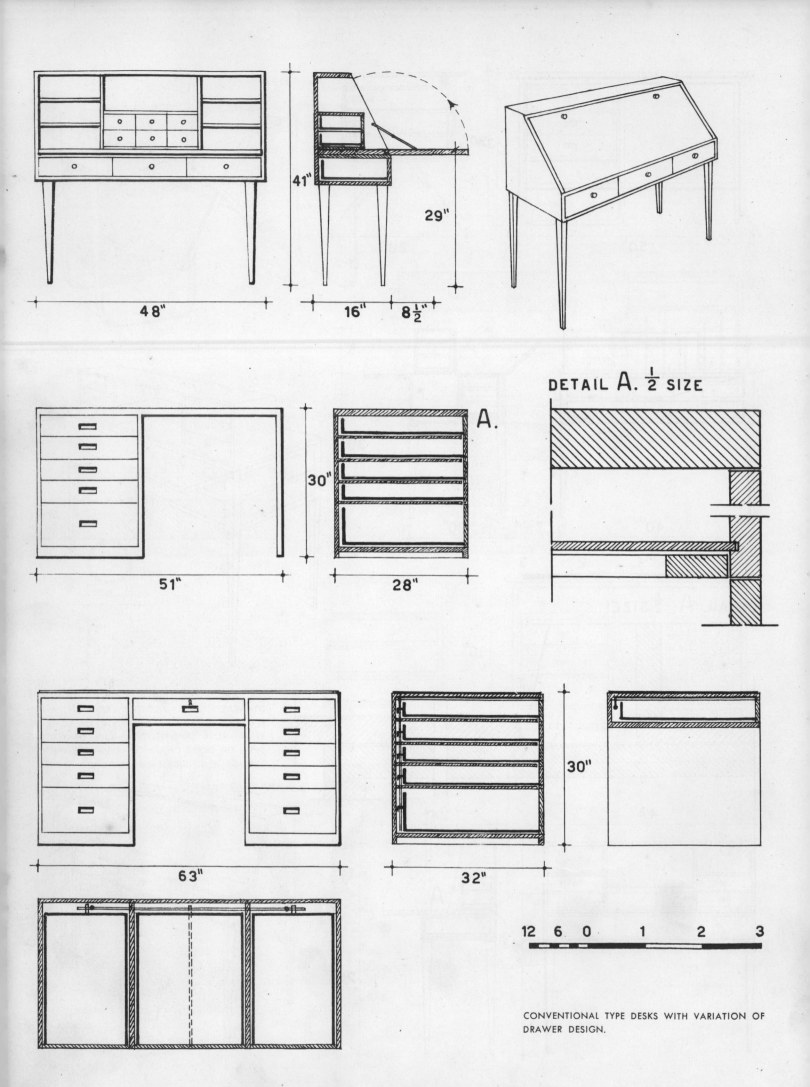

41"

29"

48"

16" 8½"

30"

51"

A.

28"

DETAIL A. ½ SIZE

63"

30"

32"

12 6 0 1 2 3

CONVENTIONAL TYPE DESKS WITH VARIATION OF
DRAWER DESIGN.

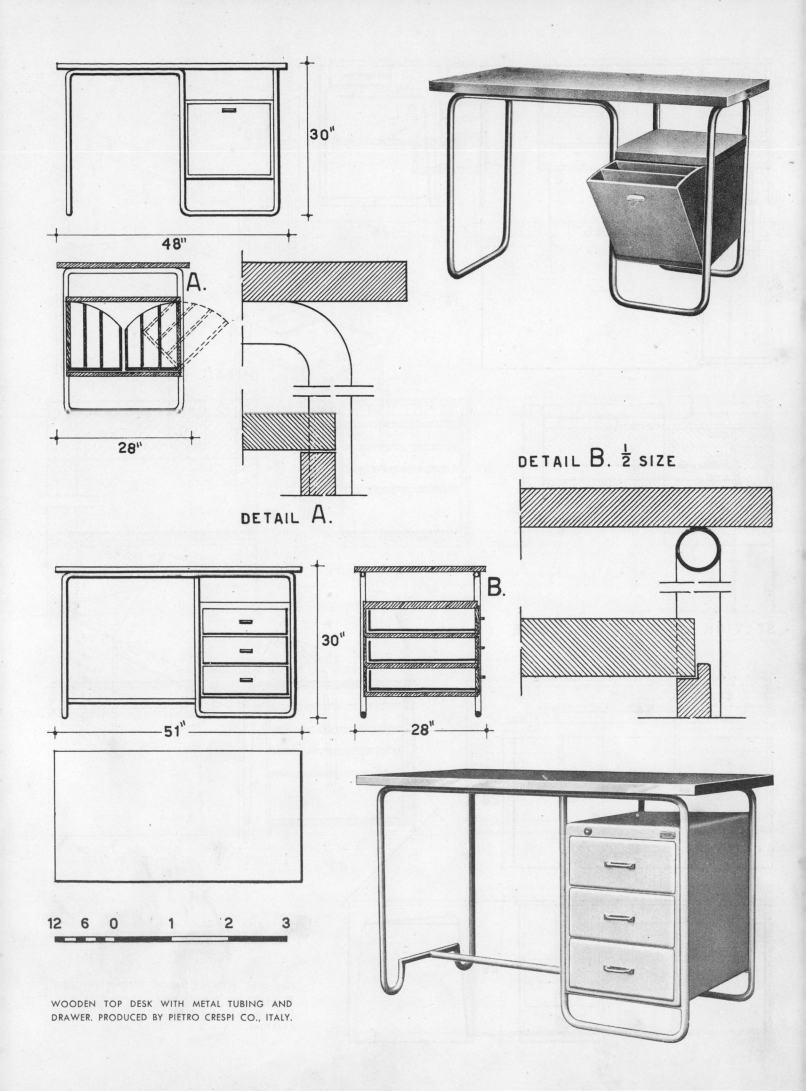

30"

48"

A.

28"

DETAIL A.

DETAIL B. ½ SIZE

B.

30"

51"

28"

12 6 0 1 2 3

WOODEN TOP DESK WITH METAL TUBING AND
DRAWER. PRODUCED BY PIETRO CRESPI CO., ITALY.

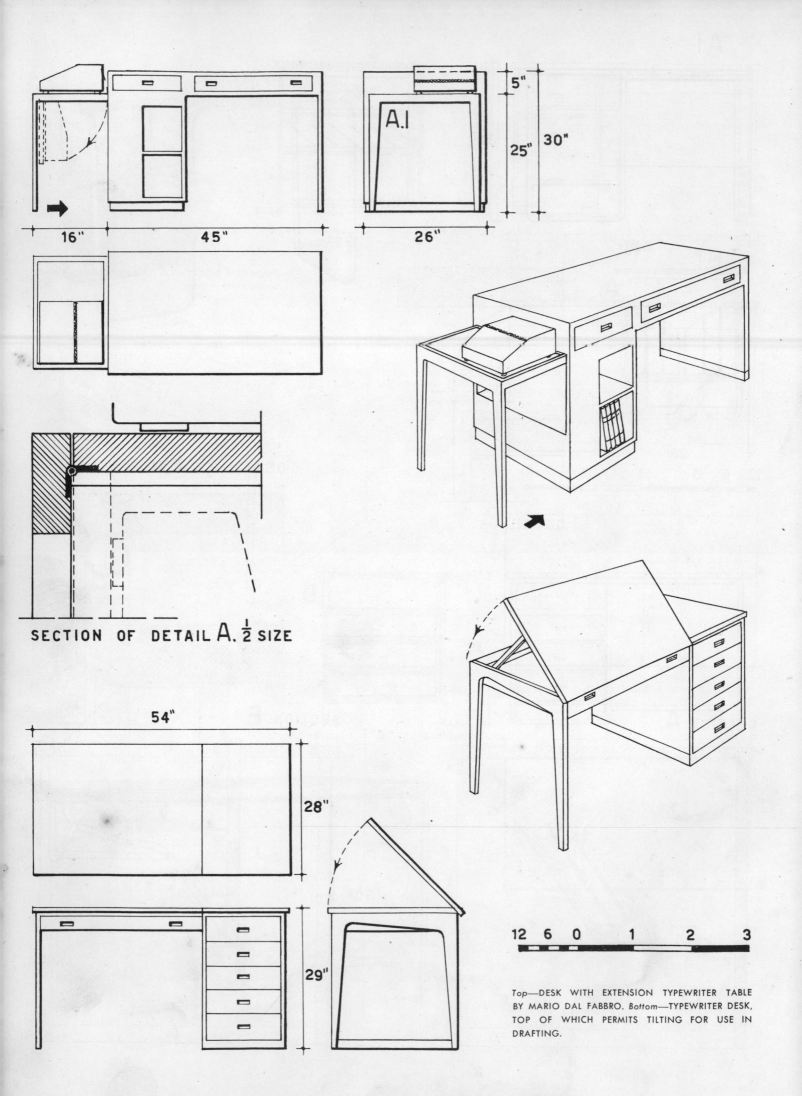

SECTION OF DETAIL A. ½ SIZE

16" **45"** **26"** **5"** **25"** **30"**

A.I

54" **28"** **29"**

12 6 0 1 2 3

Top—DESK WITH EXTENSION TYPEWRITER TABLE BY MARIO DAL FABBRO. *Bottom*—TYPEWRITER DESK, TOP OF WHICH PERMITS TILTING FOR USE IN DRAFTING.

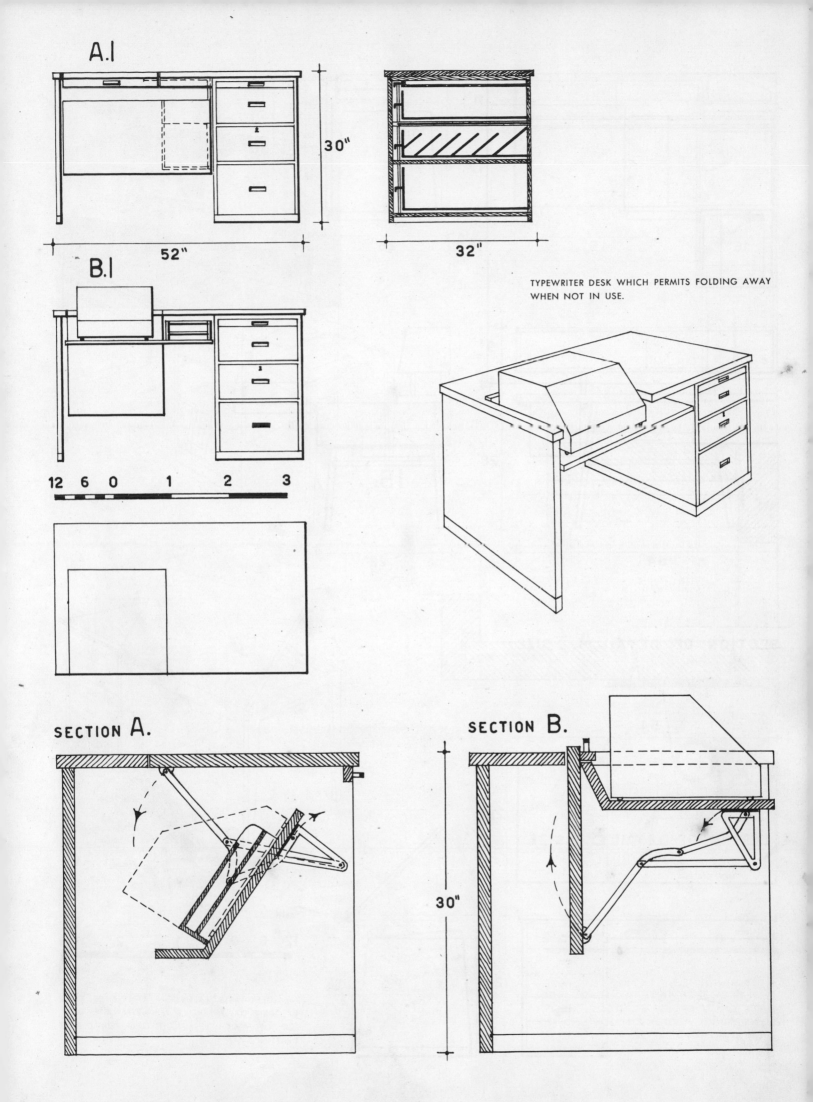

A.I

30"

52"

32"

B.I

12 6 0 1 2 3

TYPEWRITER DESK WHICH PERMITS FOLDING AWAY WHEN NOT IN USE.

SECTION A.

SECTION B.

30"

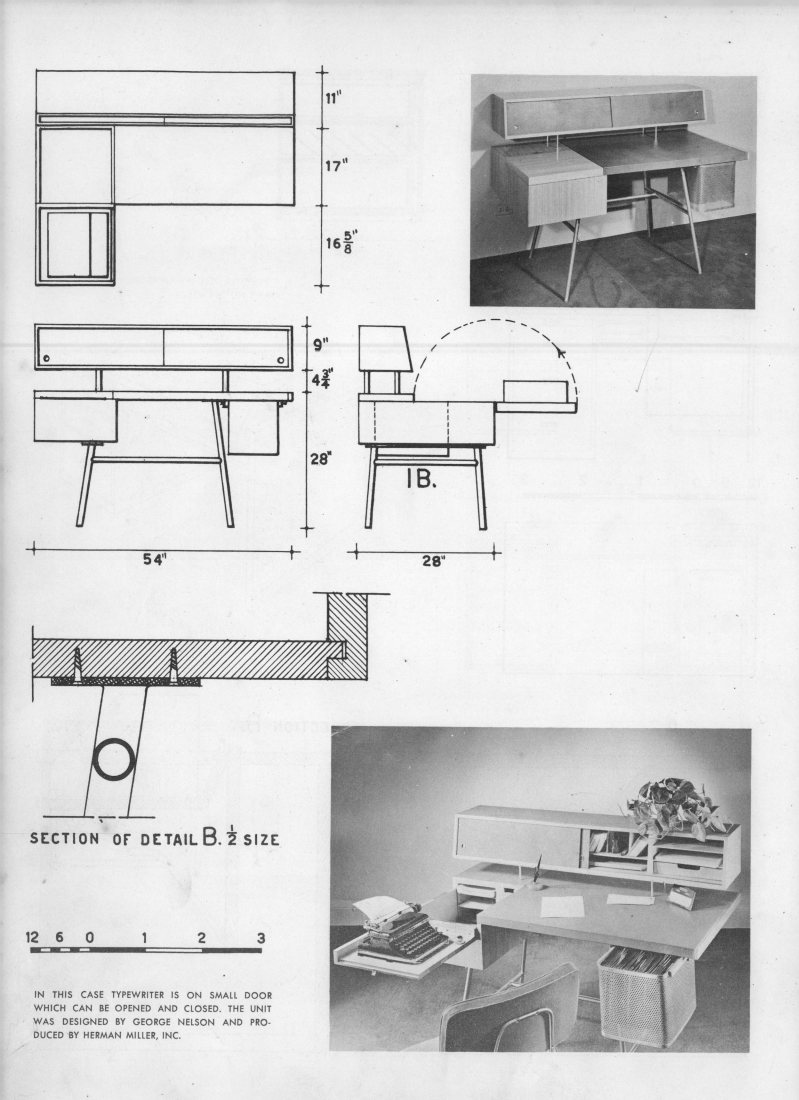

11"

17"

16 5/8"

9"

4 3/4"

28"

54"

28"

1B.

SECTION OF DETAIL B. 1/2 SIZE

12 6 0   0   1   2   3

IN THIS CASE TYPEWRITER IS ON SMALL DOOR
WHICH CAN BE OPENED AND CLOSED. THE UNIT
WAS DESIGNED BY GEORGE NELSON AND PRO-
DUCED BY HERMAN MILLER, INC.

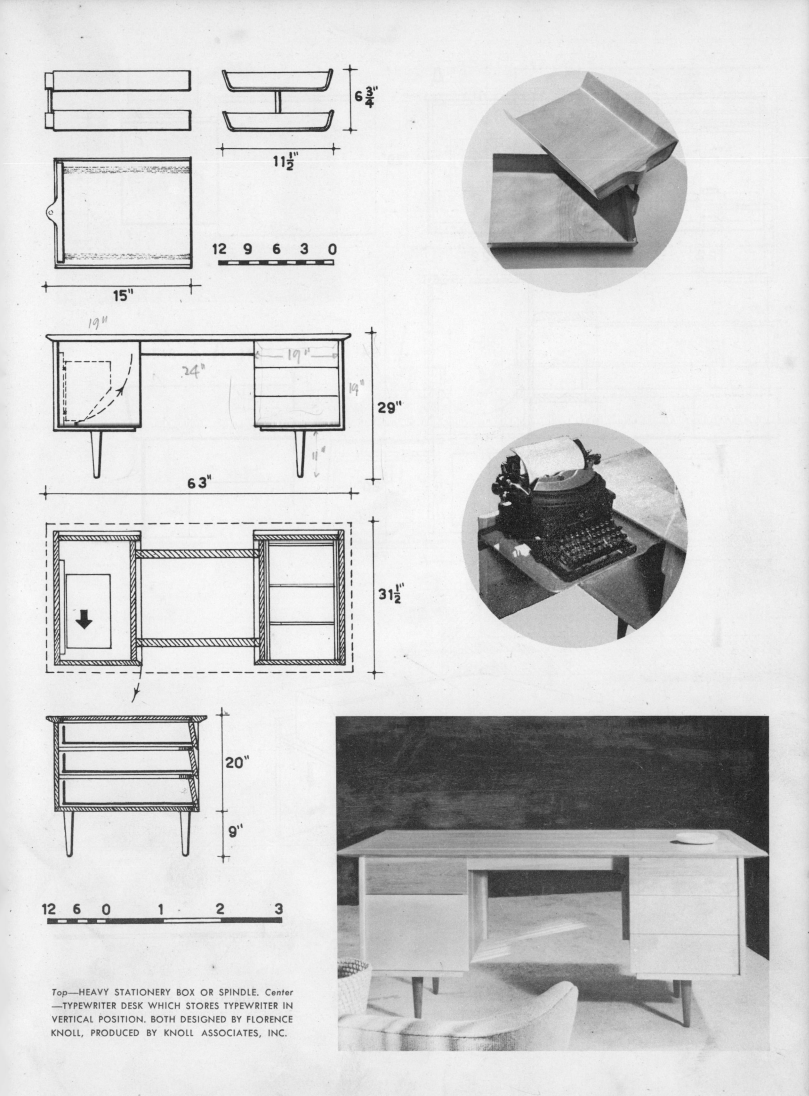

6 ¾"

11 ½"

12 9 6 3 0

15"

19"

24"

19"

19"

29"

11"

63"

31 ½"

20"

9"

12 6 0 1 2 3

Top—HEAVY STATIONERY BOX OR SPINDLE. *Center*—TYPEWRITER DESK WHICH STORES TYPEWRITER IN VERTICAL POSITION. BOTH DESIGNED BY FLORENCE KNOLL, PRODUCED BY KNOLL ASSOCIATES, INC.

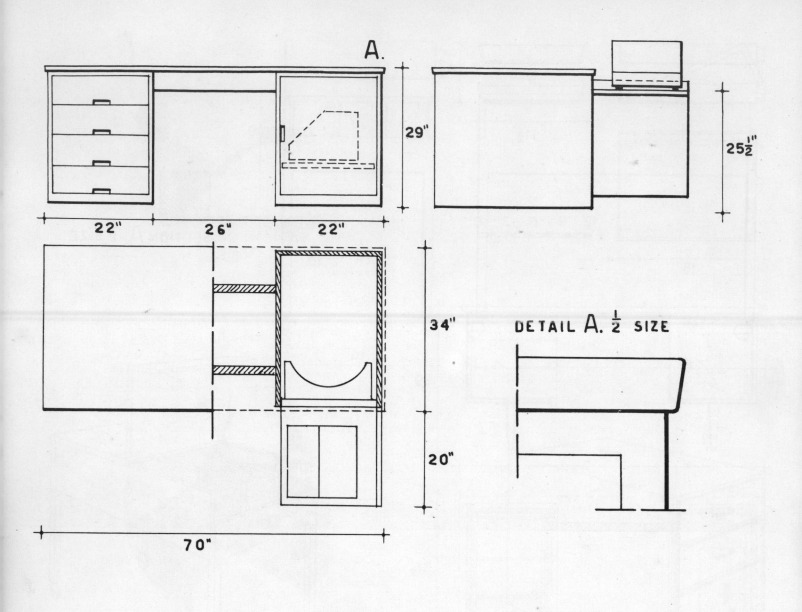

A.

29"

25½"

22"   26"   22"

34"

20"

70"

DETAIL A. ½ SIZE

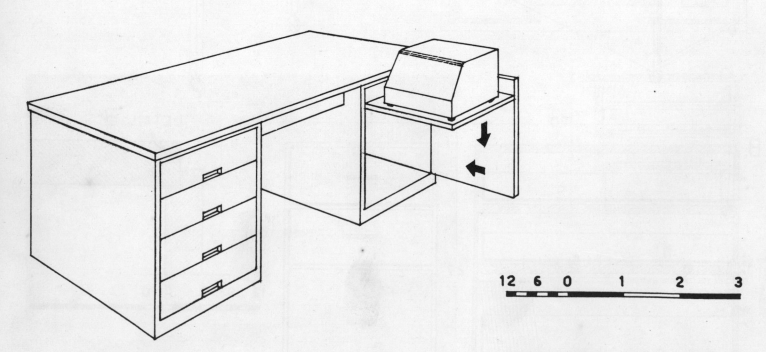

12 6 0   1   2   3

DESK WITH ATTACHED TYPEWRITER WHICH RE-
MAINS IN HORIZONTAL POSITION.

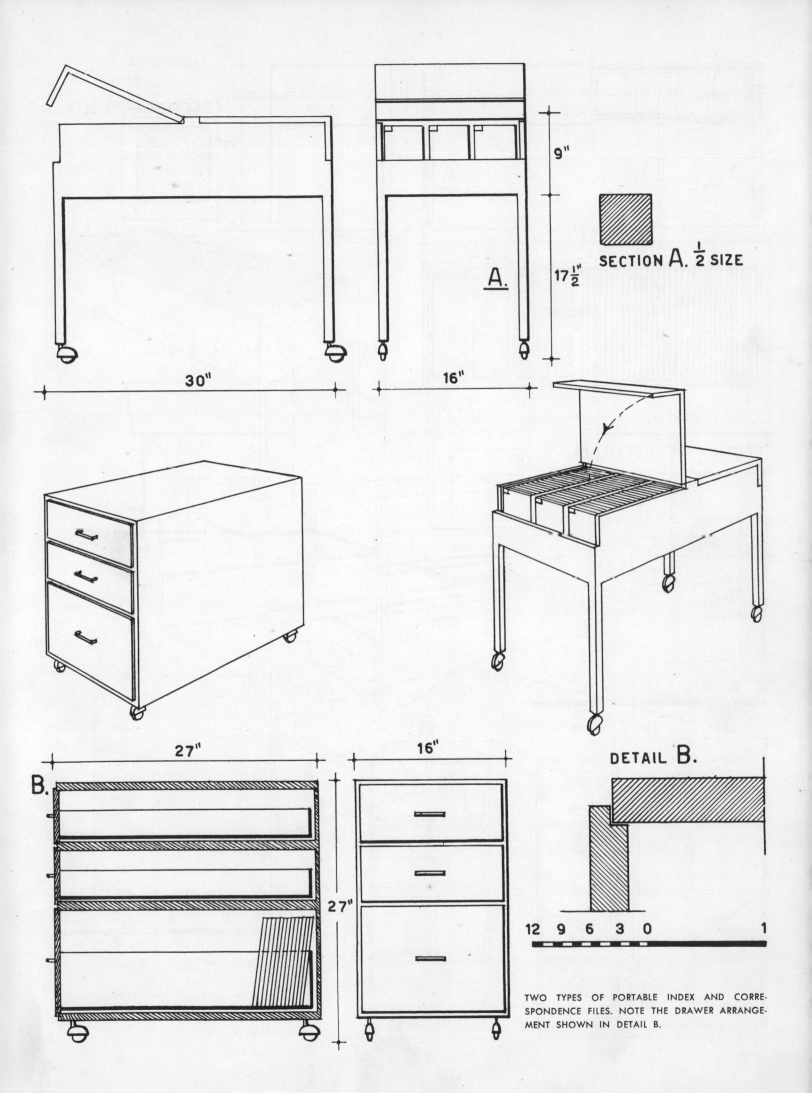

9"

17 1/2"

30"

16"

A.

SECTION A. 1/2 SIZE

27"

B.

16"

27"

DETAIL B.

12 9 6 3 0   1

TWO TYPES OF PORTABLE INDEX AND CORRE-
SPONDENCE FILES. NOTE THE DRAWER ARRANGE-
MENT SHOWN IN DETAIL B.

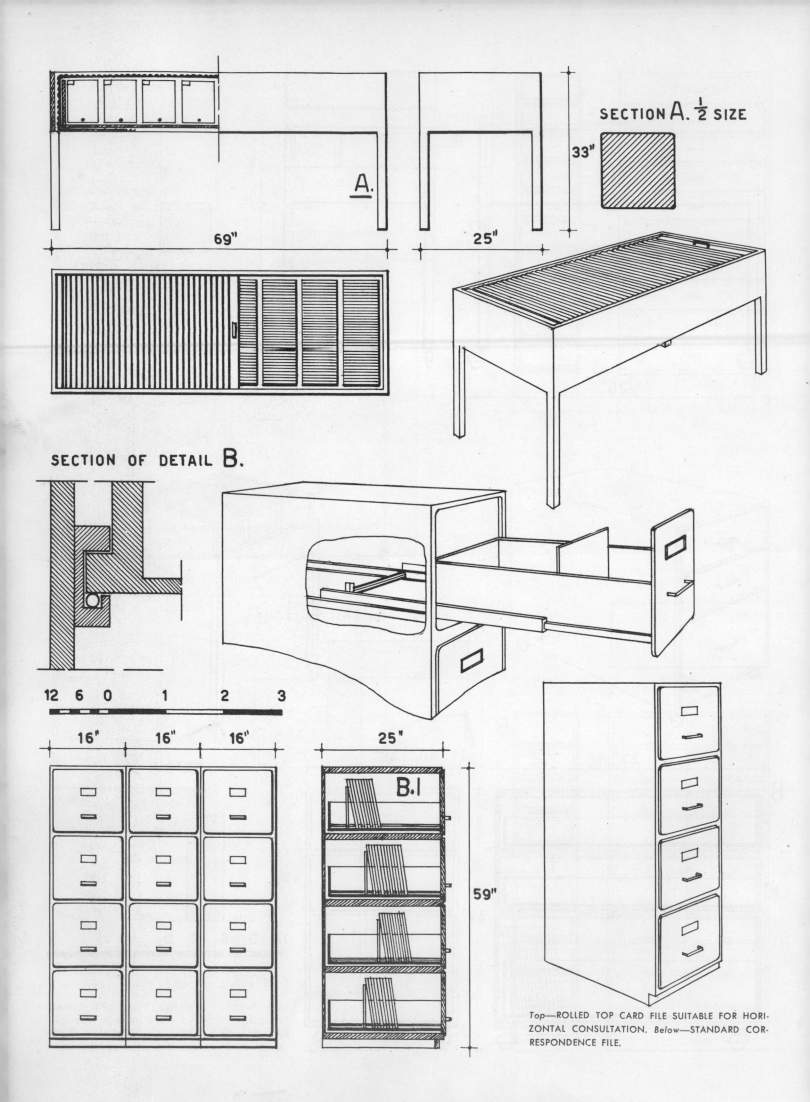

SECTION A. ½ SIZE

33"

69"

25"

A.

SECTION OF DETAIL B.

12 6 0 1 2 3

16" 16" 16"

25"

B.1

59"

Top—ROLLED TOP CARD FILE SUITABLE FOR HORIZONTAL CONSULTATION. *Below*—STANDARD CORRESPONDENCE FILE.

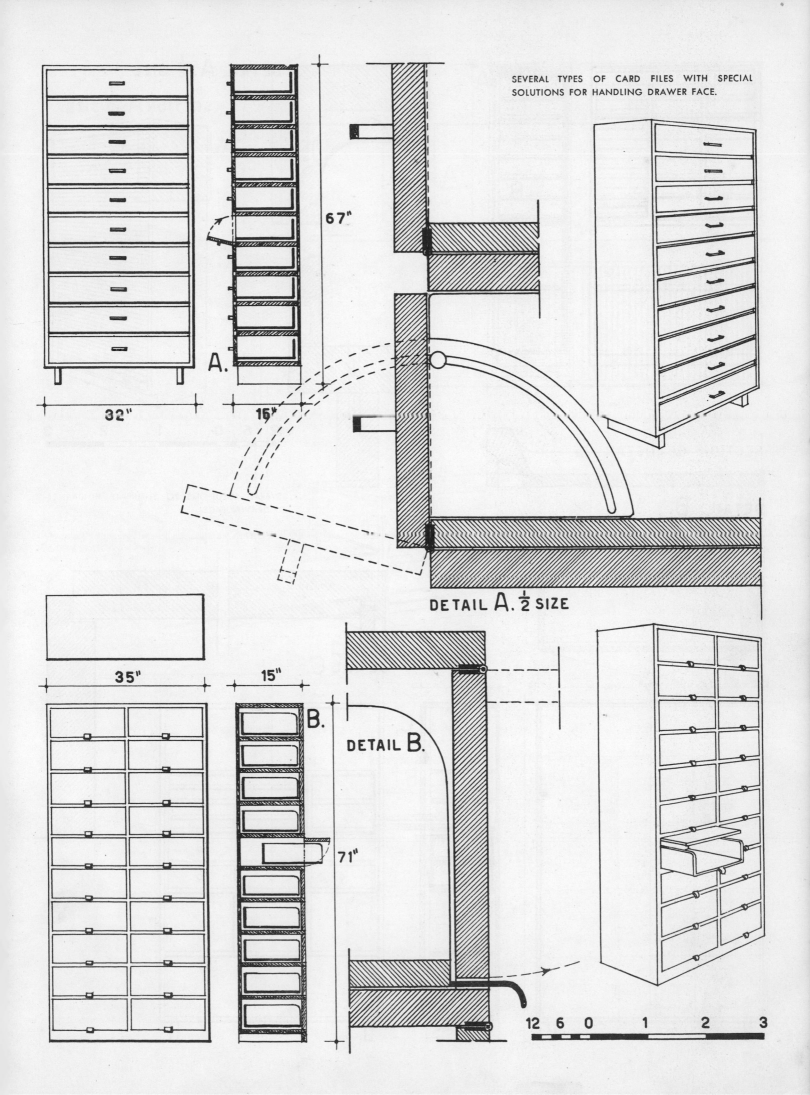

SEVERAL TYPES OF CARD FILES WITH SPECIAL
SOLUTIONS FOR HANDLING DRAWER FACE.

A.

32"

15"

67"

DETAIL A. ½ SIZE

35"

15"

B.

DETAIL B.

71"

12 6 0 1 2 3

85

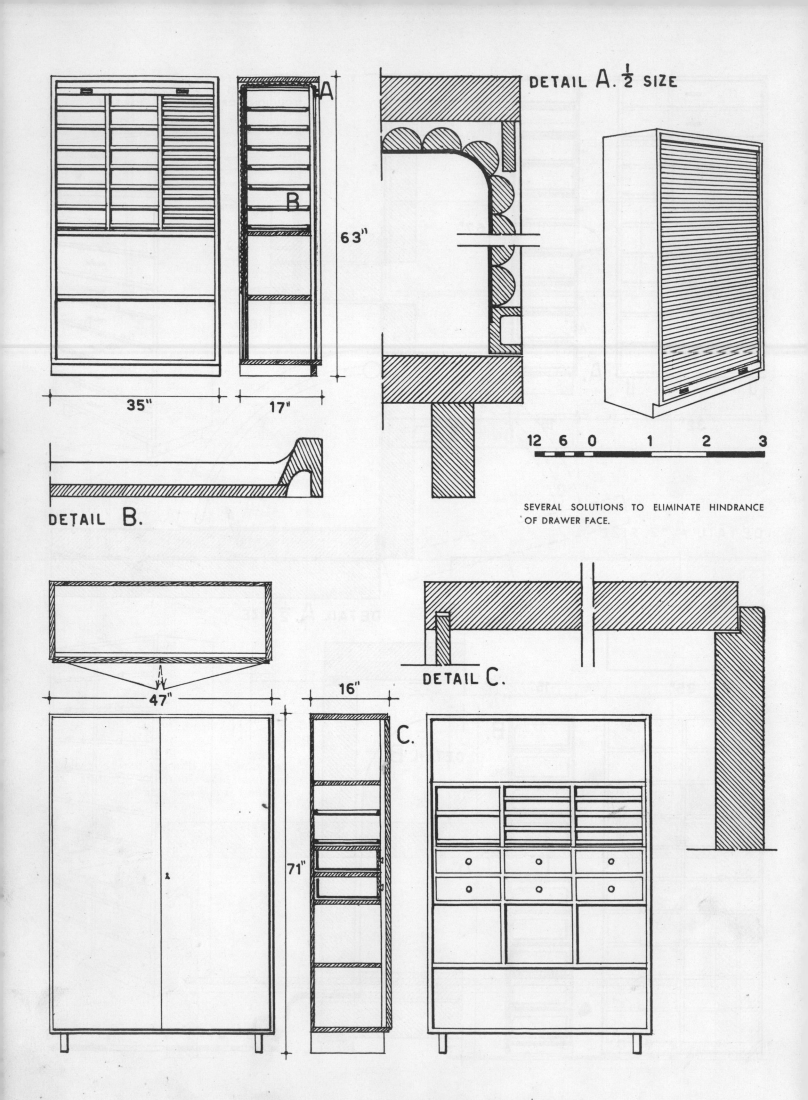

DETAIL A. ½ SIZE

63"

35"   17"

DETAIL B.

12 6 0   1   2   3

SEVERAL SOLUTIONS TO ELIMINATE HINDRANCE
OF DRAWER FACE.

DETAIL C.

47"   16"

71"

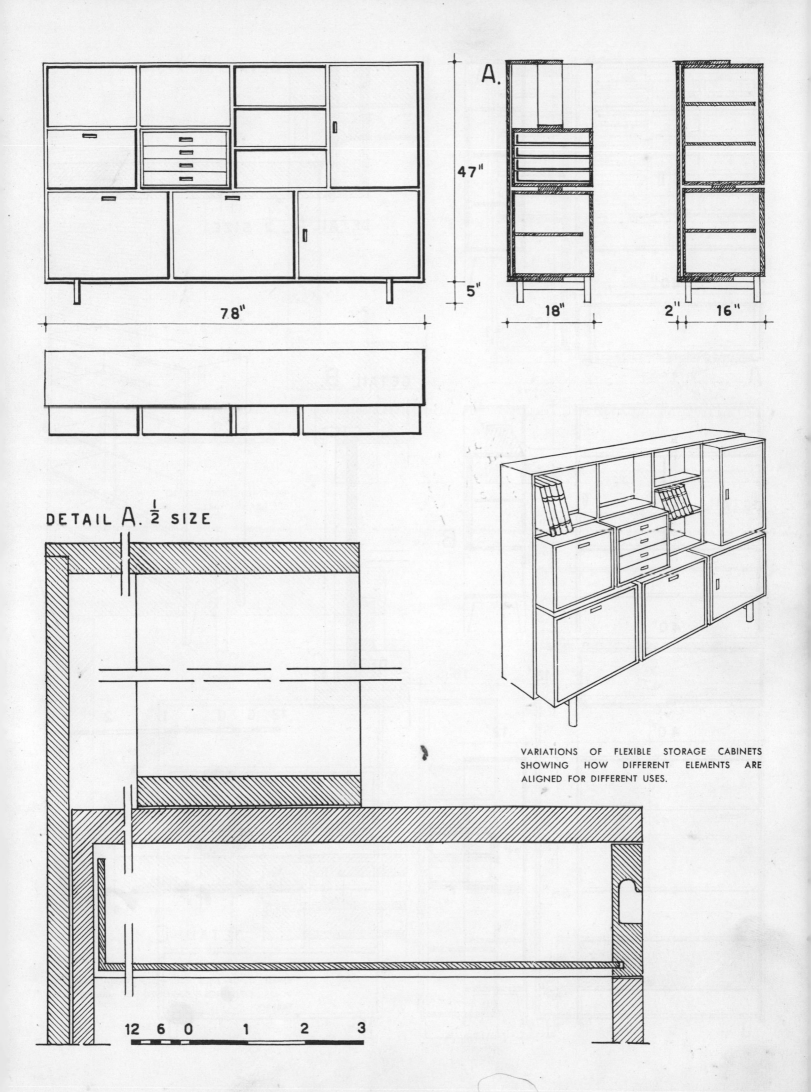

A.

47"

5"

78"

18"

2" 16"

DETAIL A. $\frac{1}{2}$ SIZE

VARIATIONS OF FLEXIBLE STORAGE CABINETS
SHOWING HOW DIFFERENT ELEMENTS ARE
ALIGNED FOR DIFFERENT USES.

12 6 0 1 2 3

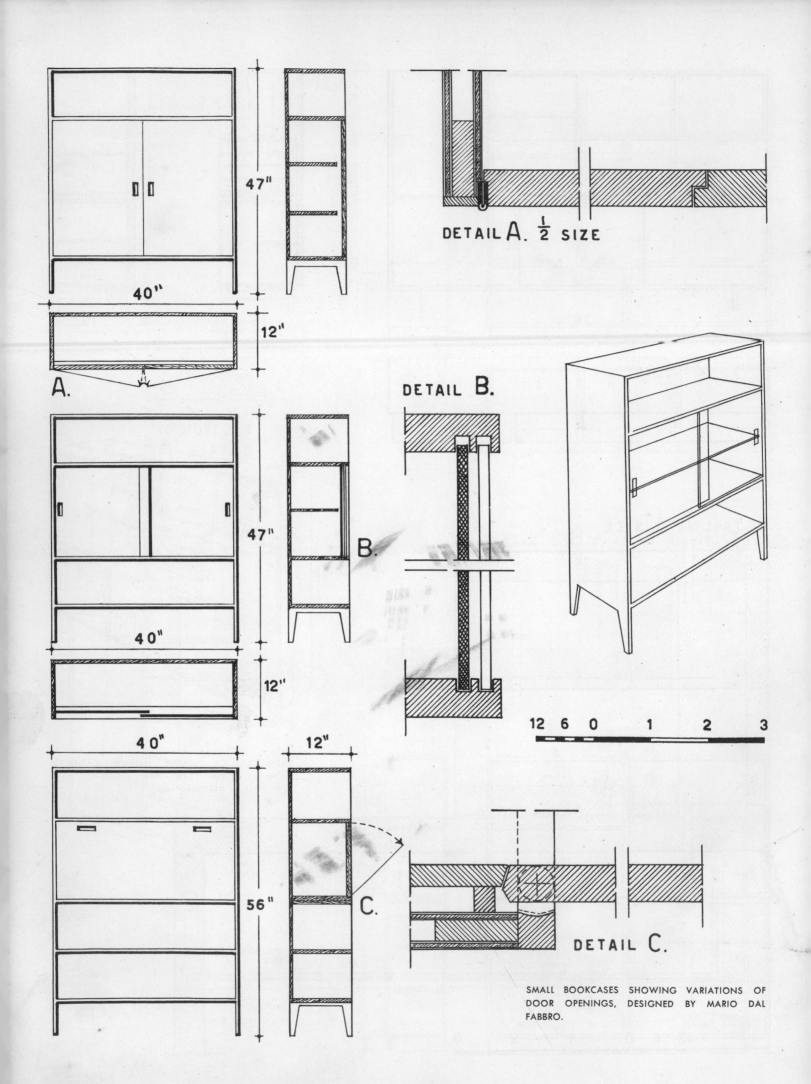

47"

40"

12"

A.

47"

40"

12"

B.

40"

56"

12"

C.

DETAIL A. $\frac{1}{2}$ SIZE

DETAIL B.

12 6 0 1 2 3

DETAIL C.

SMALL BOOKCASES SHOWING VARIATIONS OF
DOOR OPENINGS, DESIGNED BY MARIO DAL
FABBRO.

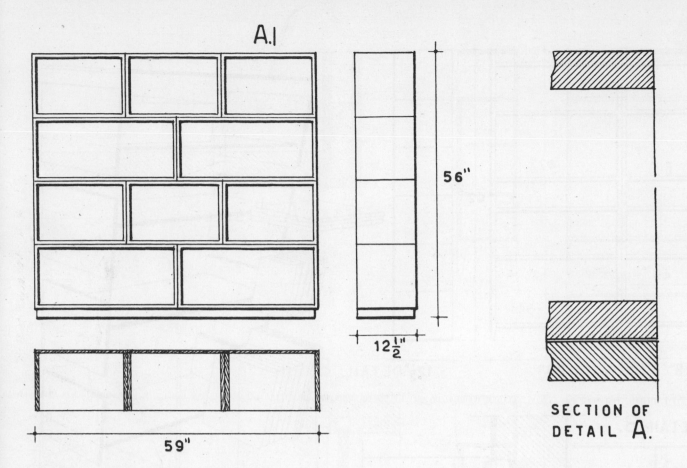

A.1

56"

12½"

59"

SECTION OF
DETAIL A.

SECTION OF DETAIL B. ½ SIZE

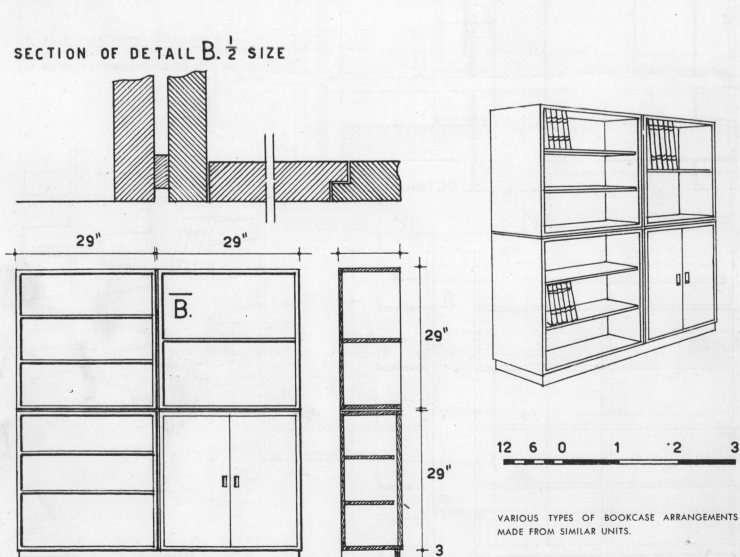

29"   29"

B.

29"

29"

3

12 6 0   1   2   3

VARIOUS TYPES OF BOOKCASE ARRANGEMENTS
MADE FROM SIMILAR UNITS.

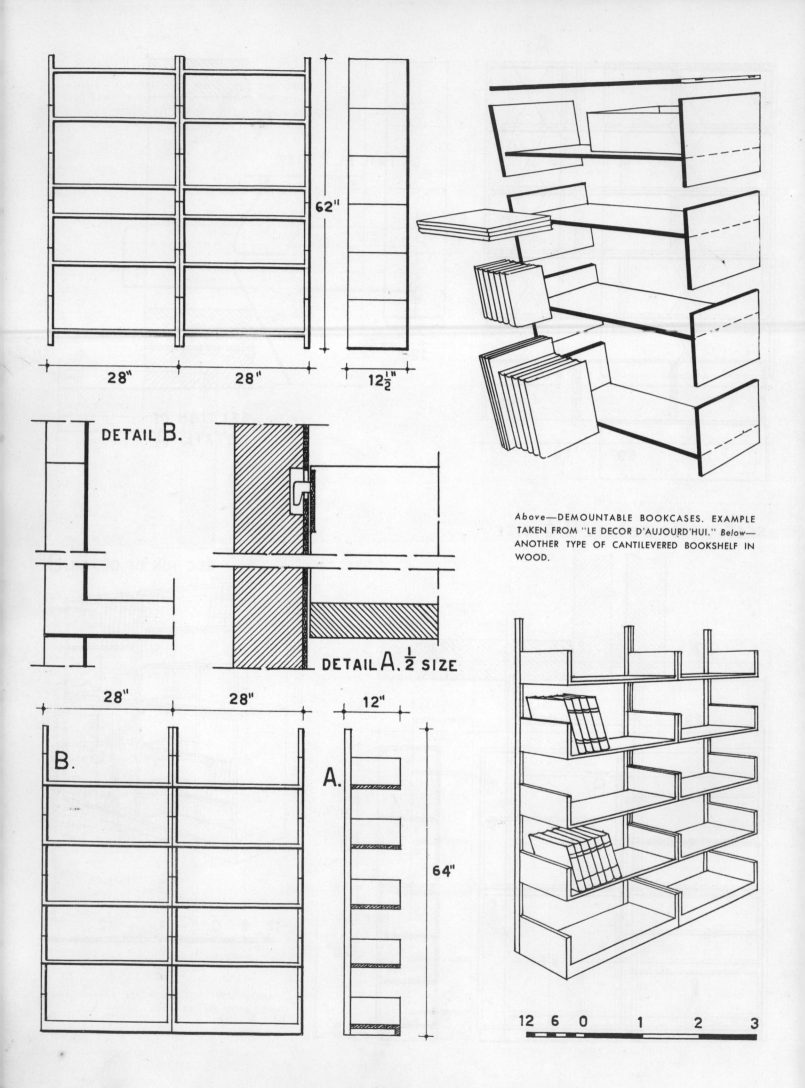

62"

28"   28"   12½"

DETAIL B.

DETAIL A. ½ SIZE

28"   28"   12"

B.   A.   64"

Above—DEMOUNTABLE BOOKCASES. EXAMPLE TAKEN FROM "LE DECOR D'AUJOURD'HUI." Below—ANOTHER TYPE OF CANTILEVERED BOOKSHELF IN WOOD.

12 6 0   1   2   3

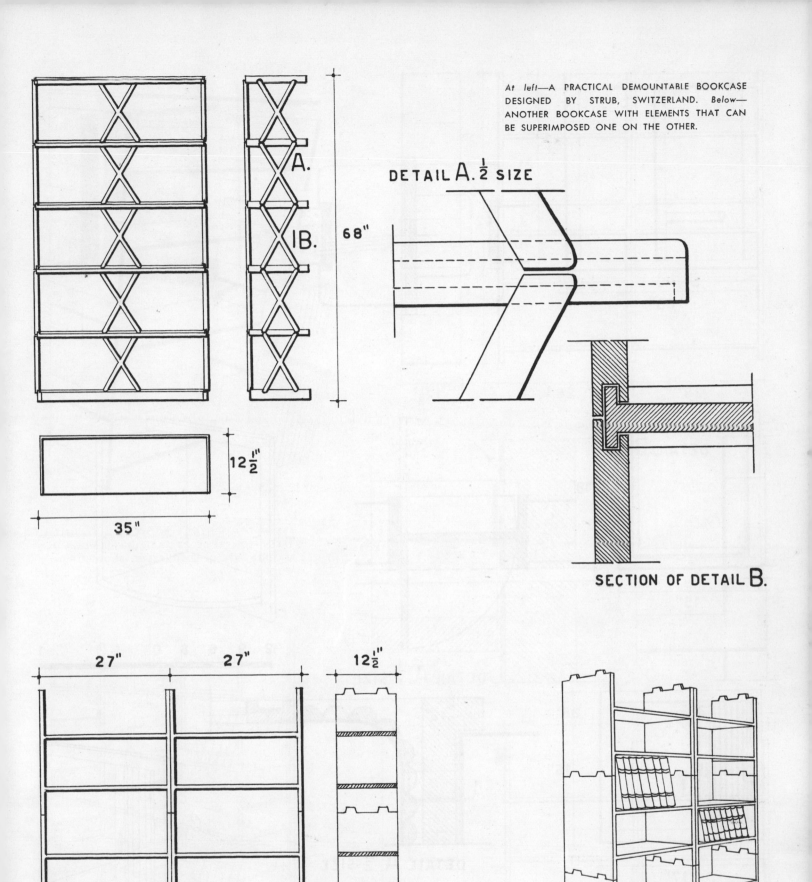

68"

12 1/2"

35"

A.

IB.

At left—A PRACTICAL DEMOUNTABLE BOOKCASE
DESIGNED BY STRUB, SWITZERLAND. Below—
ANOTHER BOOKCASE WITH ELEMENTS THAT CAN
BE SUPERIMPOSED ONE ON THE OTHER.

DETAIL A. 1/2 SIZE

SECTION OF DETAIL B.

27"   27"

12 1/2"

27"

12 6 0   1   2   3

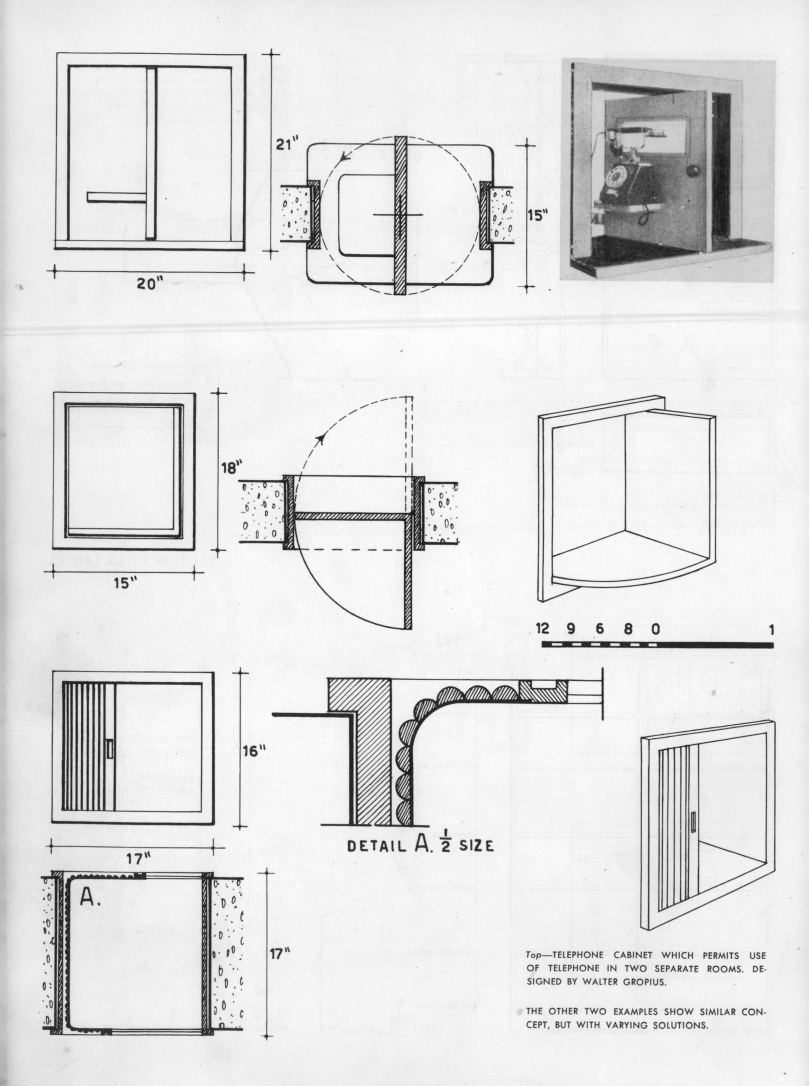

21"

20"

15"

18"

15"

16"

17"

17"

A.

12 9 6 8 0 1

DETAIL A. ½ SIZE

Top—TELEPHONE CABINET WHICH PERMITS USE OF TELEPHONE IN TWO SEPARATE ROOMS. DESIGNED BY WALTER GROPIUS.

THE OTHER TWO EXAMPLES SHOW SIMILAR CONCEPT, BUT WITH VARYING SOLUTIONS.

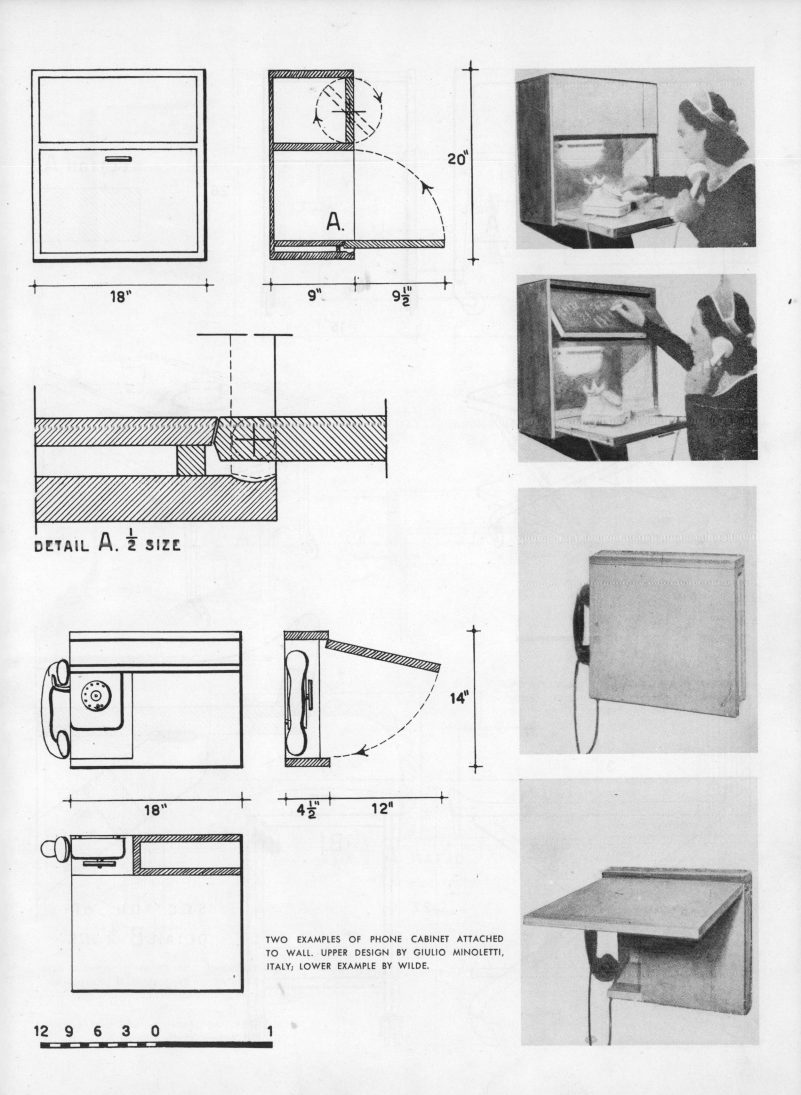

20"

18"

9" 9½"

DETAIL A. ½ SIZE

18"

4½" 12"

14"

TWO EXAMPLES OF PHONE CABINET ATTACHED
TO WALL. UPPER DESIGN BY GIULIO MINOLETTI,
ITALY; LOWER EXAMPLE BY WILDE.

12 9 6 3 0   1

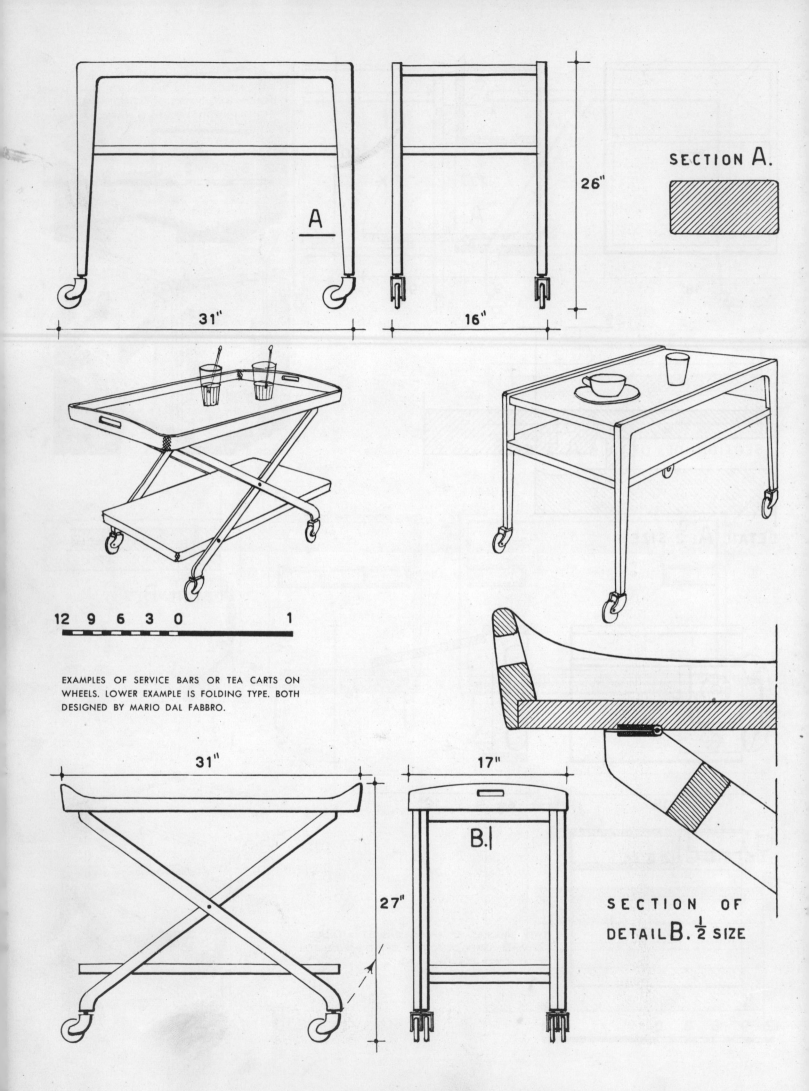

SECTION A.

26"

31"

16"

12 9 6 3 0   1

EXAMPLES OF SERVICE BARS OR TEA CARTS ON
WHEELS. LOWER EXAMPLE IS FOLDING TYPE. BOTH
DESIGNED BY MARIO DAL FABBRO.

31"

17"

27"

A

B.

SECTION OF
DETAIL B. $\frac{1}{2}$ SIZE

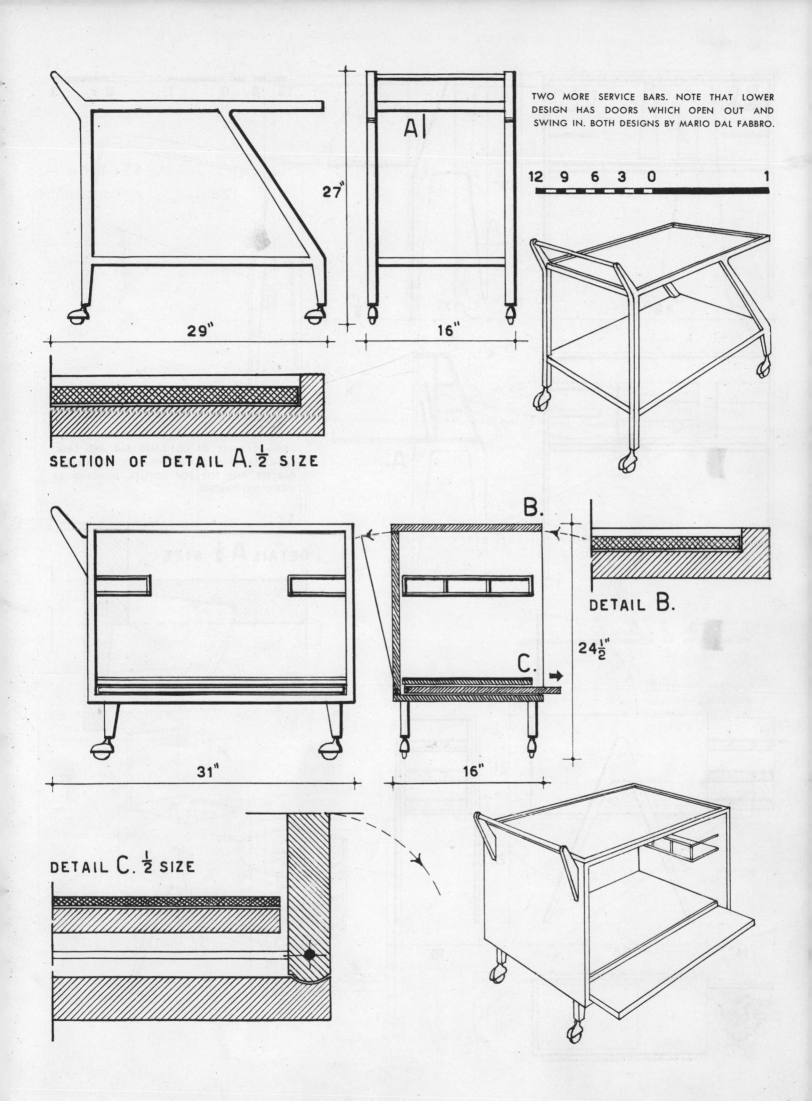

27"

A|

29"

16"

TWO MORE SERVICE BARS. NOTE THAT LOWER
DESIGN HAS DOORS WHICH OPEN OUT AND
SWING IN. BOTH DESIGNS BY MARIO DAL FABBRO.

12 9 6 3 0   1

SECTION OF DETAIL A. ½ SIZE

B.

DETAIL B.

C.

24½"

31"

16"

DETAIL C. ½ SIZE

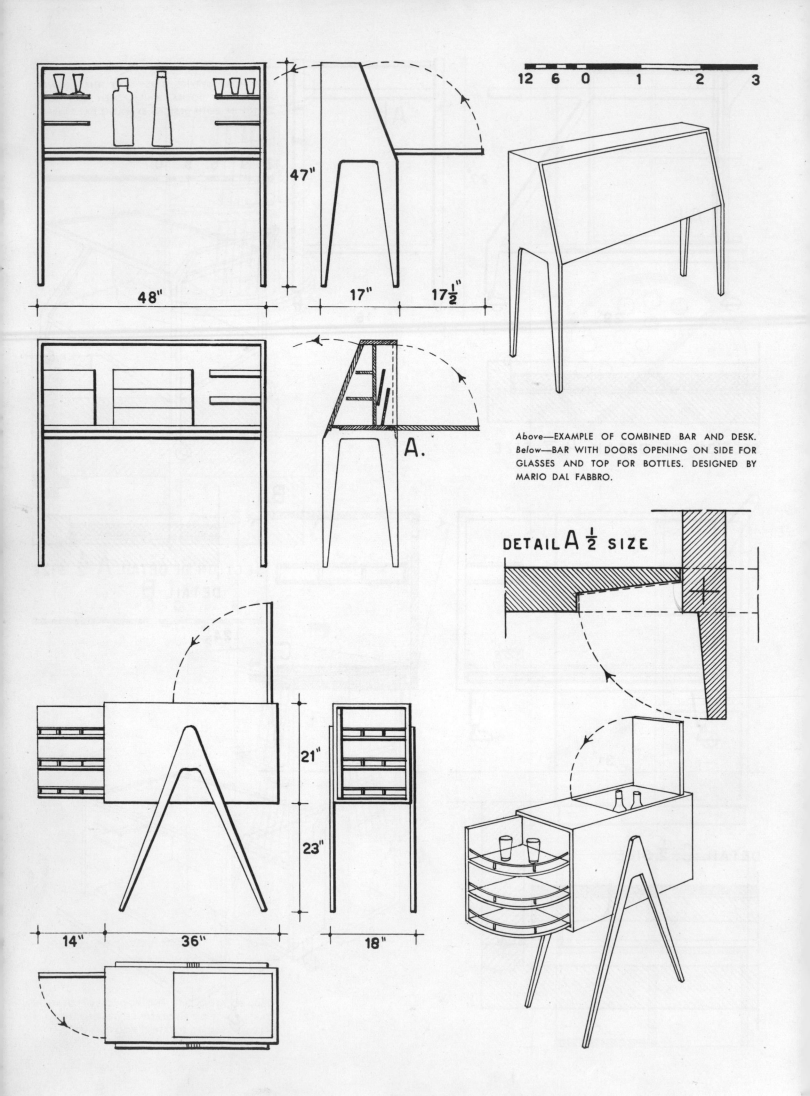

47"

48"

17"

17½"

12 6 0   1   2   3

Above—EXAMPLE OF COMBINED BAR AND DESK.
Below—BAR WITH DOORS OPENING ON SIDE FOR
GLASSES AND TOP FOR BOTTLES. DESIGNED BY
MARIO DAL FABBRO.

A.

DETAIL A ½ SIZE

21"

23"

14"

36"

18"

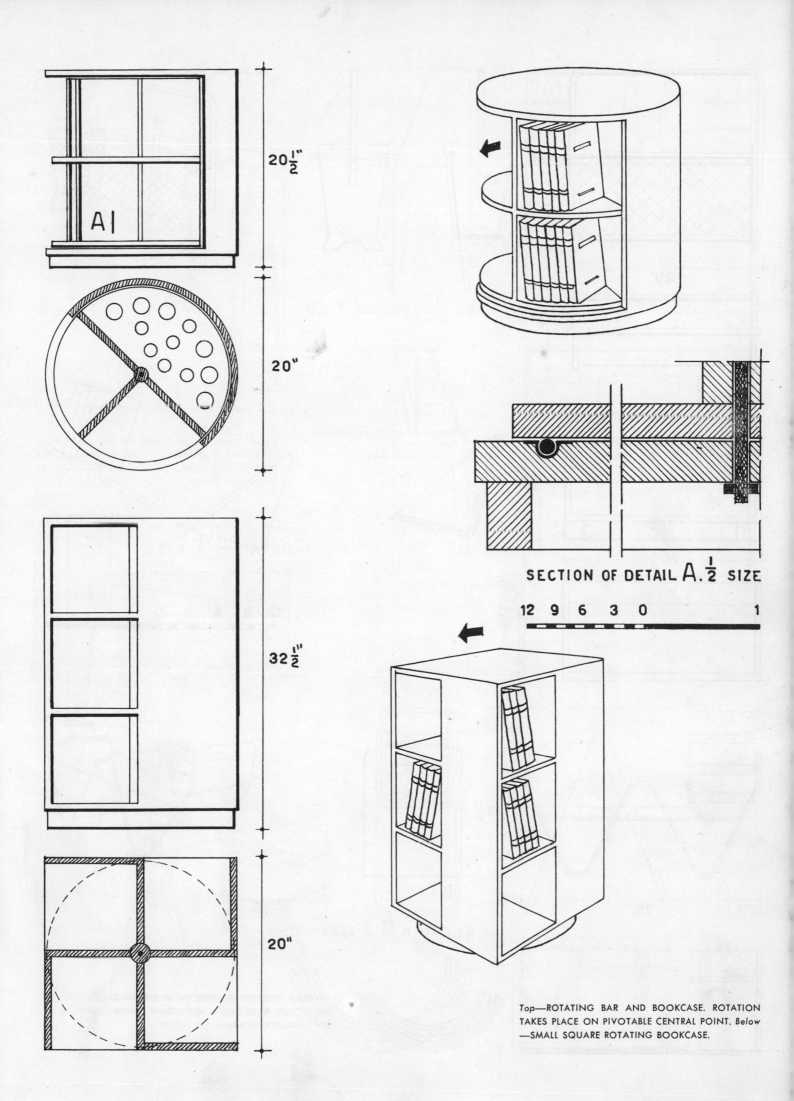

A I

$20\frac{1}{2}''$

20"

$32\frac{1}{2}''$

20"

SECTION OF DETAIL A. $\frac{1}{2}$ SIZE

12 9 6 3 0   1

Top—ROTATING BAR AND BOOKCASE. ROTATION TAKES PLACE ON PIVOTABLE CENTRAL POINT. *Below*—SMALL SQUARE ROTATING BOOKCASE.

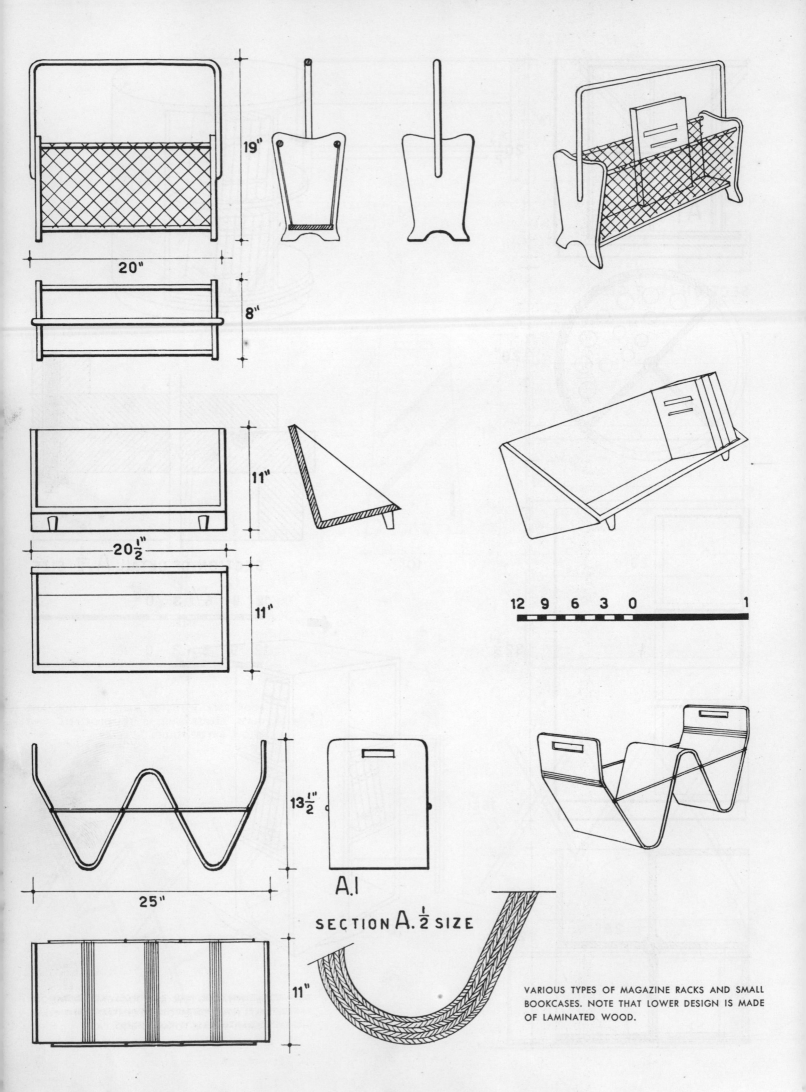

19"

20"

8"

11"

20½"

11"

13½"

25"

11"

A.I

SECTION A. ½ SIZE

12 9 6 3 0   1

VARIOUS TYPES OF MAGAZINE RACKS AND SMALL
BOOKCASES. NOTE THAT LOWER DESIGN IS MADE
OF LAMINATED WOOD.

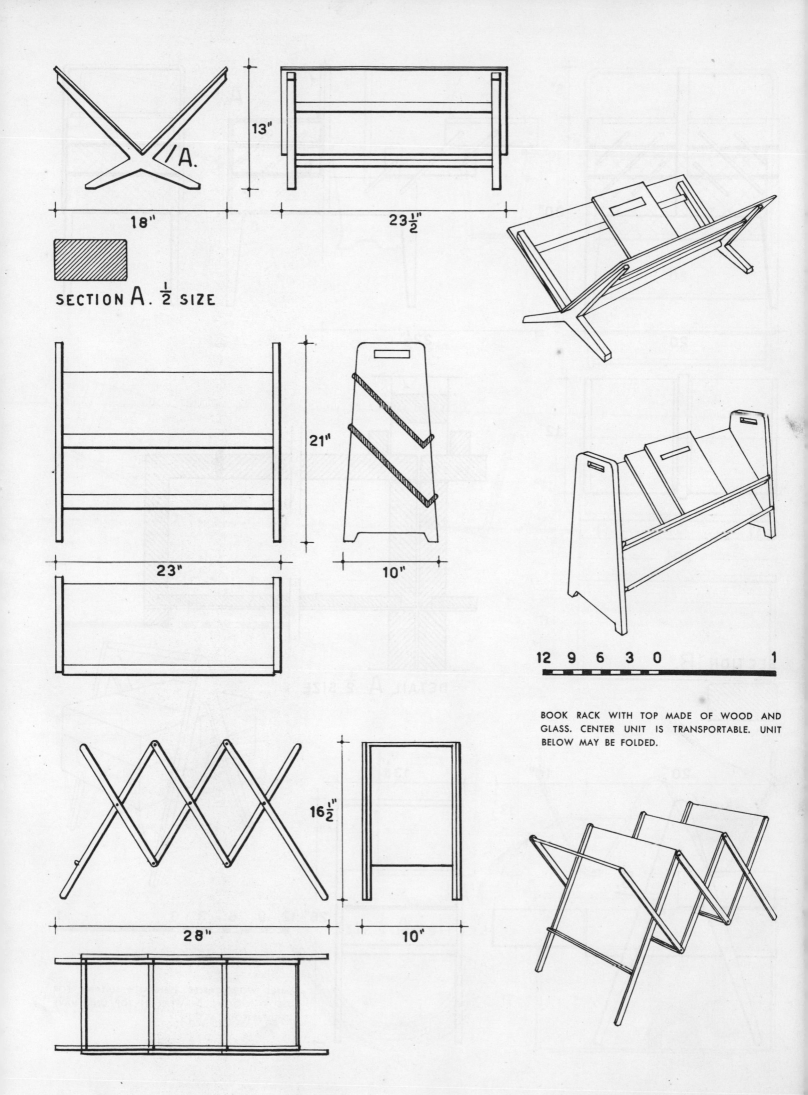

13"

18"

23½"

SECTION A. ½ SIZE

21"

23"

10"

12 9 6 3 0   1

BOOK RACK WITH TOP MADE OF WOOD AND
GLASS. CENTER UNIT IS TRANSPORTABLE. UNIT
BELOW MAY BE FOLDED.

16½"

28"

10"

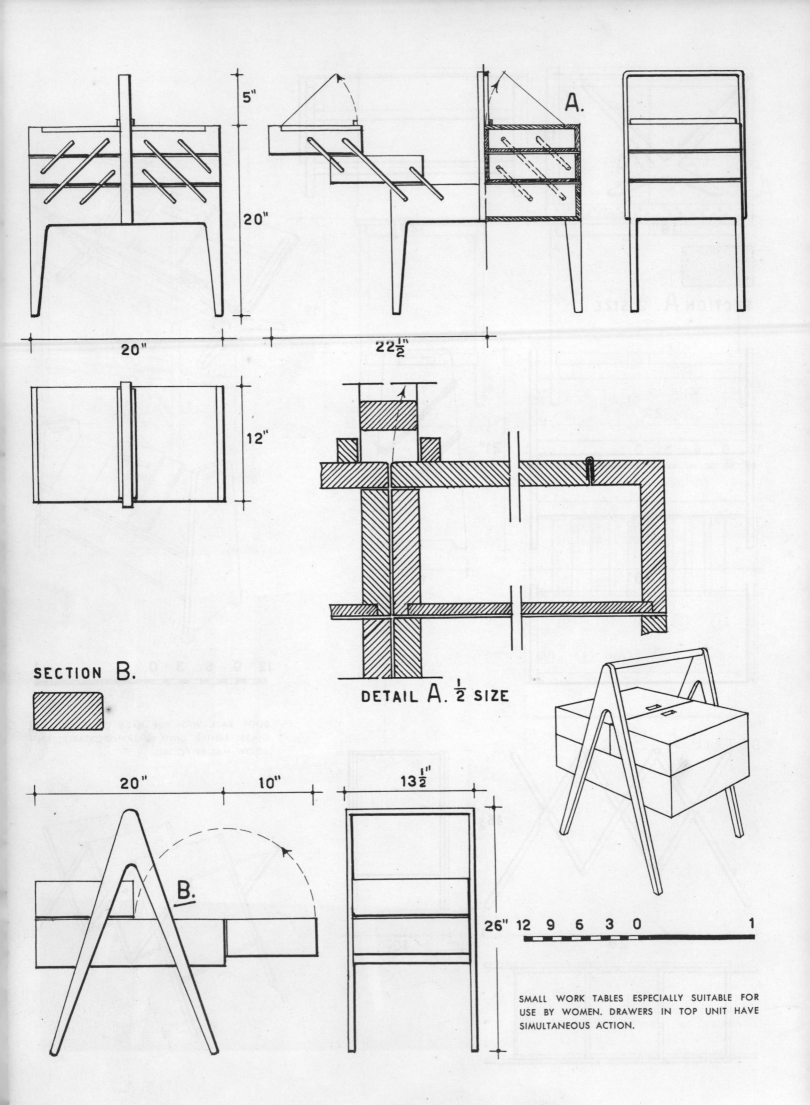

5"

20"

20"

22 1/2"

A.

12"

SECTION B.

DETAIL A. 1/2 SIZE

20"   10"   13 1/2"

B.

26" 12 9 6 3 0   1

SMALL WORK TABLES ESPECIALLY SUITABLE FOR
USE BY WOMEN. DRAWERS IN TOP UNIT HAVE
SIMULTANEOUS ACTION.

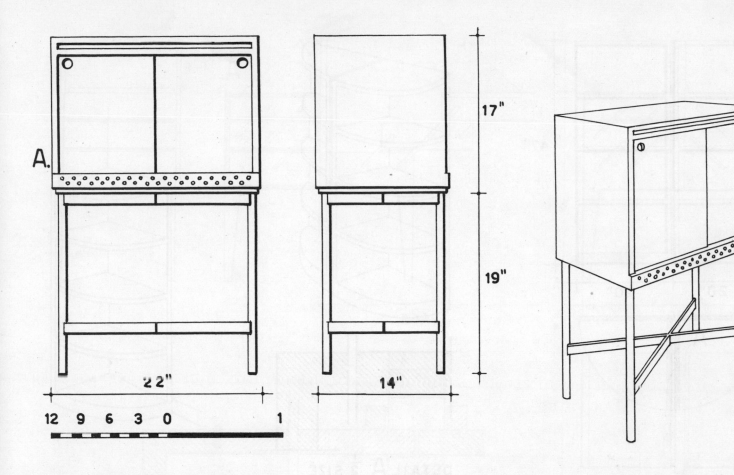

A.

17"

19"

22"

14"

12 9 6 3 0 1

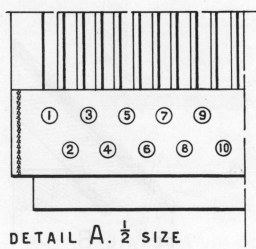

DETAIL A. ½ SIZE

A NOVEL RECORD CABINET DESIGNED BY MARIO
DAL FABBRO. DESIRED RECORD CAN BE SELECTED
BY PRESSING THE NUMBERED BUTTONS.

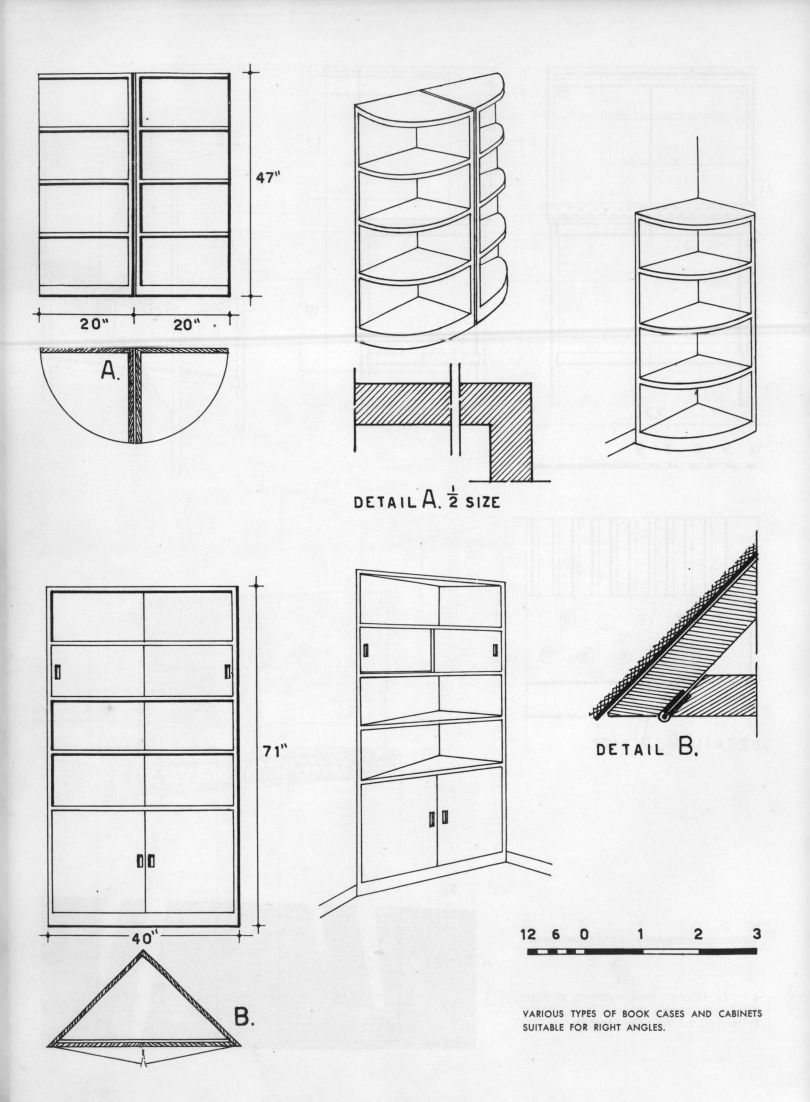

47"

20"   20"

A.

DETAIL A. ½ SIZE

71"

40"

B.

DETAIL B.

12 6 0   1   2   3

VARIOUS TYPES OF BOOK CASES AND CABINETS
SUITABLE FOR RIGHT ANGLES.

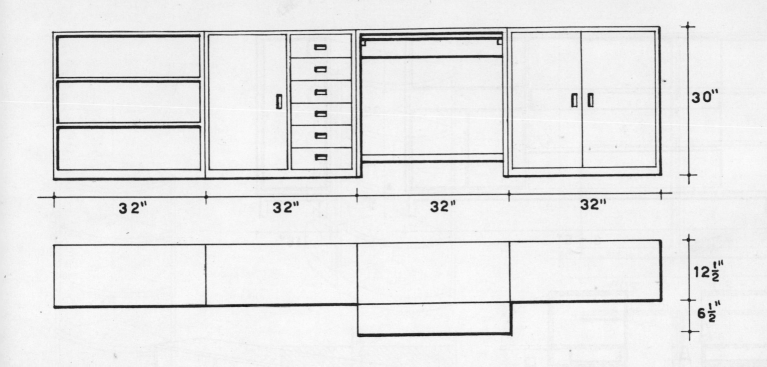

30"

32" 32" 32" 32"

12 1/2"

6 1/2"

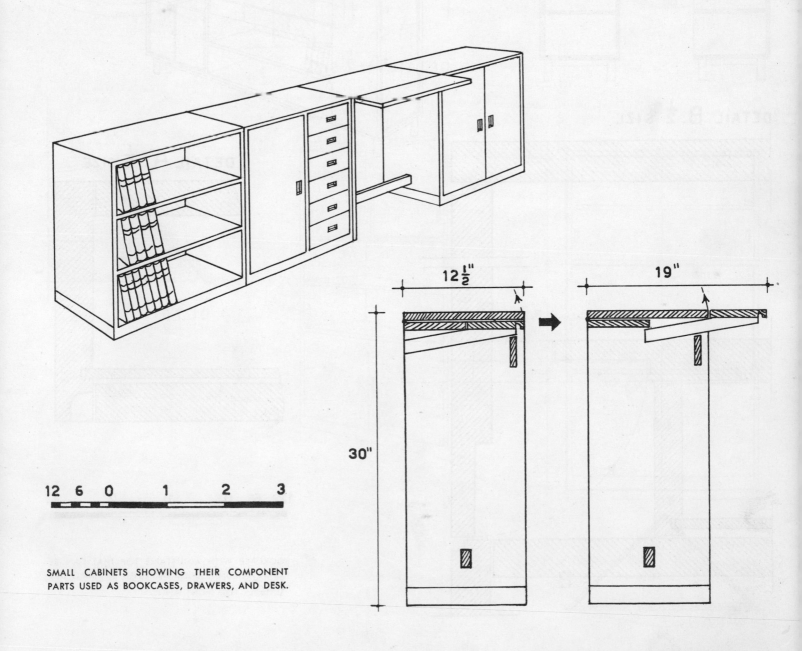

12 1/2"   19"

30"

12 6 0   1   2   3

SMALL CABINETS SHOWING THEIR COMPONENT
PARTS USED AS BOOKCASES, DRAWERS, AND DESK.

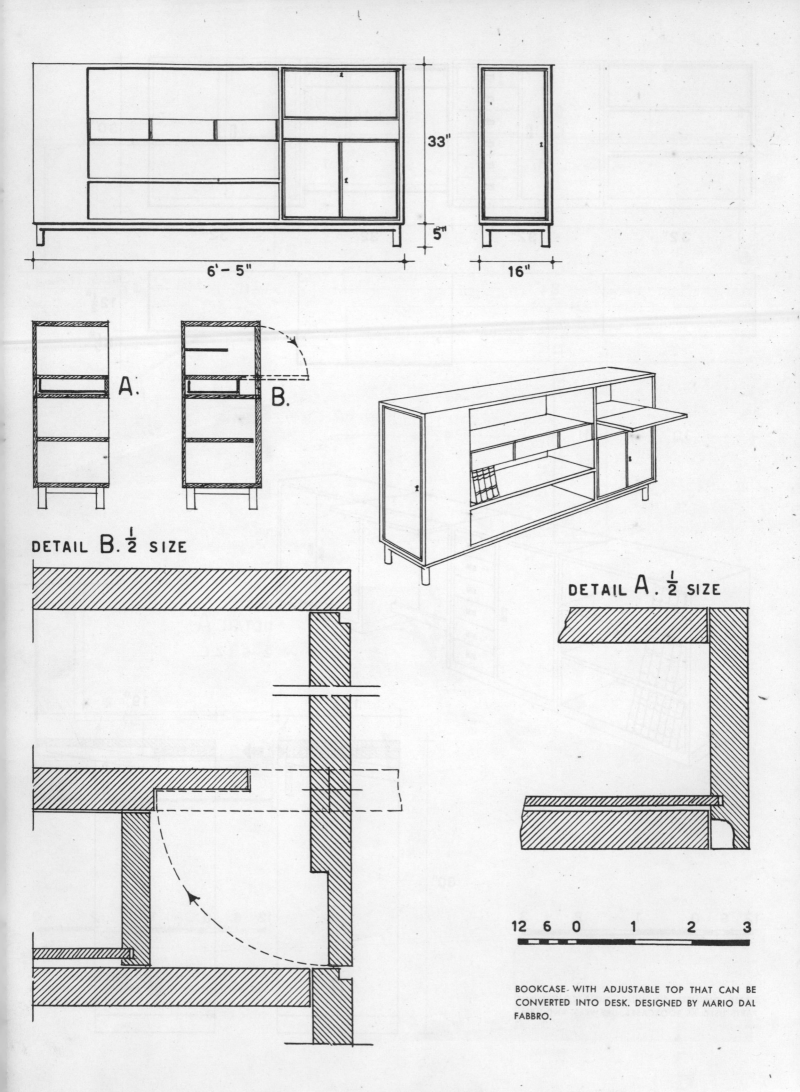

33"

5"

6'- 5"

16"

A.

B.

DETAIL B. $\frac{1}{2}$ SIZE

DETAIL A. $\frac{1}{2}$ SIZE

12 6 0   1   2   3

BOOKCASE WITH ADJUSTABLE TOP THAT CAN BE
CONVERTED INTO DESK. DESIGNED BY MARIO DAL
FABBRO.

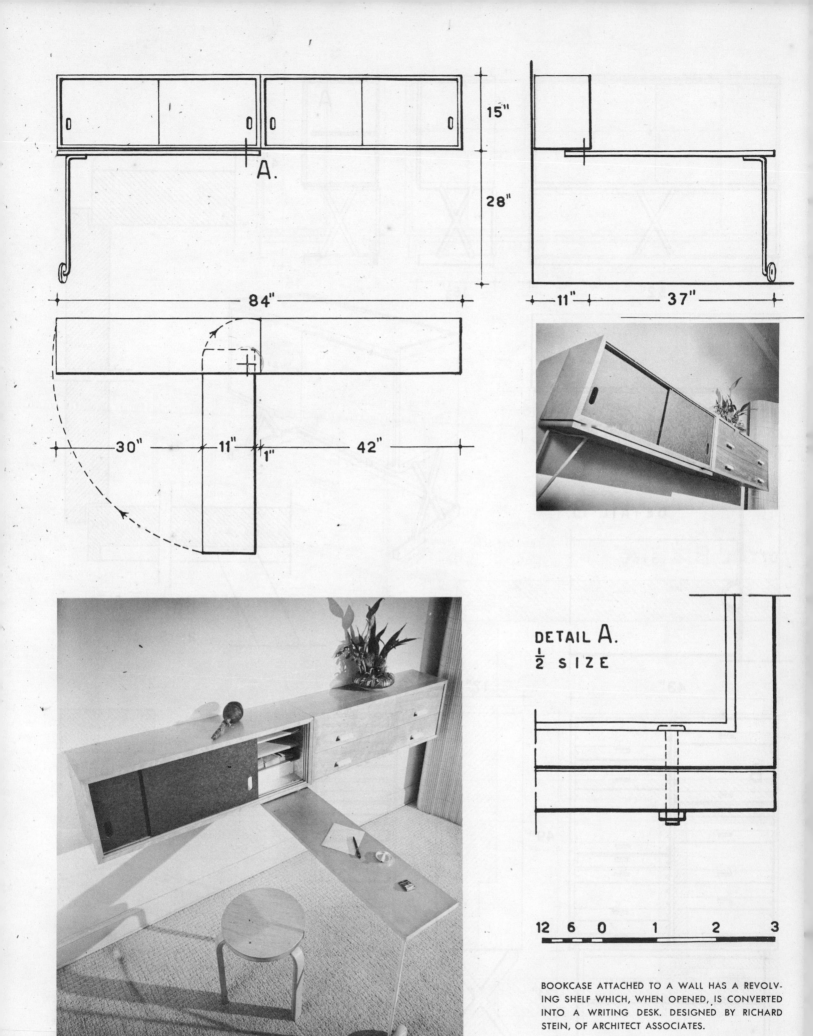

15"

28"

A.

84"

11"   37"

30"   11"   1"   42"

DETAIL A.
½ SIZE

12 6 0 1 2 3

BOOKCASE ATTACHED TO A WALL HAS A REVOLV-
ING SHELF WHICH, WHEN OPENED, IS CONVERTED
INTO A WRITING DESK. DESIGNED BY RICHARD
STEIN, OF ARCHITECT ASSOCIATES.

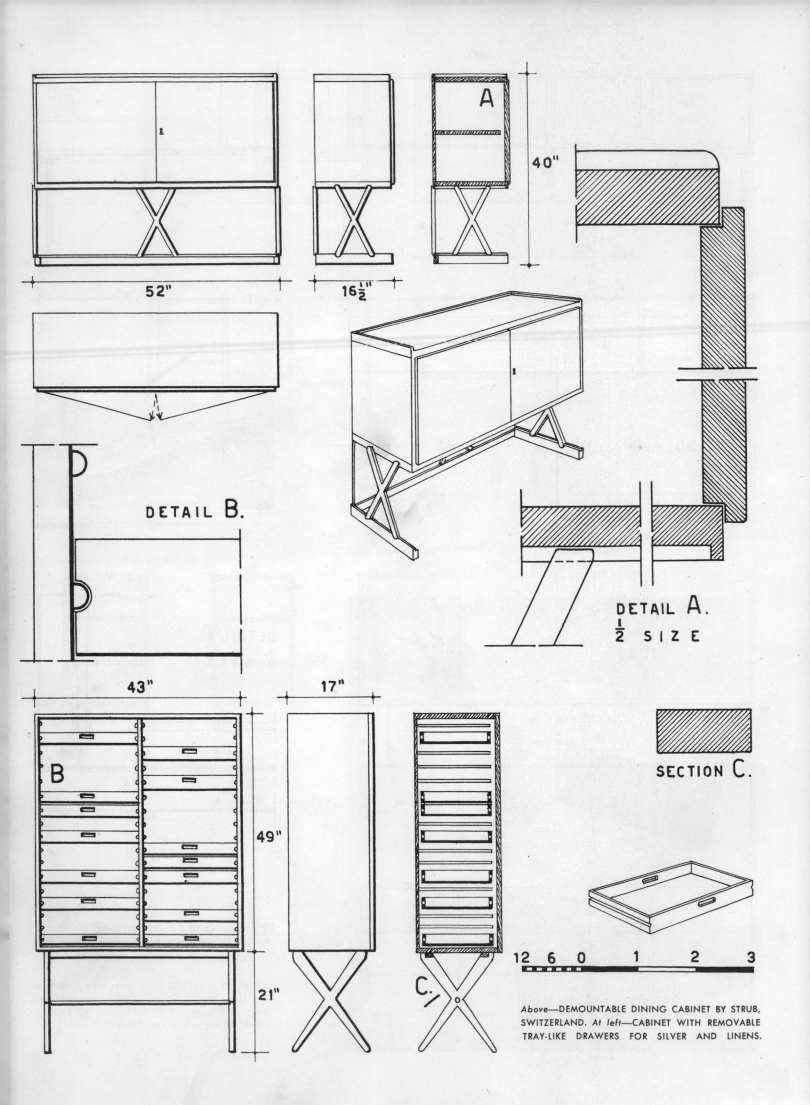

40"

52"

16½"

A

DETAIL B.

43"

17"

DETAIL A.
½ SIZE

SECTION C.

B

49"

21"

C.1

12 6 0 1 2 3

Above—DEMOUNTABLE DINING CABINET BY STRUB,
SWITZERLAND. *At left*—CABINET WITH REMOVABLE
TRAY-LIKE DRAWERS FOR SILVER AND LINENS.

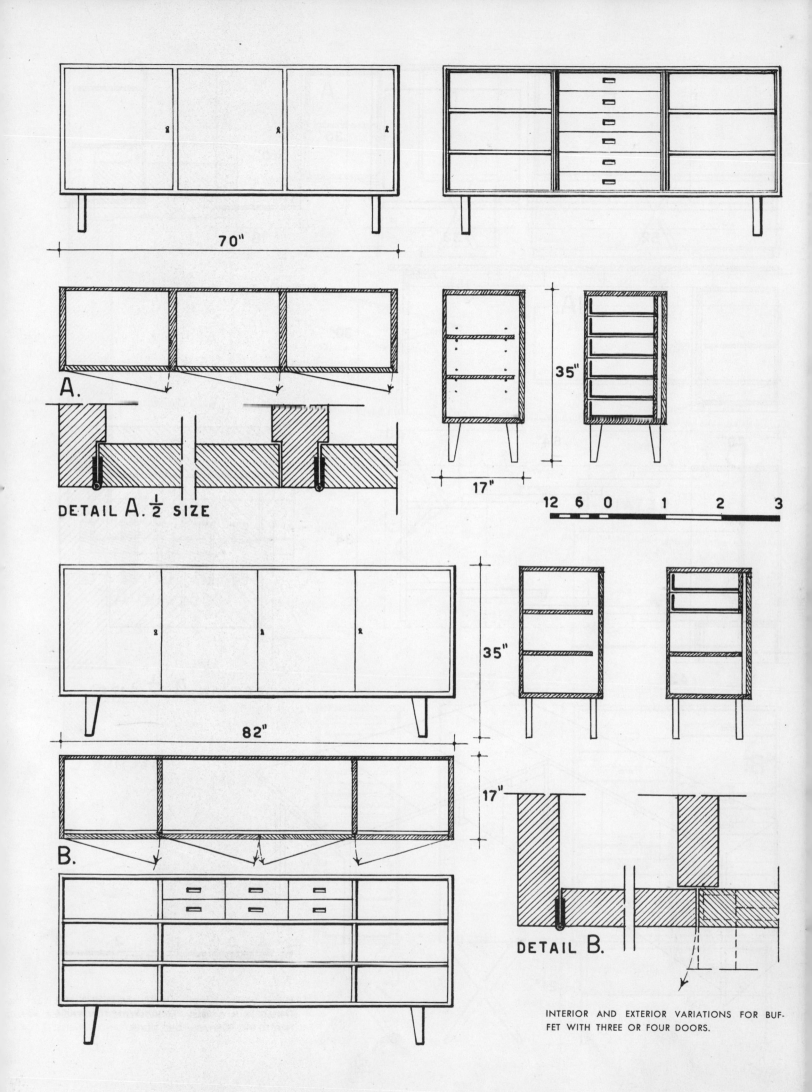

70"

A.

DETAIL A. ½ SIZE

35"

17"

12 6 0 1 2 3

82"

35"

B.

17"

DETAIL B.

INTERIOR AND EXTERIOR VARIATIONS FOR BUF-
FET WITH THREE OR FOUR DOORS.

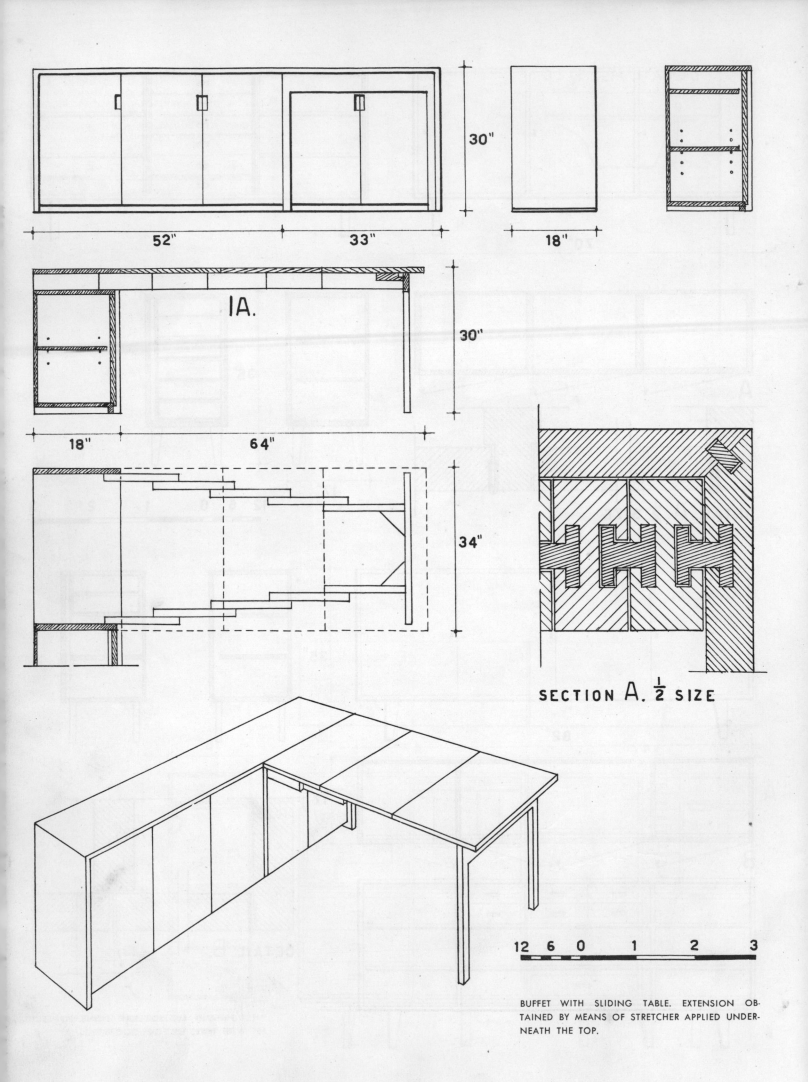

30"

52"   33"   18"

IA.

30"

18"   64"

34"

SECTION A. ½ SIZE

12 6 0 1 2 3

BUFFET WITH SLIDING TABLE. EXTENSION OB-
TAINED BY MEANS OF STRETCHER APPLIED UNDER-
NEATH THE TOP.

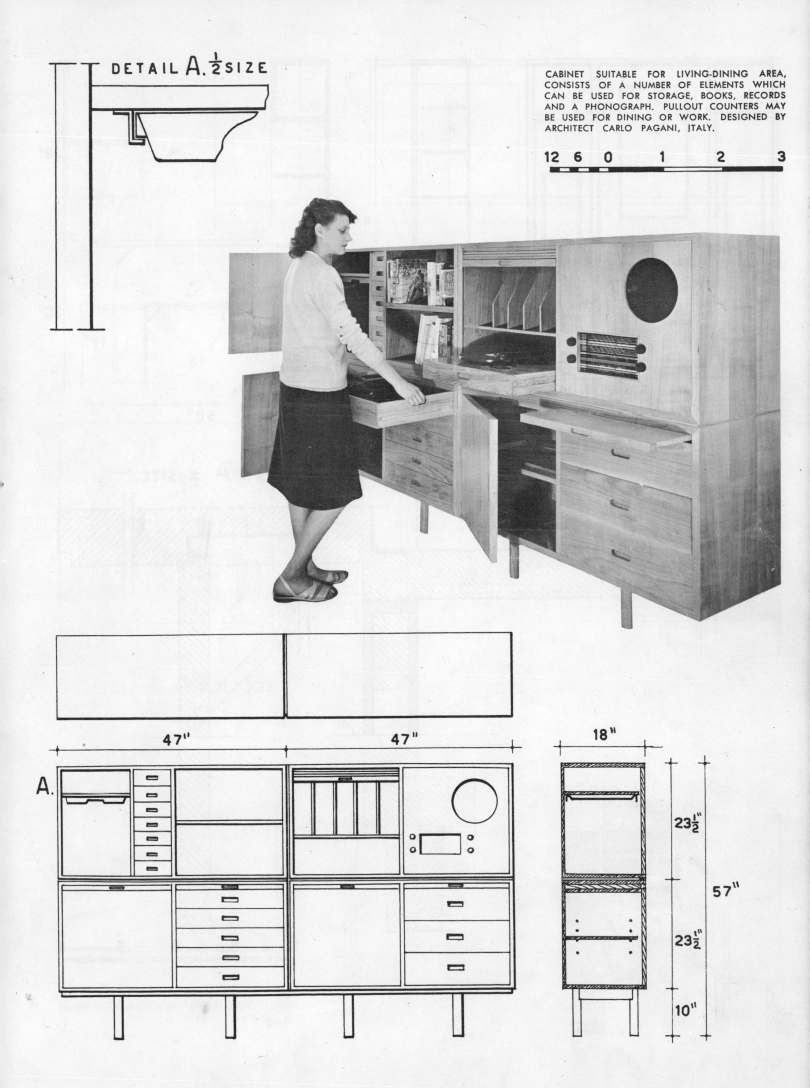

DETAIL A. ½ SIZE

CABINET SUITABLE FOR LIVING-DINING AREA, CONSISTS OF A NUMBER OF ELEMENTS WHICH CAN BE USED FOR STORAGE, BOOKS, RECORDS AND A PHONOGRAPH. PULLOUT COUNTERS MAY BE USED FOR DINING OR WORK. DESIGNED BY ARCHITECT CARLO PAGANI, ITALY.

12 6 0 1 2 3

A.

47" 47" 18"

23½" 57" 23½" 10"

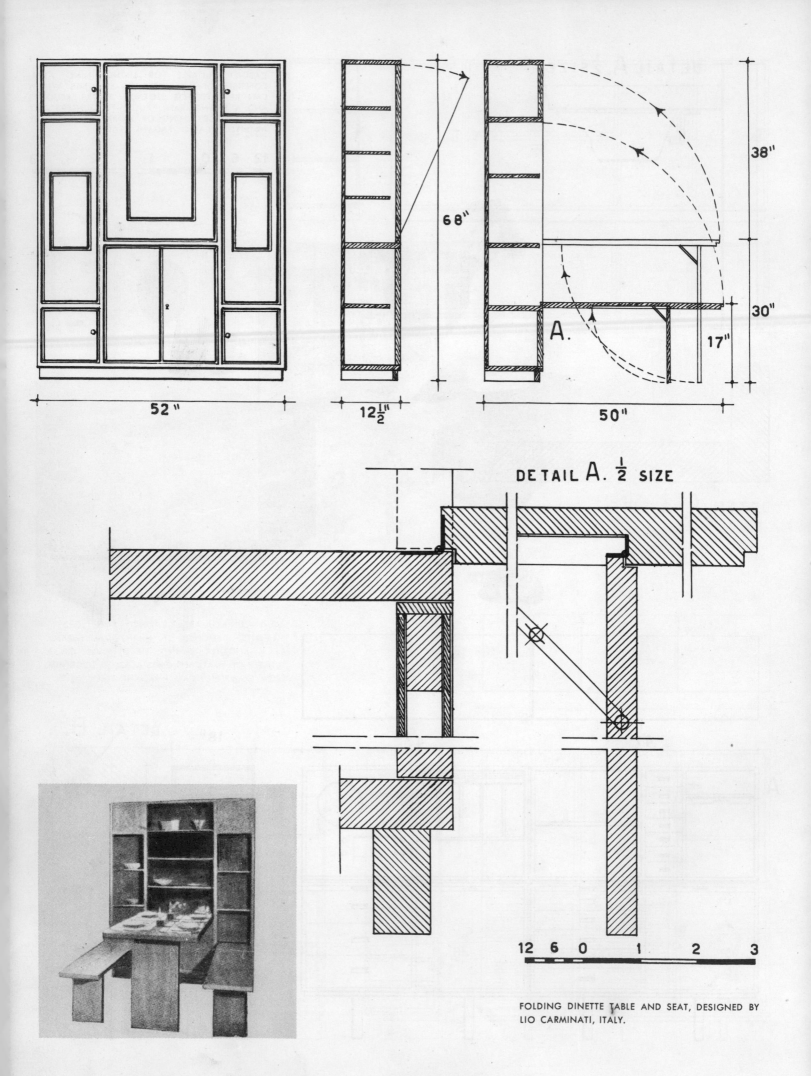

52"

12 1/2"

50"

68"

38"

30"

17"

A.

DETAIL A. ½ SIZE

12 6 0 1 2 3

FOLDING DINETTE TABLE AND SEAT, DESIGNED BY LIO CARMINATI, ITALY.

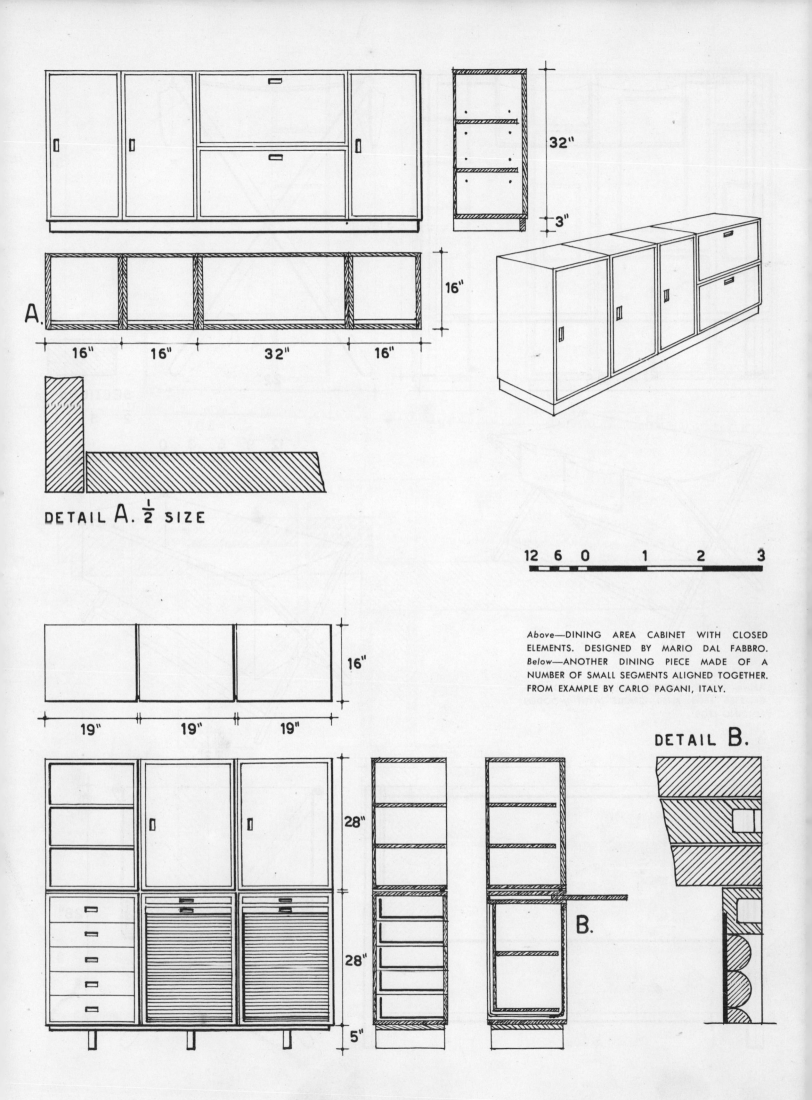

A.

32"

3"

16"

16"   16"   32"   16"

DETAIL A. ½ SIZE

12 6 0   1   2   3

Above—DINING AREA CABINET WITH CLOSED
ELEMENTS. DESIGNED BY MARIO DAL FABBRO.
Below—ANOTHER DINING PIECE MADE OF A
NUMBER OF SMALL SEGMENTS ALIGNED TOGETHER.
FROM EXAMPLE BY CARLO PAGANI, ITALY.

DETAIL **B.**

16"

19"   19"   19"

28"

28"

5"

B.

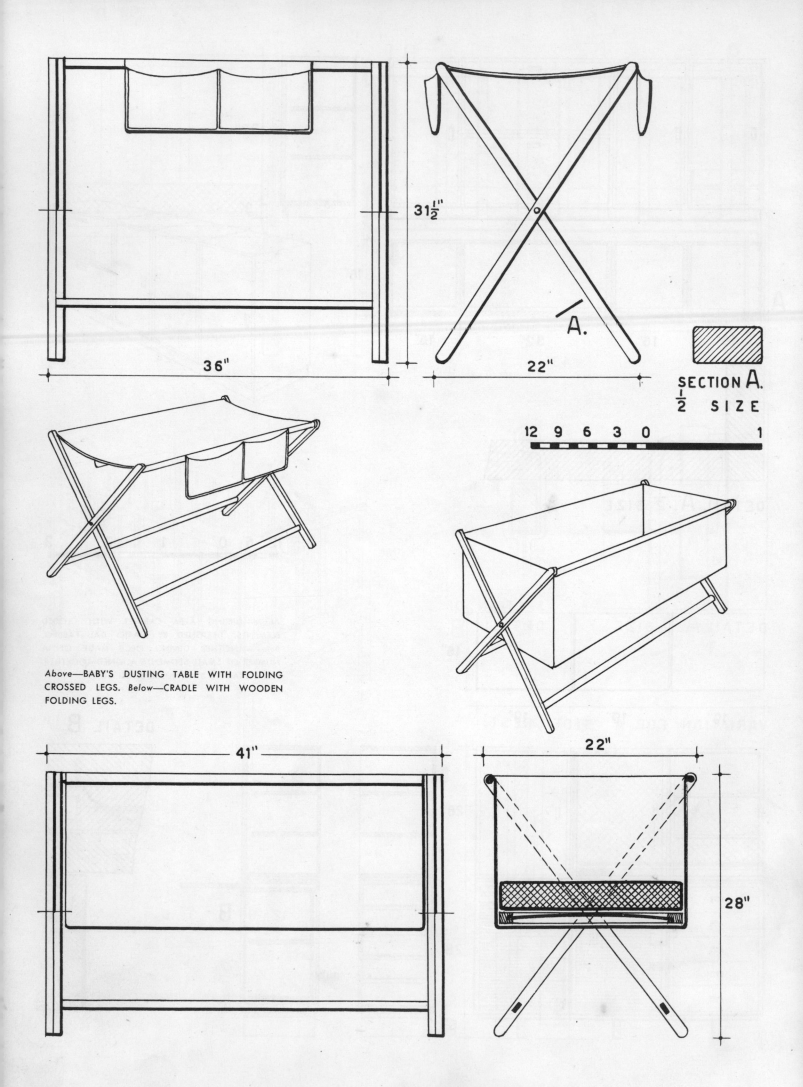

31½"

36"

22"

SECTION A.
½ SIZE

12 9 6 3 0 1

A.

Above—BABY'S DUSTING TABLE WITH FOLDING
CROSSED LEGS. *Below*—CRADLE WITH WOODEN
FOLDING LEGS.

41"

22"

28"

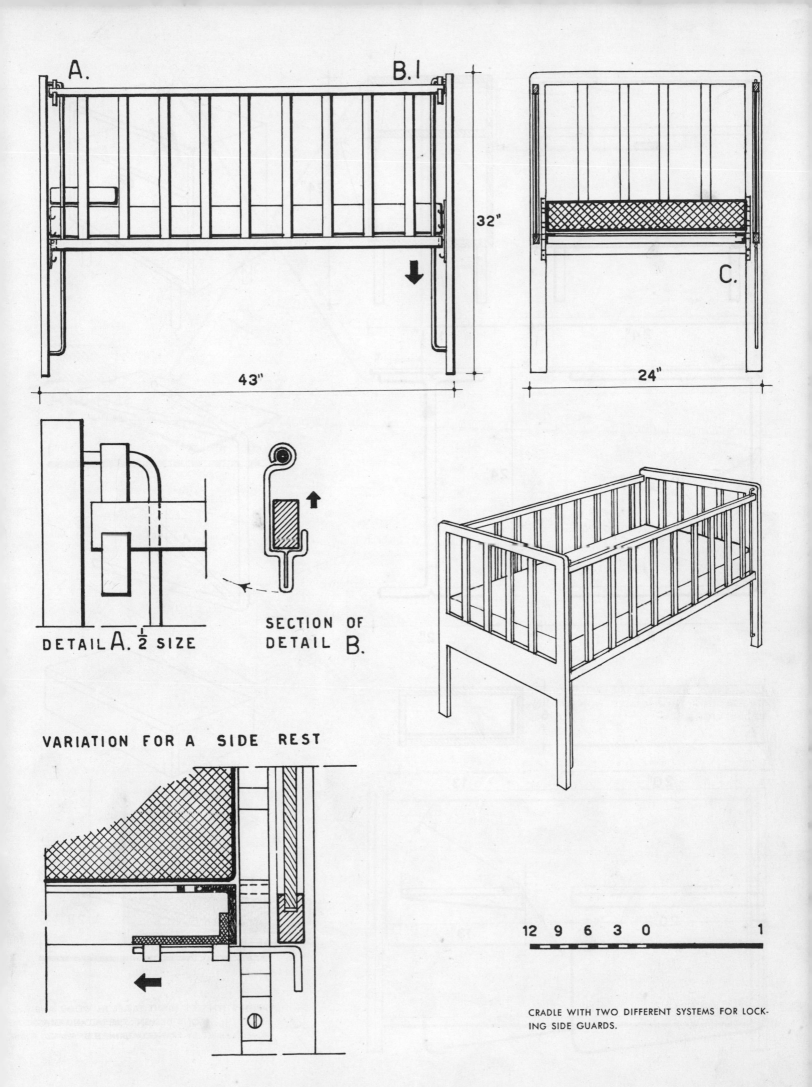

A.

B.I

32"

43"

DETAIL A. ½ SIZE

SECTION OF DETAIL B.

C.

24"

VARIATION FOR A SIDE REST

12 9 6 3 0   1

CRADLE WITH TWO DIFFERENT SYSTEMS FOR LOCKING SIDE GUARDS.

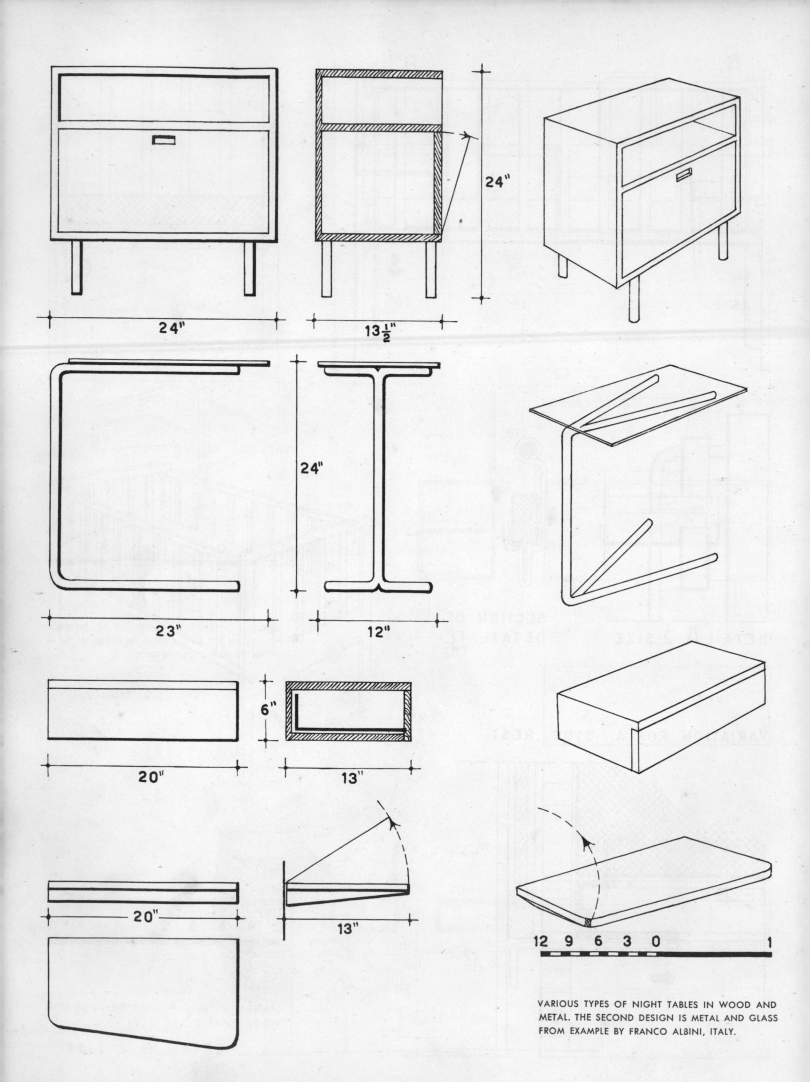

24"

24"

13½"

24"

23"

12"

6"

20"

13"

20"

13"

12 9 6 3 0 1

VARIOUS TYPES OF NIGHT TABLES IN WOOD AND METAL. THE SECOND DESIGN IS METAL AND GLASS FROM EXAMPLE BY FRANCO ALBINI, ITALY.

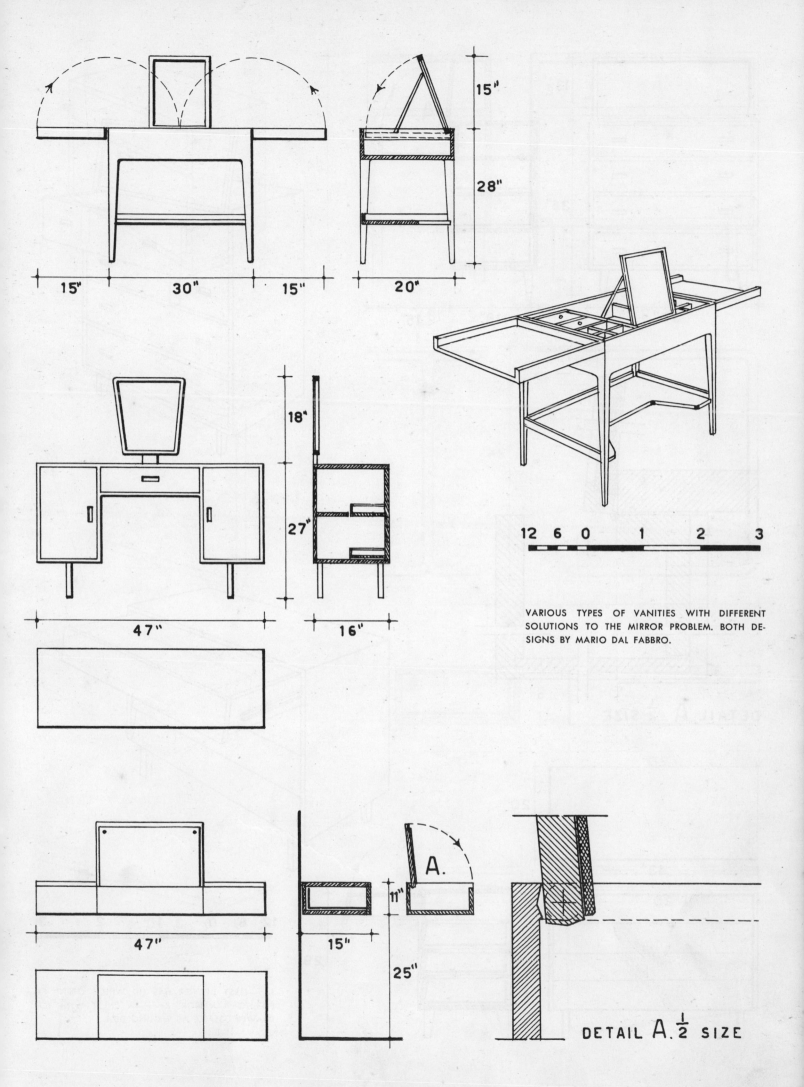

15"   30"   15"

15"

28"

20"

18"

27"

47"

16"

12 6 0 1 2 3

VARIOUS TYPES OF VANITIES WITH DIFFERENT
SOLUTIONS TO THE MIRROR PROBLEM. BOTH DE-
SIGNS BY MARIO DAL FABBRO.

47"

15"

11"

25"

A.

DETAIL A. ½ SIZE

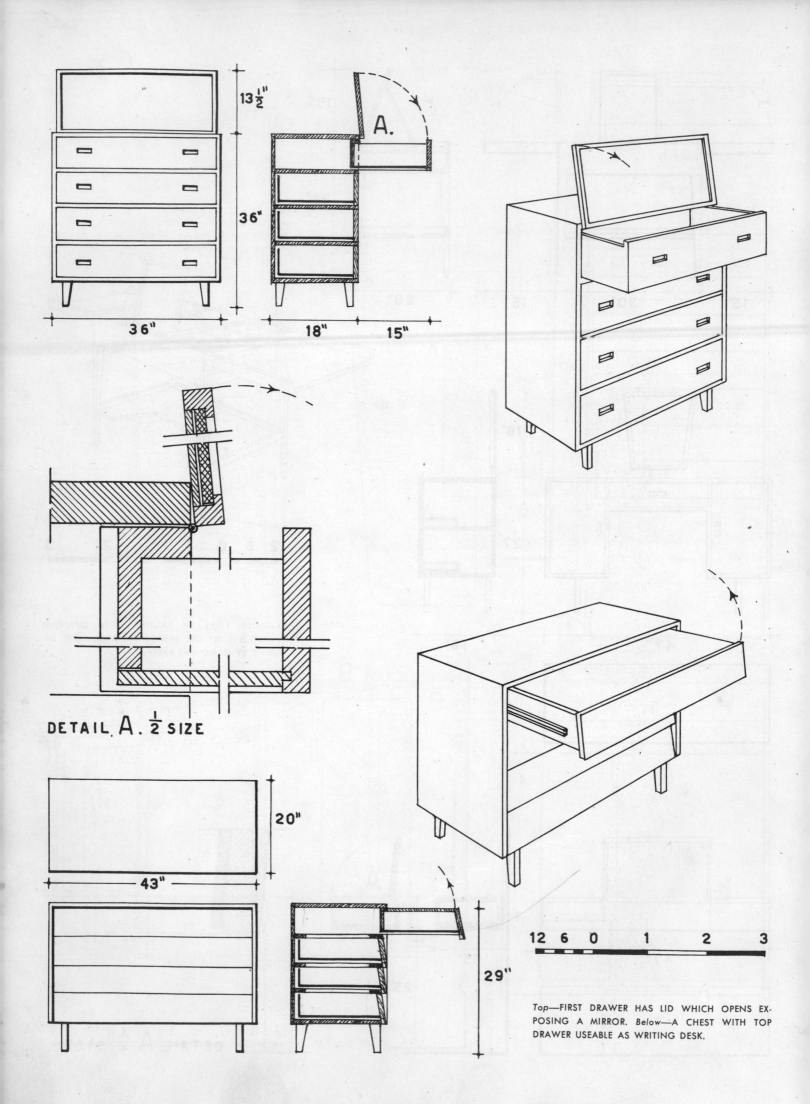

13½"

36"

36"

18"   15"

A.

DETAIL. A. ½ SIZE

20"

43"

29"

12 6 0   1   2   3

Top—FIRST DRAWER HAS LID WHICH OPENS EX-
POSING A MIRROR. *Below*—A CHEST WITH TOP
DRAWER USEABLE AS WRITING DESK.

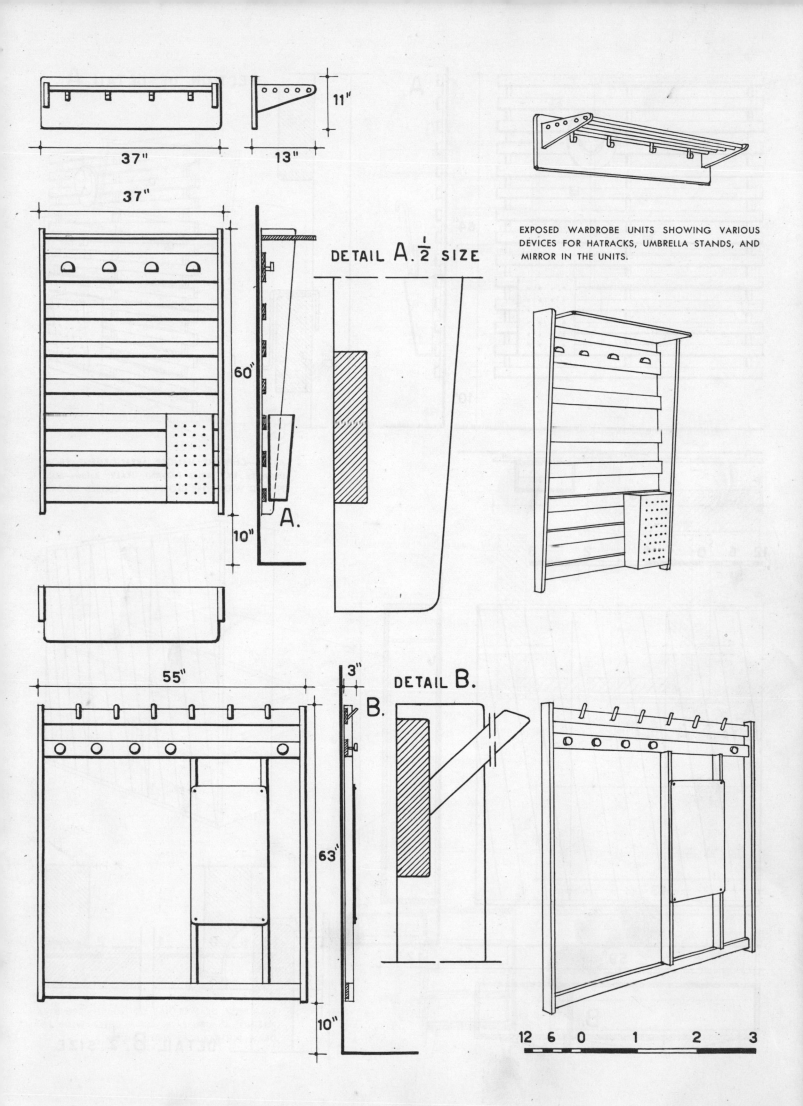

37"

13"

11"

37"

60"

10"

DETAIL A. ½ SIZE

A.

EXPOSED WARDROBE UNITS SHOWING VARIOUS
DEVICES FOR HATRACKS, UMBRELLA STANDS, AND
MIRROR IN THE UNITS.

55"

3"

DETAIL B.

B.

63"

10"

12 6 0 1 2 3

117

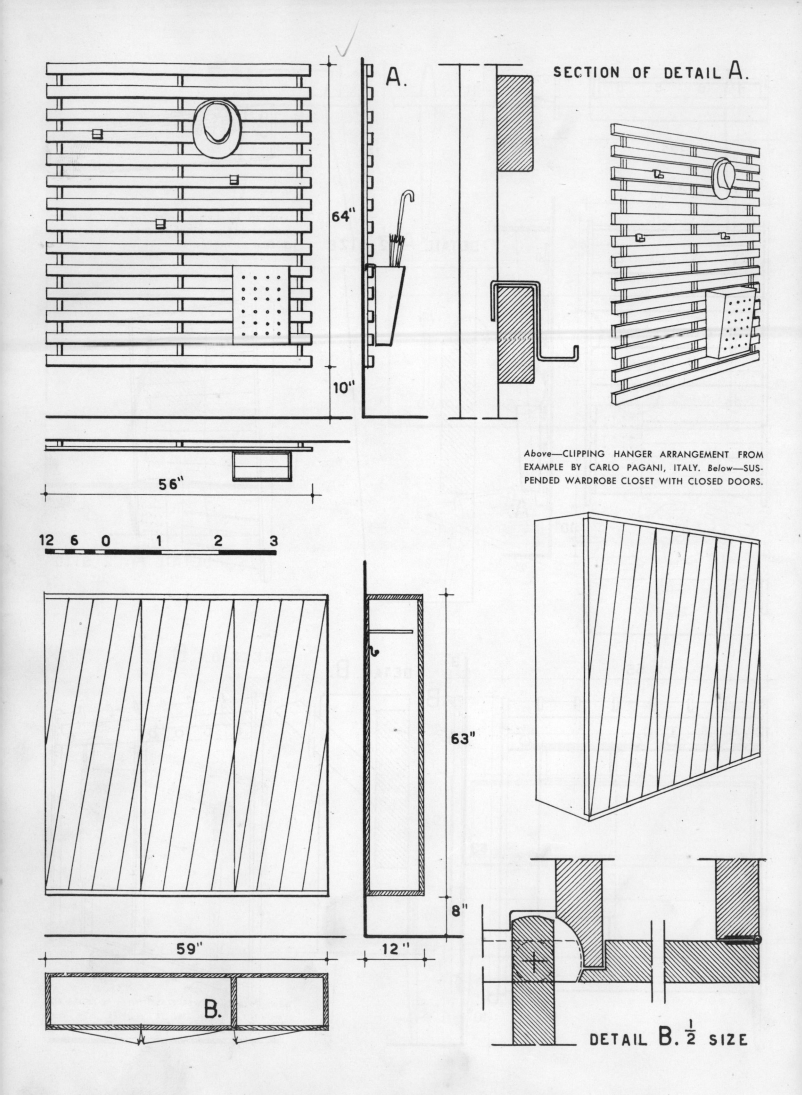

SECTION OF DETAIL A.

64"

10"

56"

12 6 0 1 2 3

A.

Above—CLIPPING HANGER ARRANGEMENT FROM EXAMPLE BY CARLO PAGANI, ITALY. *Below*—SUSPENDED WARDROBE CLOSET WITH CLOSED DOORS.

63"

8"

B.

59"

12"

DETAIL B. ½ SIZE

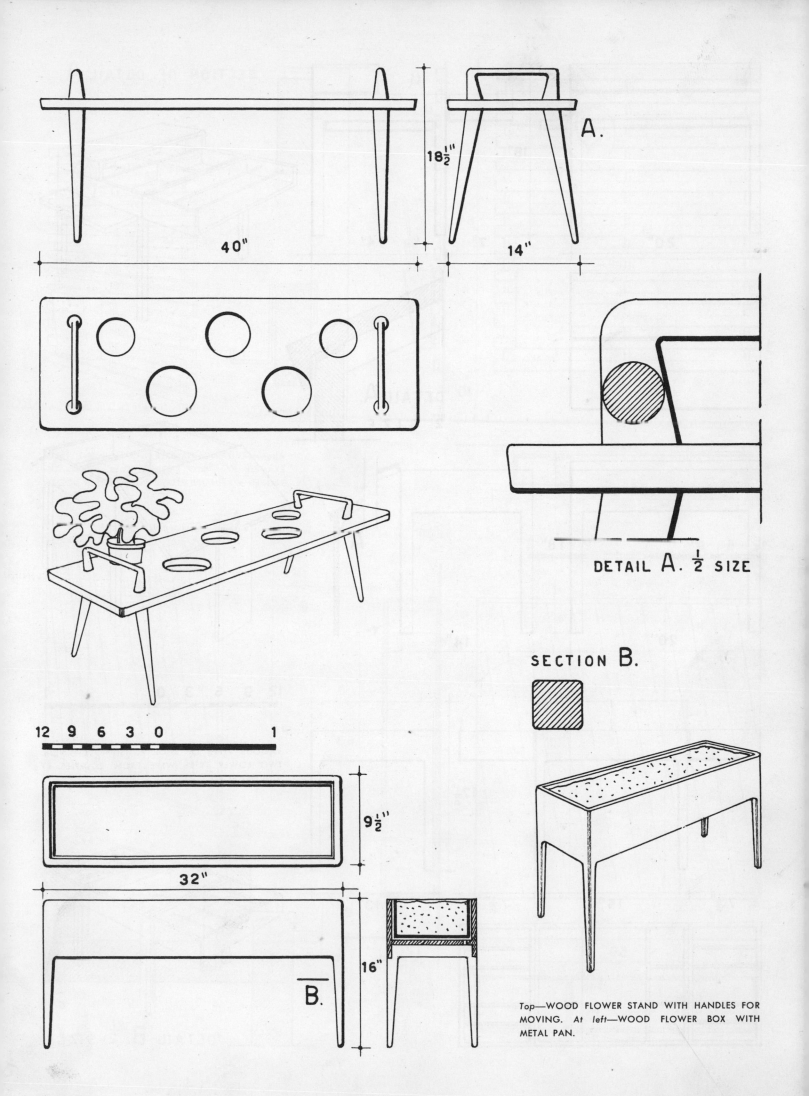

A.

18½"

40"

14"

DETAIL A. ½ SIZE

SECTION B.

12 9 6 3 0 1

9½"

32"

16"

B.

Top—WOOD FLOWER STAND WITH HANDLES FOR MOVING. At left—WOOD FLOWER BOX WITH METAL PAN.

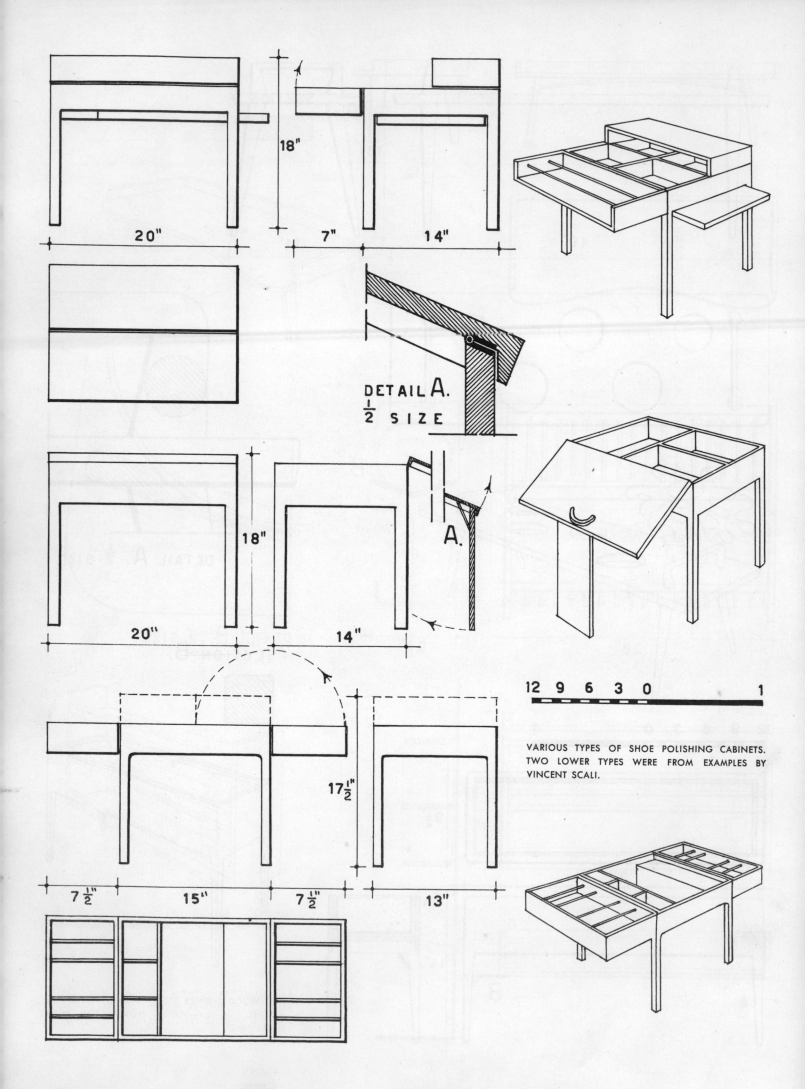

18"

20"

7"   14"

DETAIL A.
½ SIZE

18"

20"   14"

A.

17½"

7½"   15"   7½"   13"

12 9 6 3 0   1

VARIOUS TYPES OF SHOE POLISHING CABINETS.
TWO LOWER TYPES WERE FROM EXAMPLES BY
VINCENT SCALI.

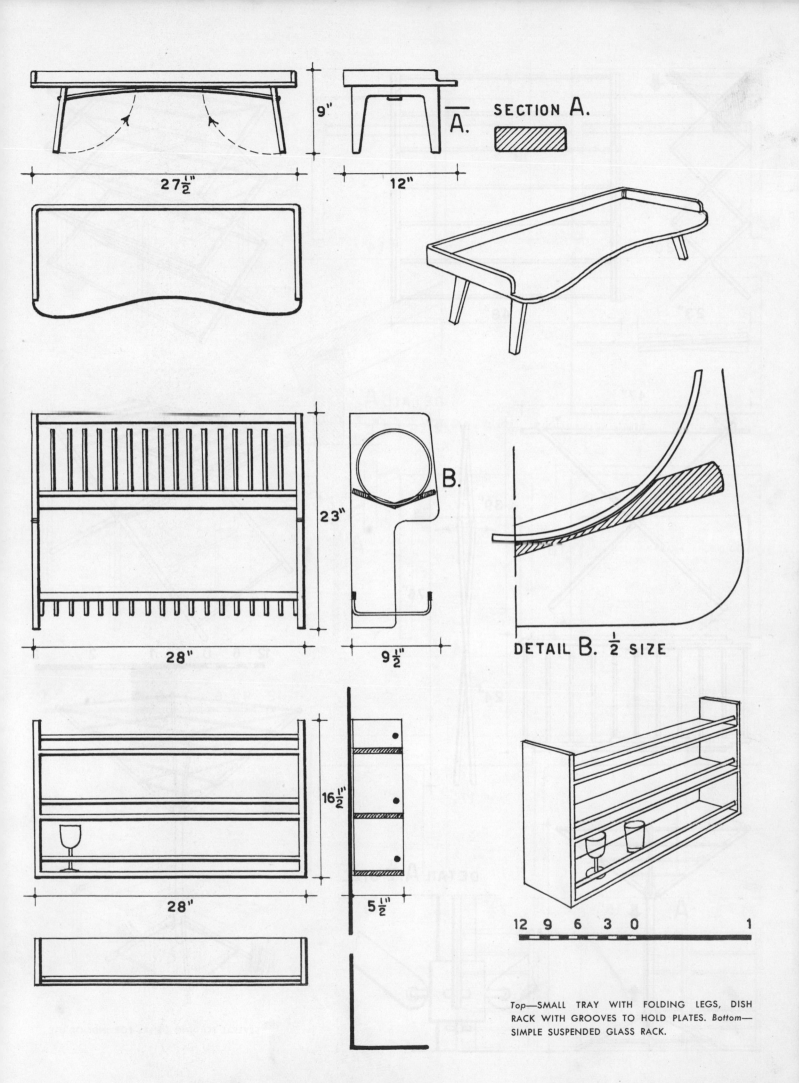

9"

27½"

12"

SECTION A.

B.

23"

28"

9½"

DETAIL B. ½ SIZE

16½"

28"

5½"

12 9 6 3 0 1

Top—SMALL TRAY WITH FOLDING LEGS, DISH RACK WITH GROOVES TO HOLD PLATES. *Bottom*—SIMPLE SUSPENDED GLASS RACK.

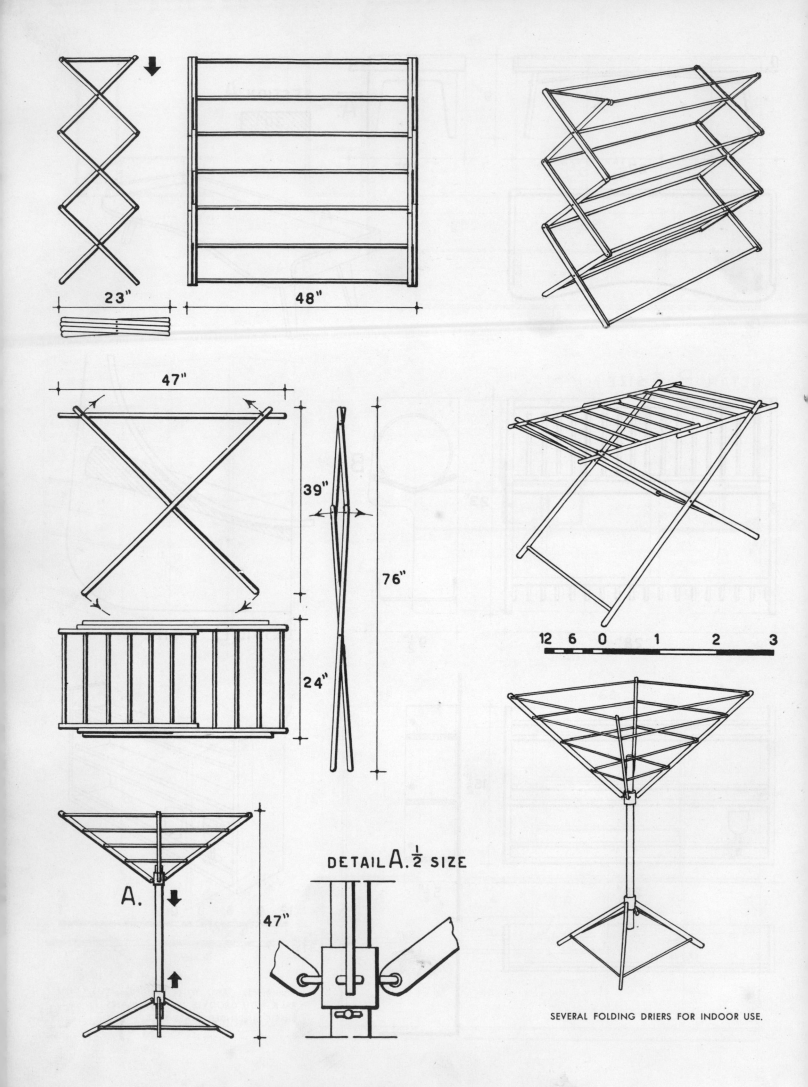

23"

48"

47"

39"

76"

24"

A.

47"

DETAIL A. ½ SIZE

12 6 0 1 2 3

SEVERAL FOLDING DRIERS FOR INDOOR USE.

122

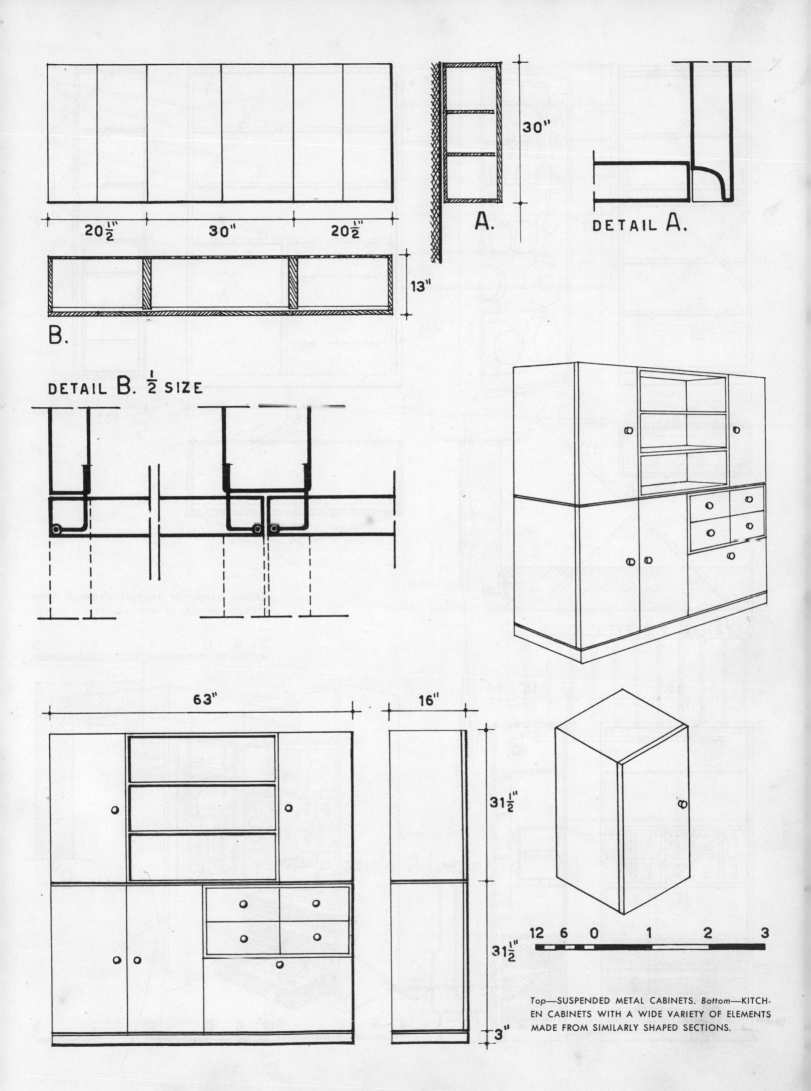

20½"   30"   20½"

13"

B.

30"

A.

DETAIL A.

DETAIL B. ½ SIZE

63"   16"

31½"

31½"

3"

12 6 0 1 2 3

Top—SUSPENDED METAL CABINETS, *Bottom*—KITCH-EN CABINETS WITH A WIDE VARIETY OF ELEMENTS MADE FROM SIMILARLY SHAPED SECTIONS.

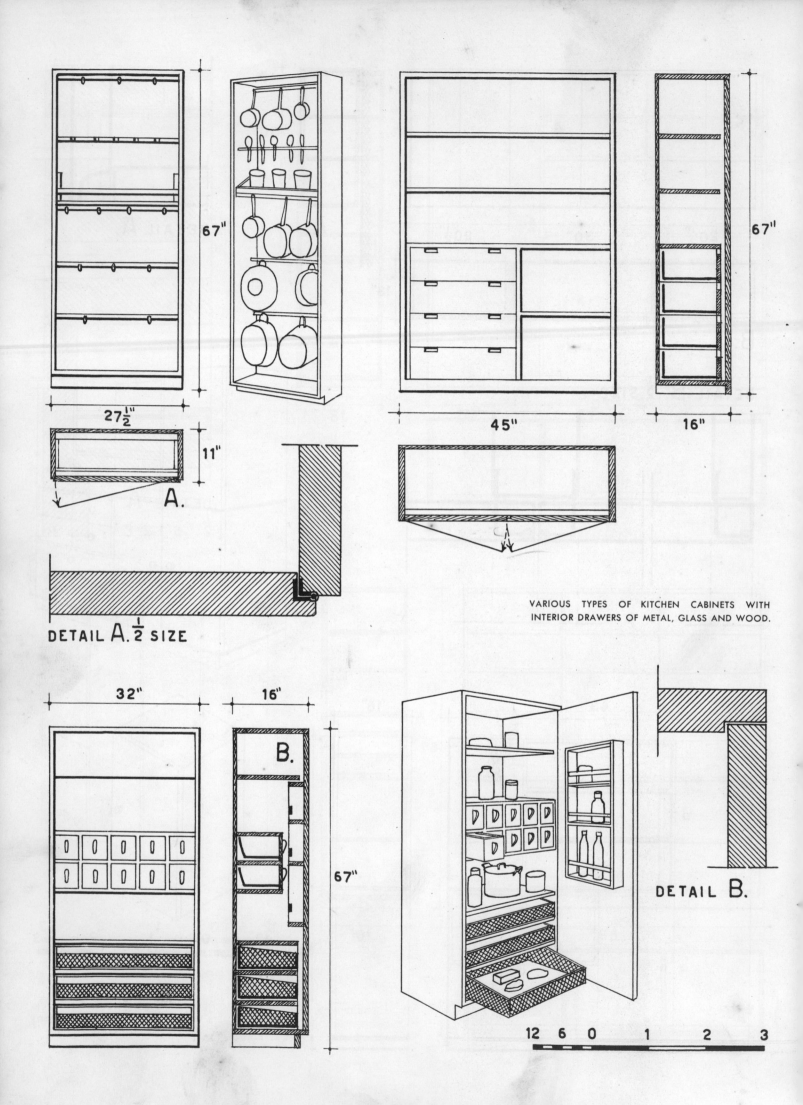

67"

27½"

11"

A.

DETAIL A. ½ SIZE

45"

16"

67"

VARIOUS TYPES OF KITCHEN CABINETS WITH
INTERIOR DRAWERS OF METAL, GLASS AND WOOD.

32"

16"

B.

67"

DETAIL B.

12 6 0 1 2 3

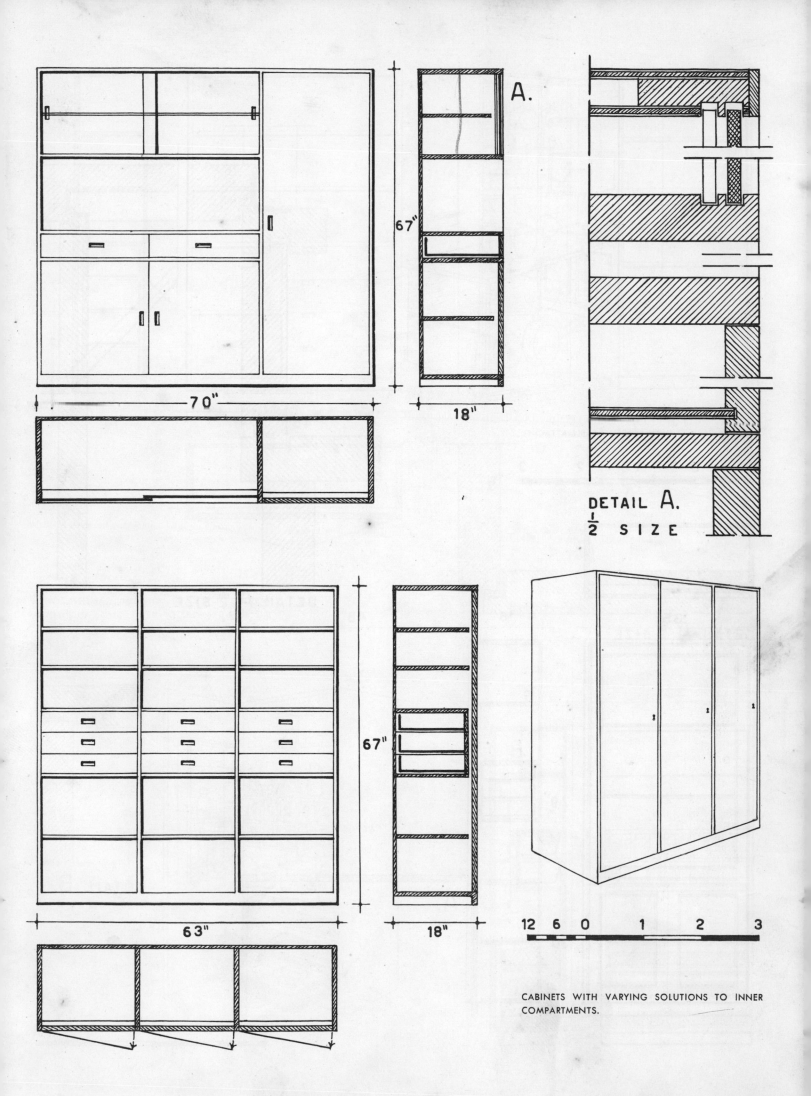

70"

67"

18"

A.

DETAIL A.
½ SIZE

63"

67"

18"

12 6 0 1 2 3

CABINETS WITH VARYING SOLUTIONS TO INNER
COMPARTMENTS.

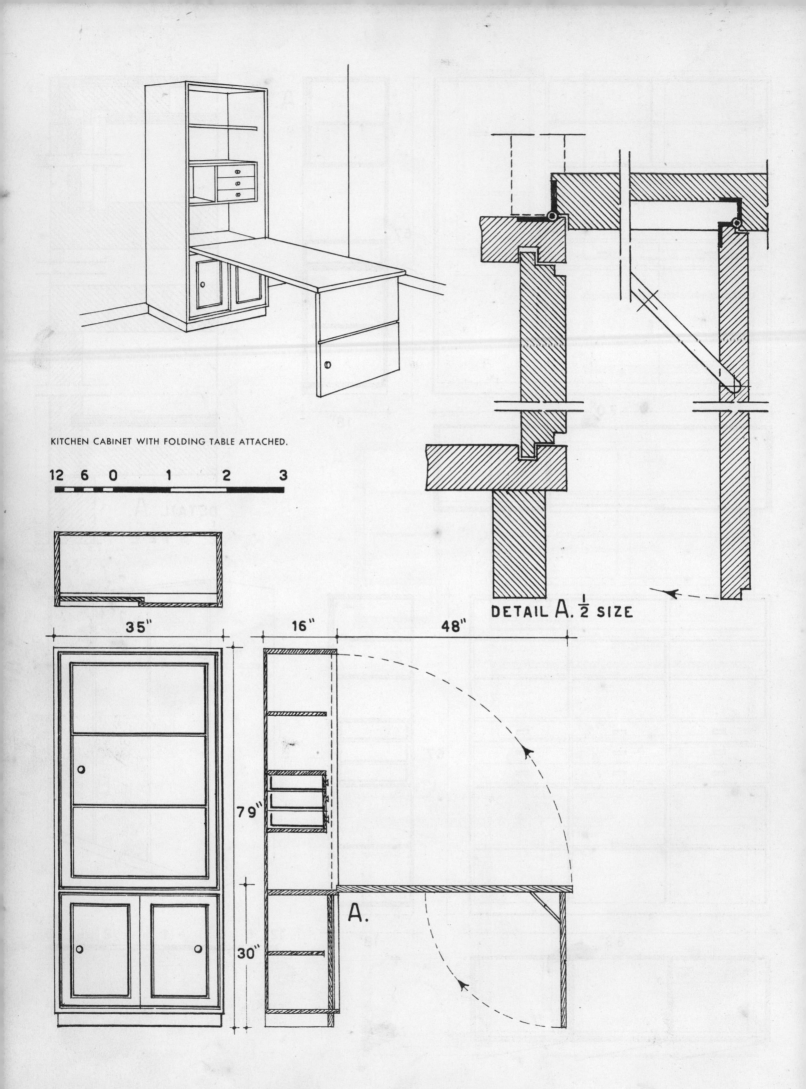

KITCHEN CABINET WITH FOLDING TABLE ATTACHED.

12 6 0 1 2 3

DETAIL A. ½ SIZE

35"

16"

48"

79"

30"

A.

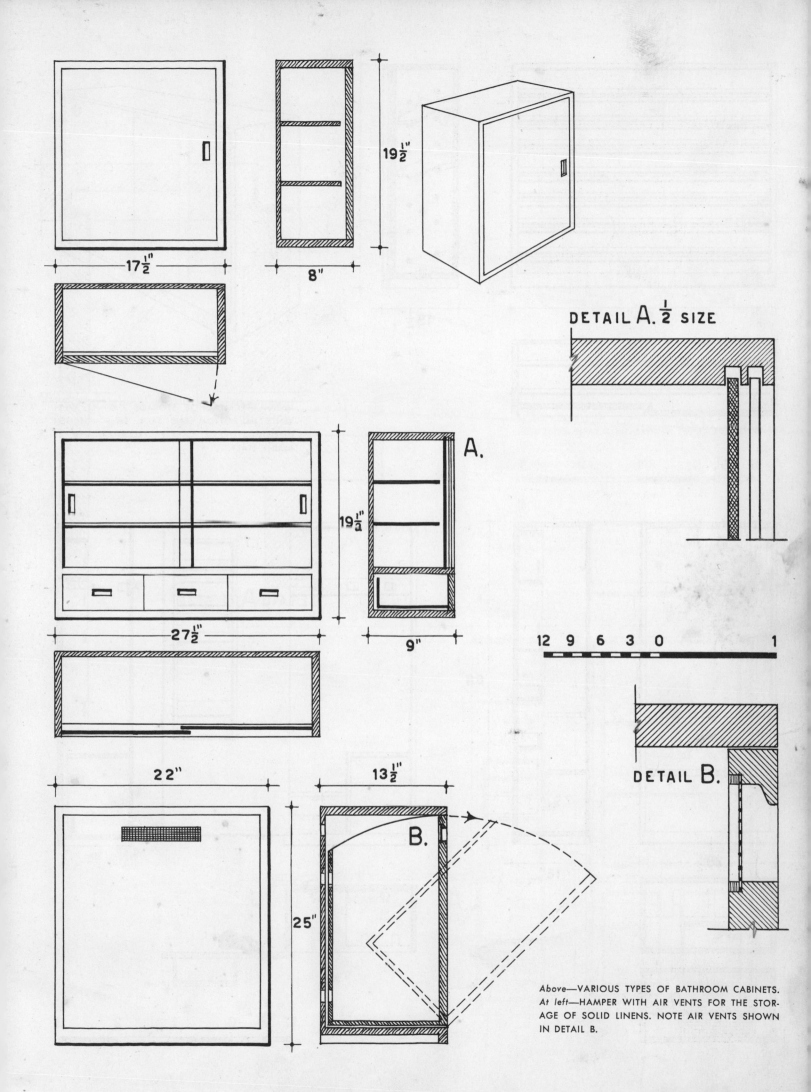

$17\frac{1}{2}$"

8"

$19\frac{1}{2}$"

DETAIL A. $\frac{1}{2}$ SIZE

A.

$19\frac{1}{4}$"

$27\frac{1}{2}$"

9"

12 9 6 3 0 1

DETAIL B.

22"

$13\frac{1}{2}$"

B.

25"

Above—VARIOUS TYPES OF BATHROOM CABINETS. At left—HAMPER WITH AIR VENTS FOR THE STORAGE OF SOLID LINENS. NOTE AIR VENTS SHOWN IN DETAIL B.

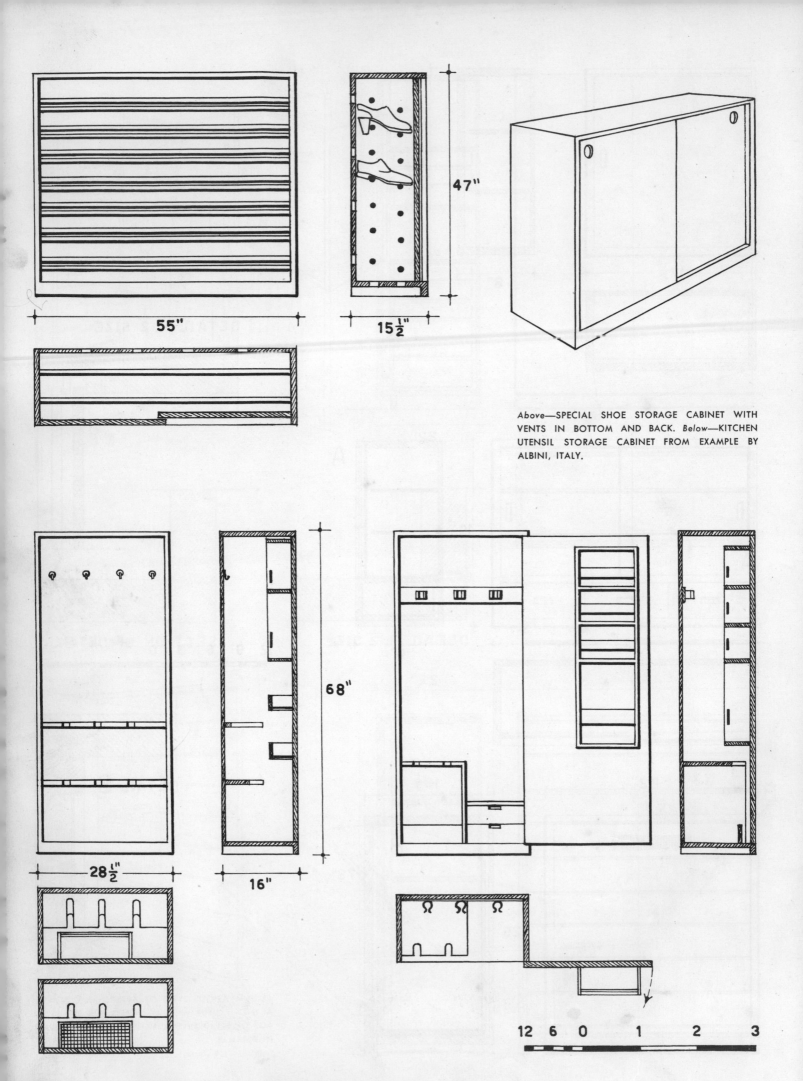

55"

15½"

47"

Above—SPECIAL SHOE STORAGE CABINET WITH VENTS IN BOTTOM AND BACK. *Below*—KITCHEN UTENSIL STORAGE CABINET FROM EXAMPLE BY ALBINI, ITALY.

28½"

16"

68"

12 6 0 1 2 3

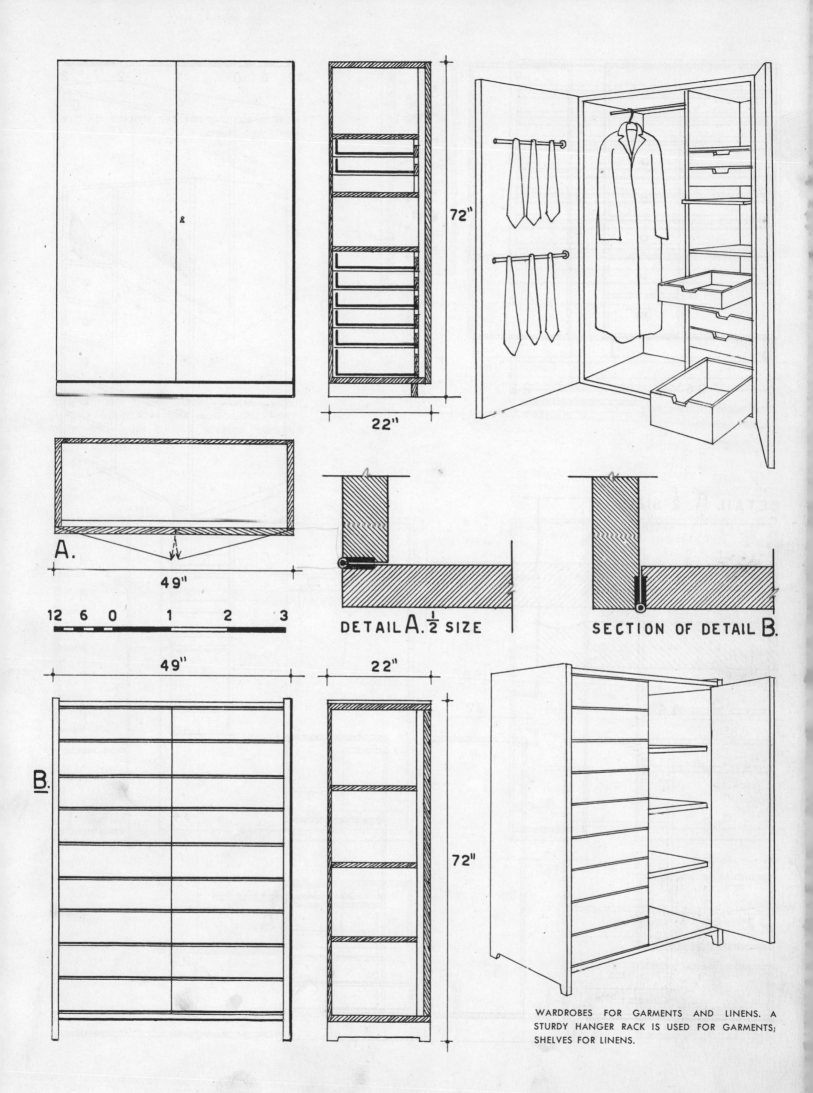

A.

49"

12 6 0 1 2 3

72"

22"

DETAIL A. ½ SIZE

SECTION OF DETAIL B.

49"

B.

22"

72"

WARDROBES FOR GARMENTS AND LINENS. A
STURDY HANGER RACK IS USED FOR GARMENTS;
SHELVES FOR LINENS.

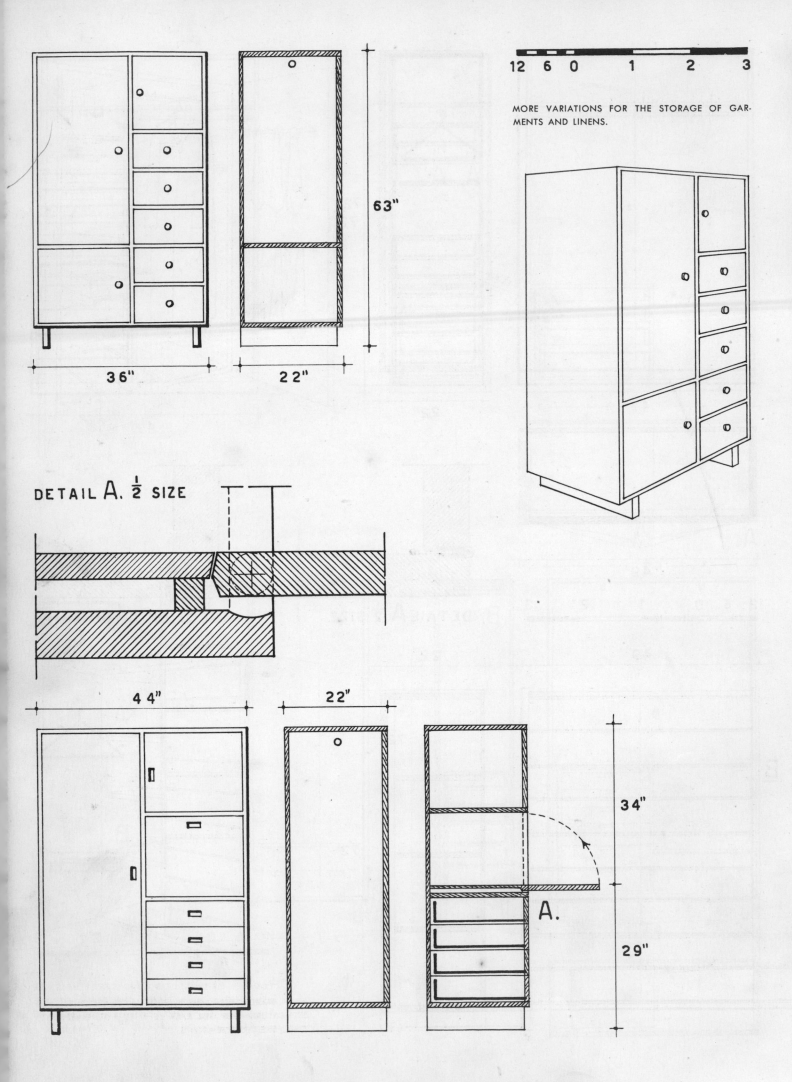

63"

36"

22"

DETAIL A. ½ SIZE

44"

22"

34"

A.

29"

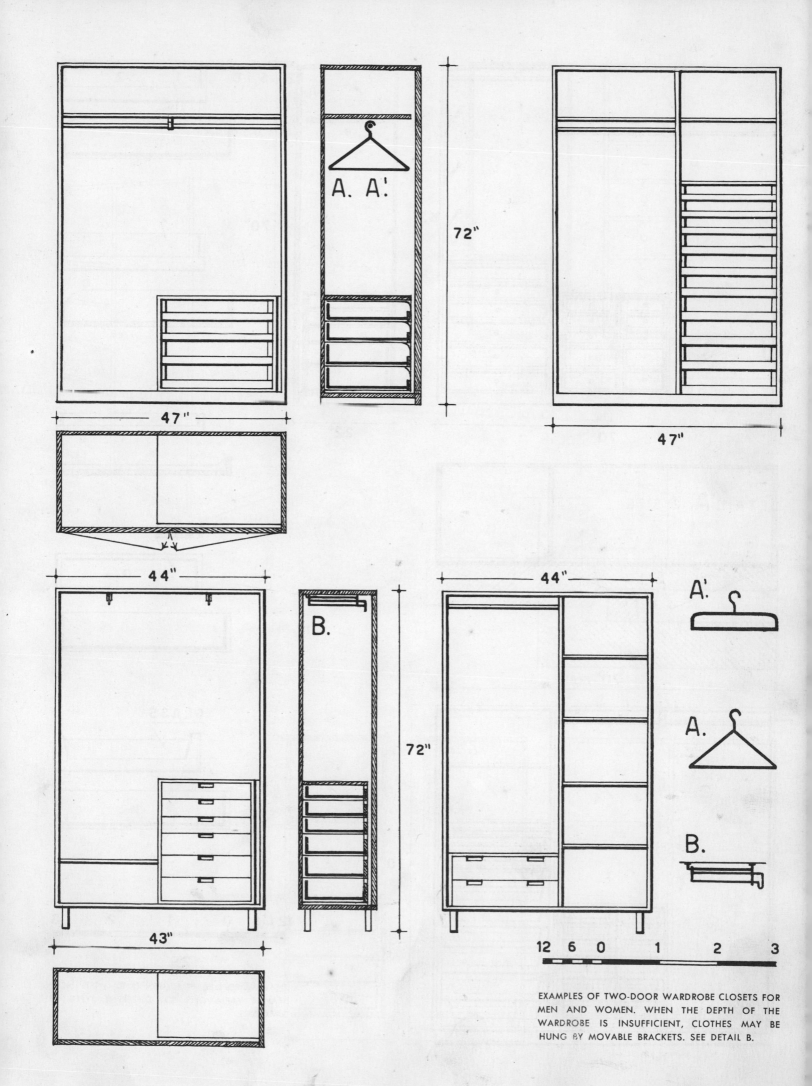

72"

A. A'.

47"

B.

72"

44"

A'.

A.

B.

44"

43"

12 6 0 1 2 3

EXAMPLES OF TWO-DOOR WARDROBE CLOSETS FOR MEN AND WOMEN. WHEN THE DEPTH OF THE WARDROBE IS INSUFFICIENT, CLOTHES MAY BE HUNG BY MOVABLE BRACKETS. SEE DETAIL B.

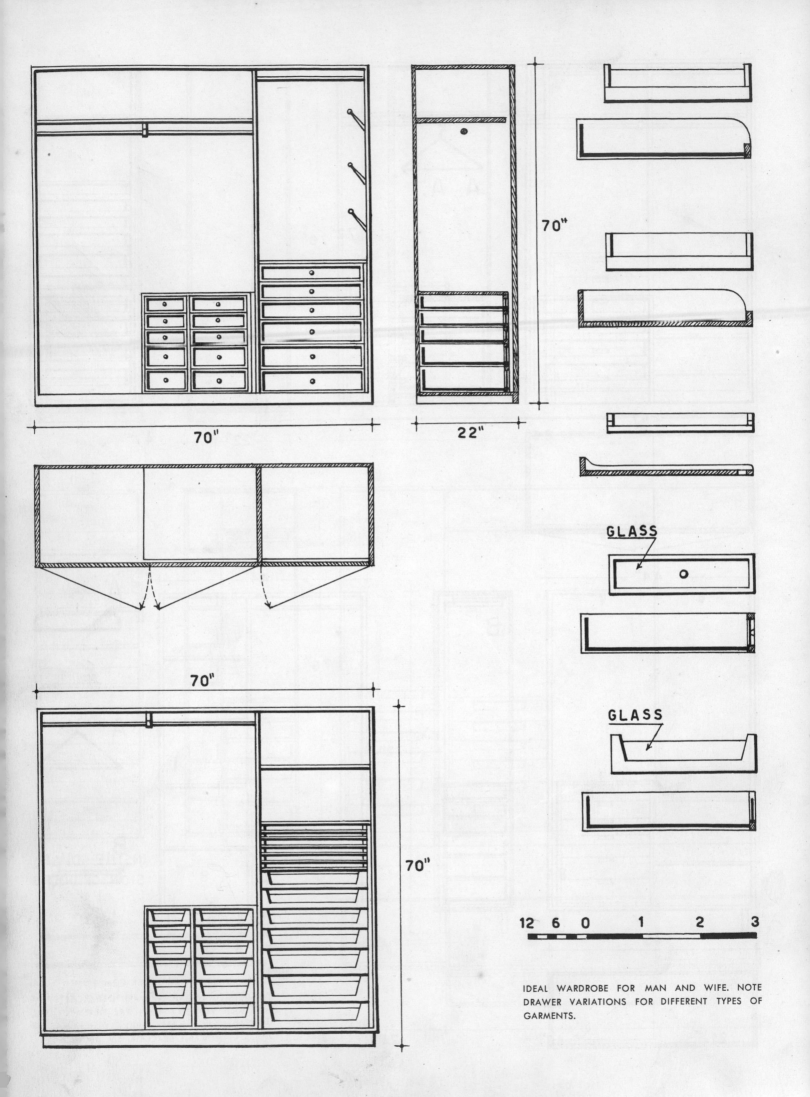

70"

70"

22"

70"

70"

GLASS

GLASS

12 6 0 1 2 3

IDEAL WARDROBE FOR MAN AND WIFE. NOTE
DRAWER VARIATIONS FOR DIFFERENT TYPES OF
GARMENTS.

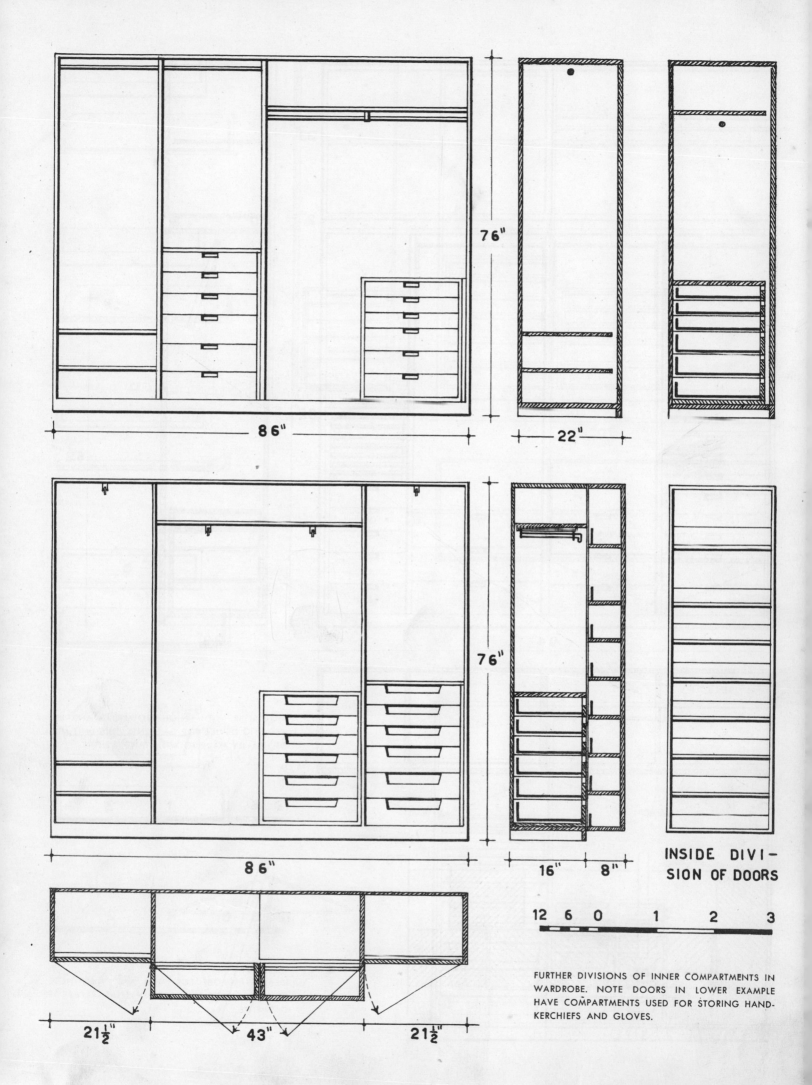

76"

86"

22"

76"

86"

16" 8"

INSIDE DIVI-
SION OF DOORS

21½"   43"   21½"

12 6 0   1   2   3

FURTHER DIVISIONS OF INNER COMPARTMENTS IN
WARDROBE. NOTE DOORS IN LOWER EXAMPLE
HAVE COMPARTMENTS USED FOR STORING HAND-
KERCHIEFS AND GLOVES.

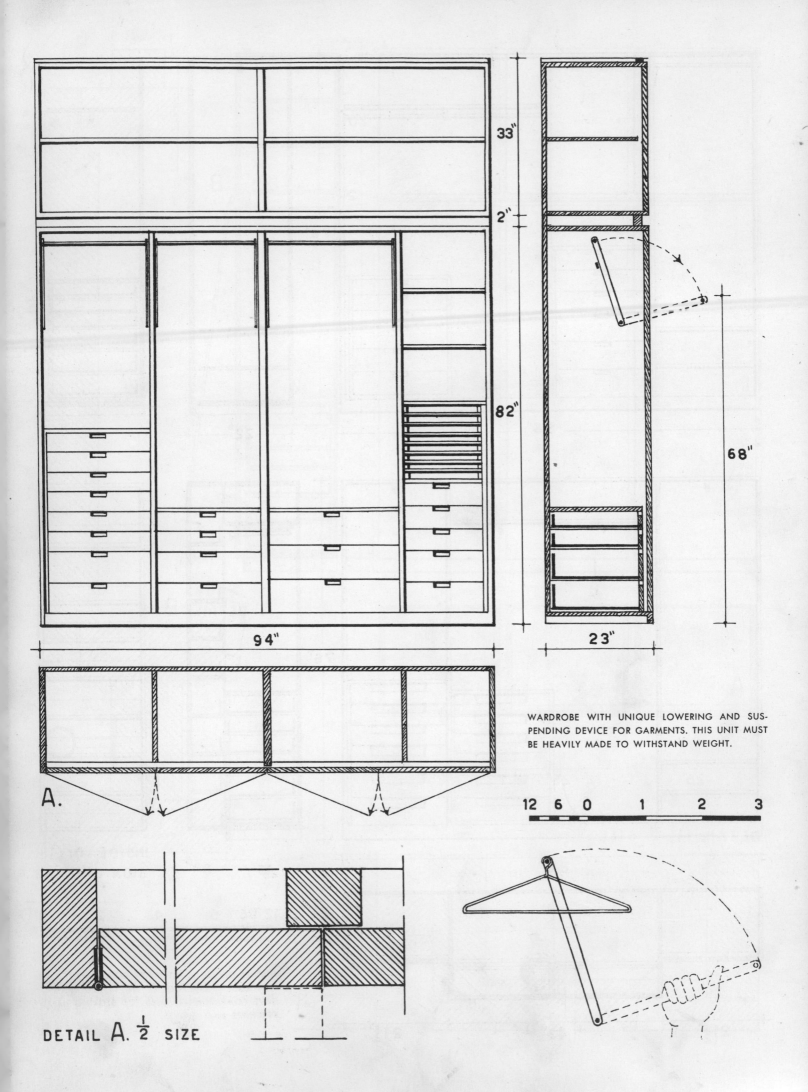

33"

2"

82"

68"

94"

23"

WARDROBE WITH UNIQUE LOWERING AND SUS-
PENDING DEVICE FOR GARMENTS. THIS UNIT MUST
BE HEAVILY MADE TO WITHSTAND WEIGHT.

12 6 0   1   2   3

A.

DETAIL A. ½ SIZE

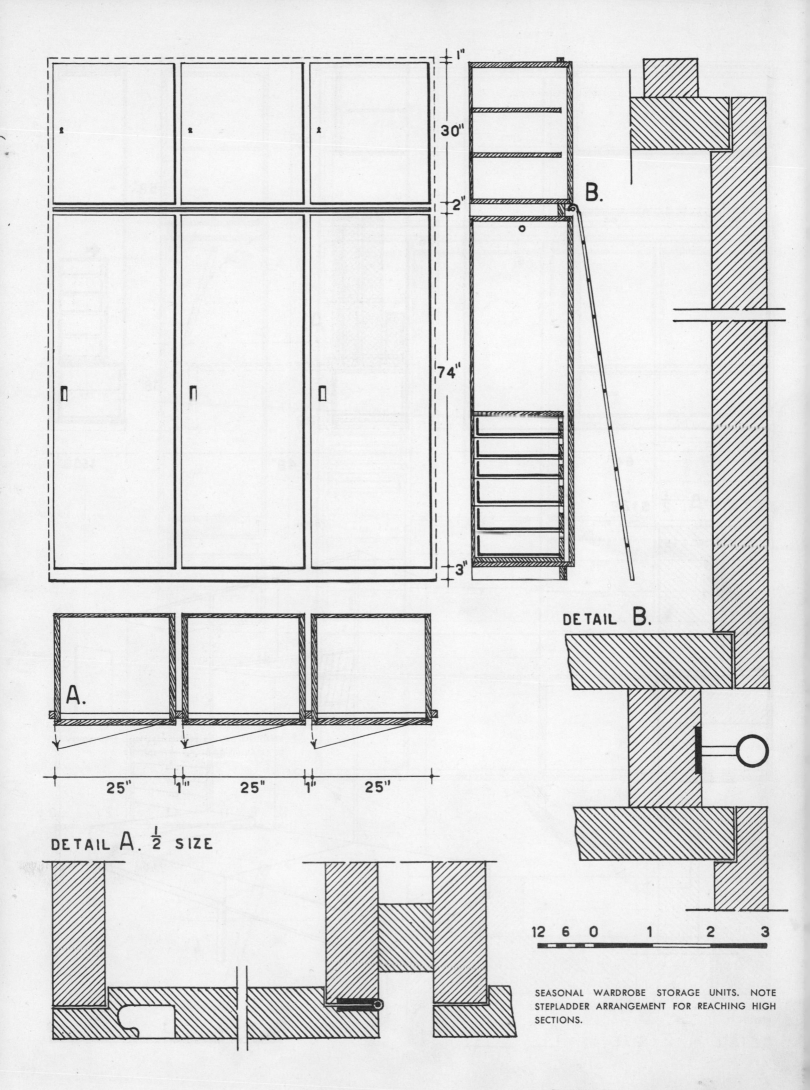

1"

30"

2"

74"

3"

25"   1"   25"   1"   25"

DETAIL A. ½ SIZE

A.

B.

DETAIL B.

12 6 0   1   2   3

SEASONAL WARDROBE STORAGE UNITS. NOTE
STEPLADDER ARRANGEMENT FOR REACHING HIGH
SECTIONS.

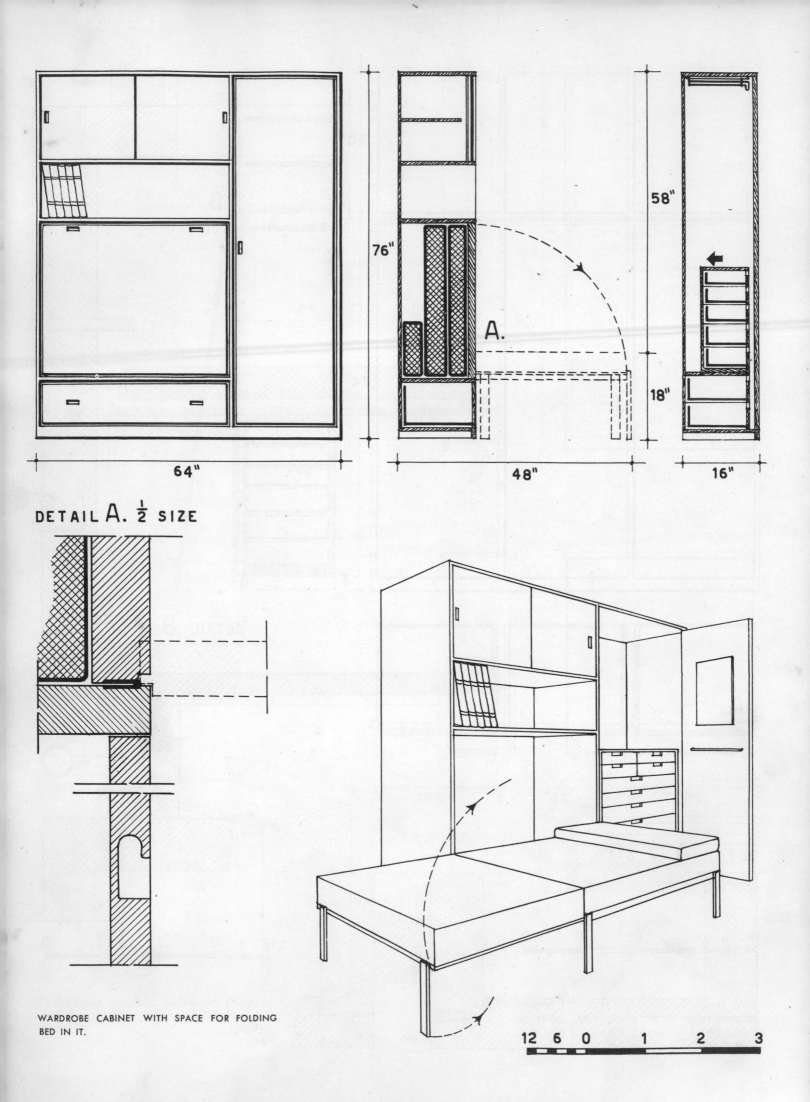

64"

76"

48"

58"

18"

16"

A.

DETAIL A. ½ SIZE

WARDROBE CABINET WITH SPACE FOR FOLDING
BED IN IT.

12 6 0 1 2 3

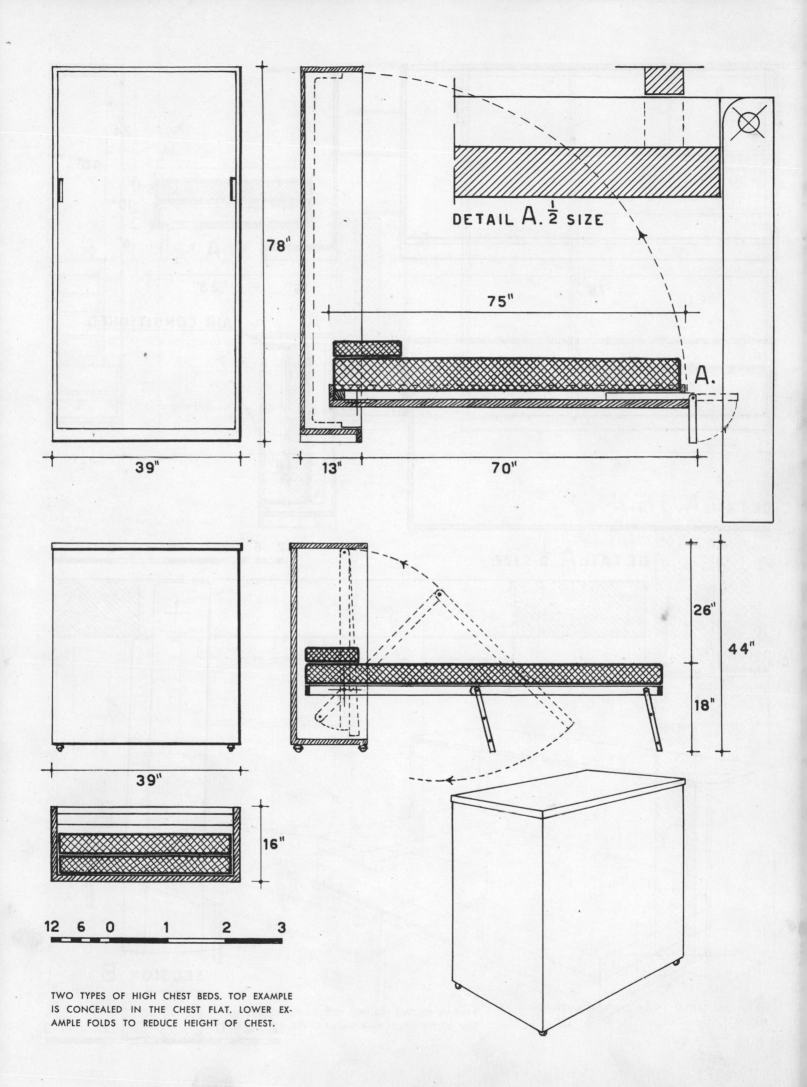

78"

39"

DETAIL A. $\frac{1}{2}$ SIZE

75"

13"   70"

A.

26"

44"

18"

39"

16"

12 6 0   1   2   3

TWO TYPES OF HIGH CHEST BEDS. TOP EXAMPLE
IS CONCEALED IN THE CHEST FLAT. LOWER EX-
AMPLE FOLDS TO REDUCE HEIGHT OF CHEST.

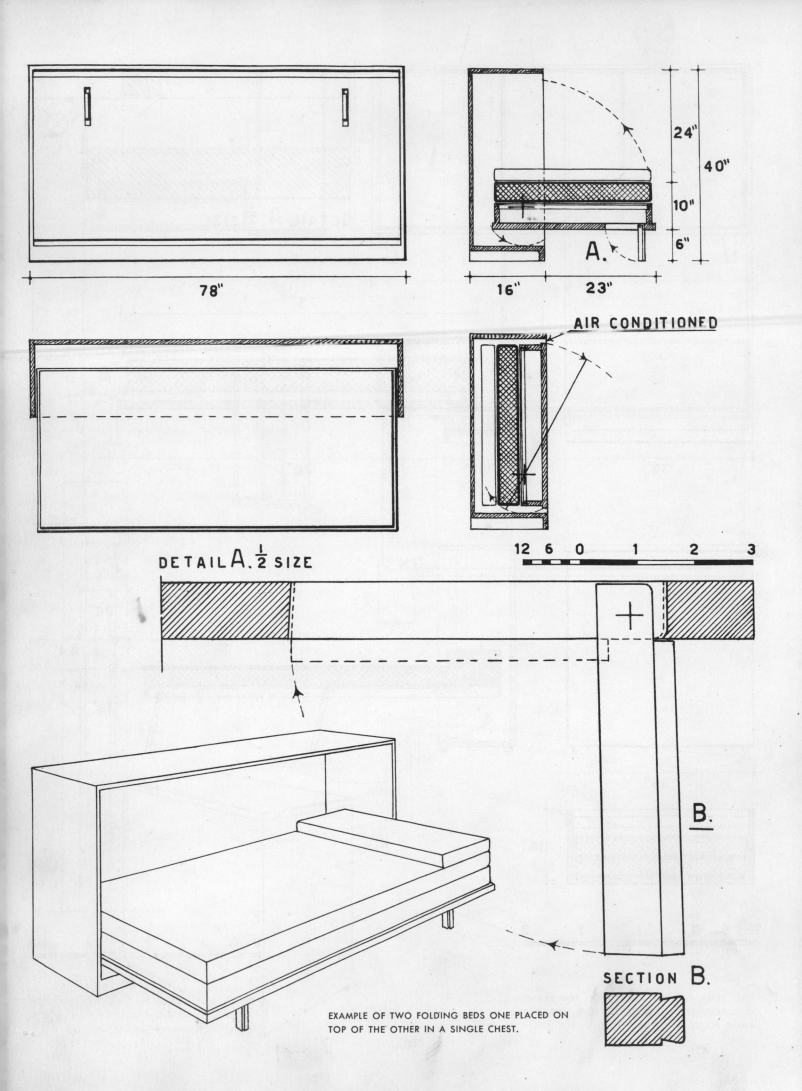

78"

24"

40"

10"

6"

16"   23"

A.

AIR CONDITIONED

12 6 0 1 2 3

DETAIL A. $\frac{1}{2}$ SIZE

B.

SECTION B.

EXAMPLE OF TWO FOLDING BEDS ONE PLACED ON
TOP OF THE OTHER IN A SINGLE CHEST.

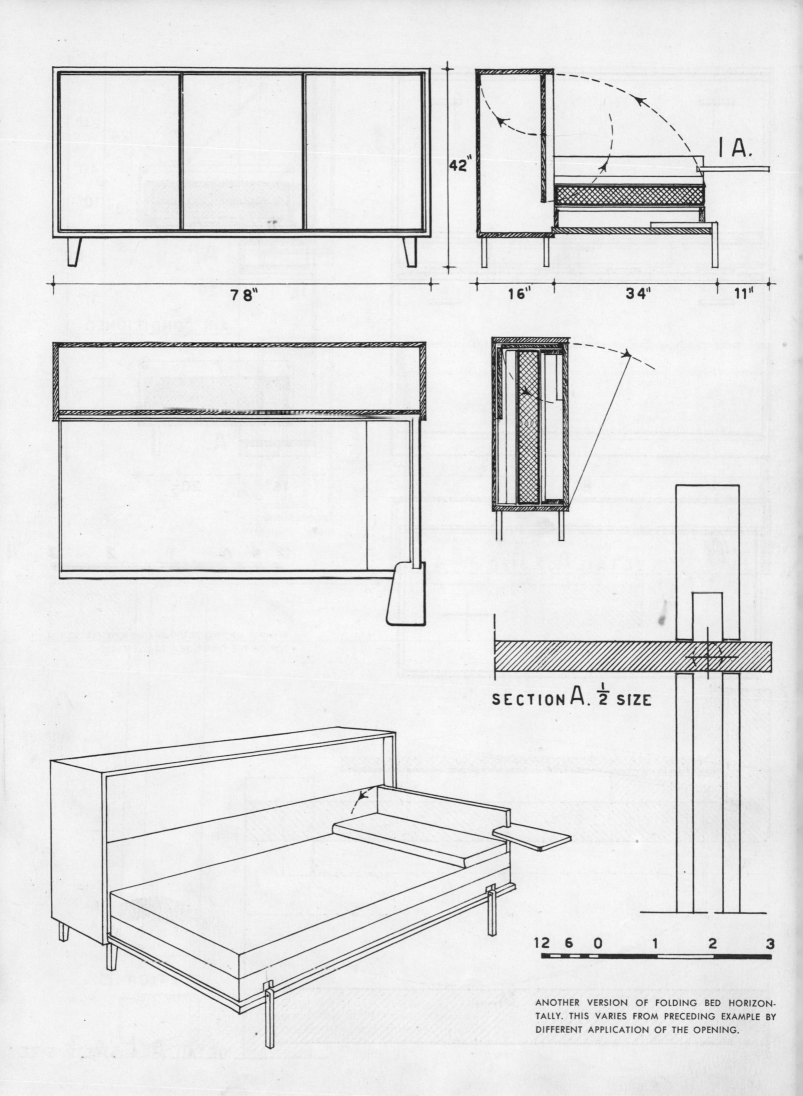

42"

78"

16"   34"   11"

1A.

SECTION A. $\frac{1}{2}$ SIZE

12 6 0 1 2 3

ANOTHER VERSION OF FOLDING BED HORIZON-
TALLY. THIS VARIES FROM PRECEDING EXAMPLE BY
DIFFERENT APPLICATION OF THE OPENING.

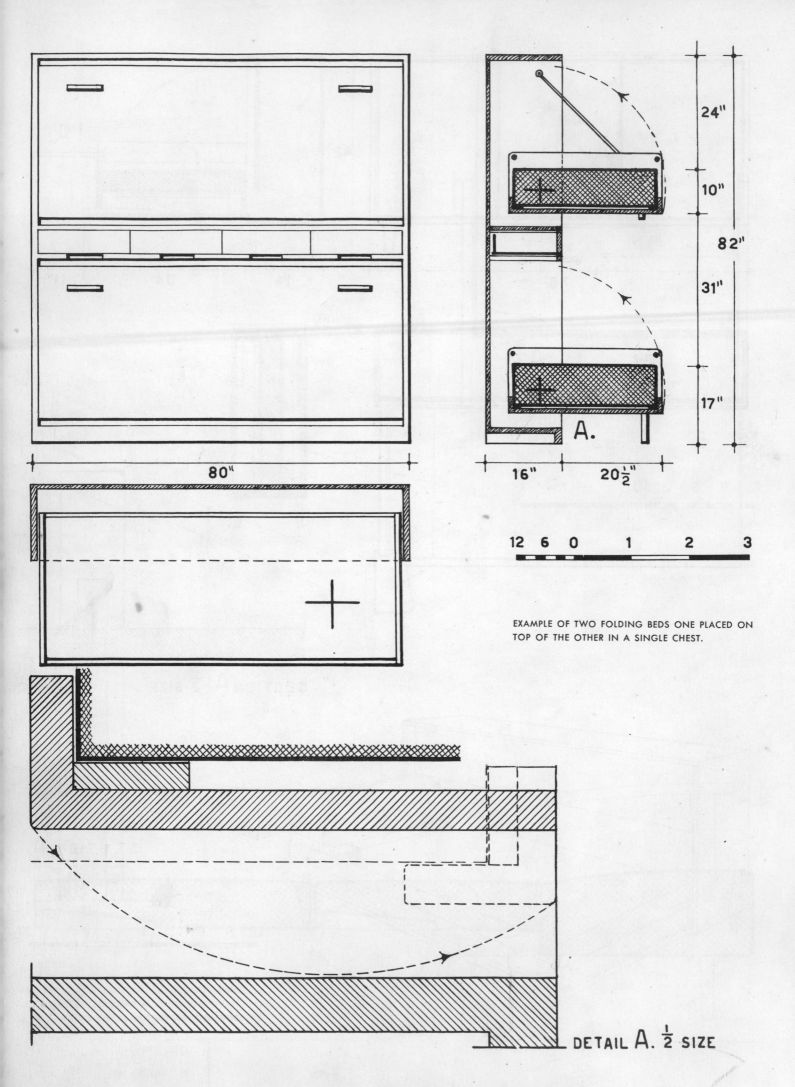

80"

24"

10"

82"

31"

17"

16"   20½"

A.

12 6 0   1   2   3

EXAMPLE OF TWO FOLDING BEDS ONE PLACED ON
TOP OF THE OTHER IN A SINGLE CHEST.

DETAIL A. ½ SIZE

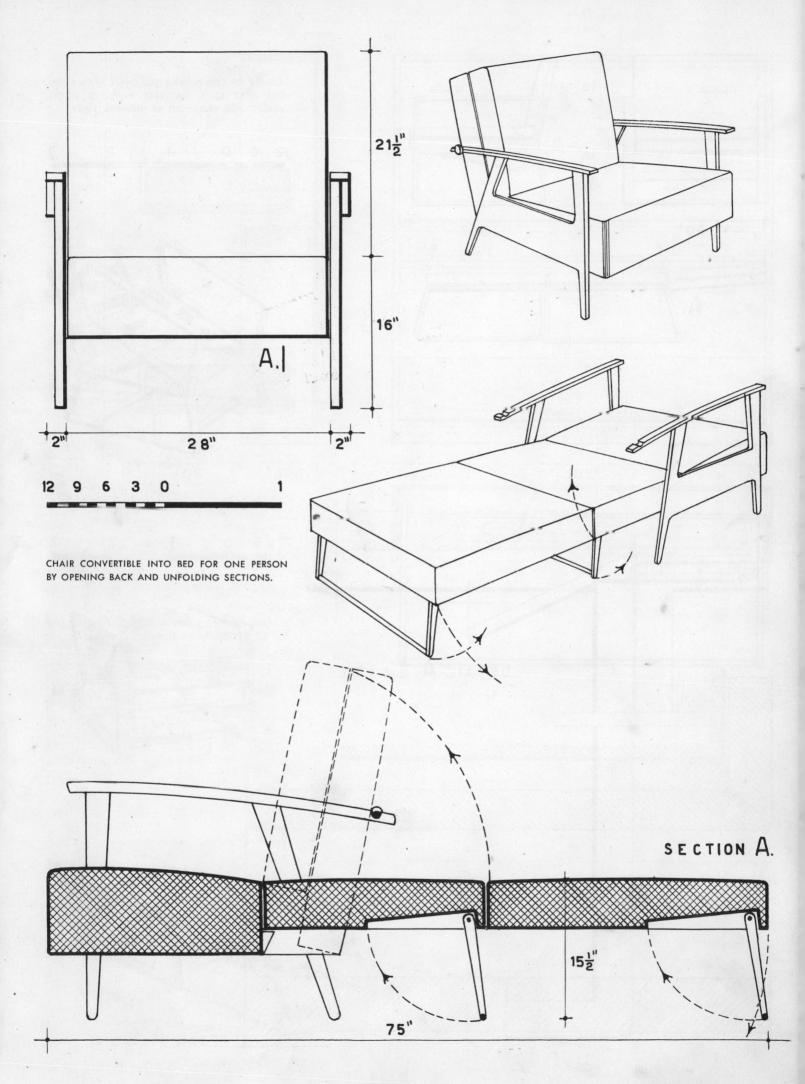

21½"

16"

A.1

2" 28" 2"

12 9 6 3 0 1

CHAIR CONVERTIBLE INTO BED FOR ONE PERSON
BY OPENING BACK AND UNFOLDING SECTIONS.

SECTION A.

15½"

75"

141

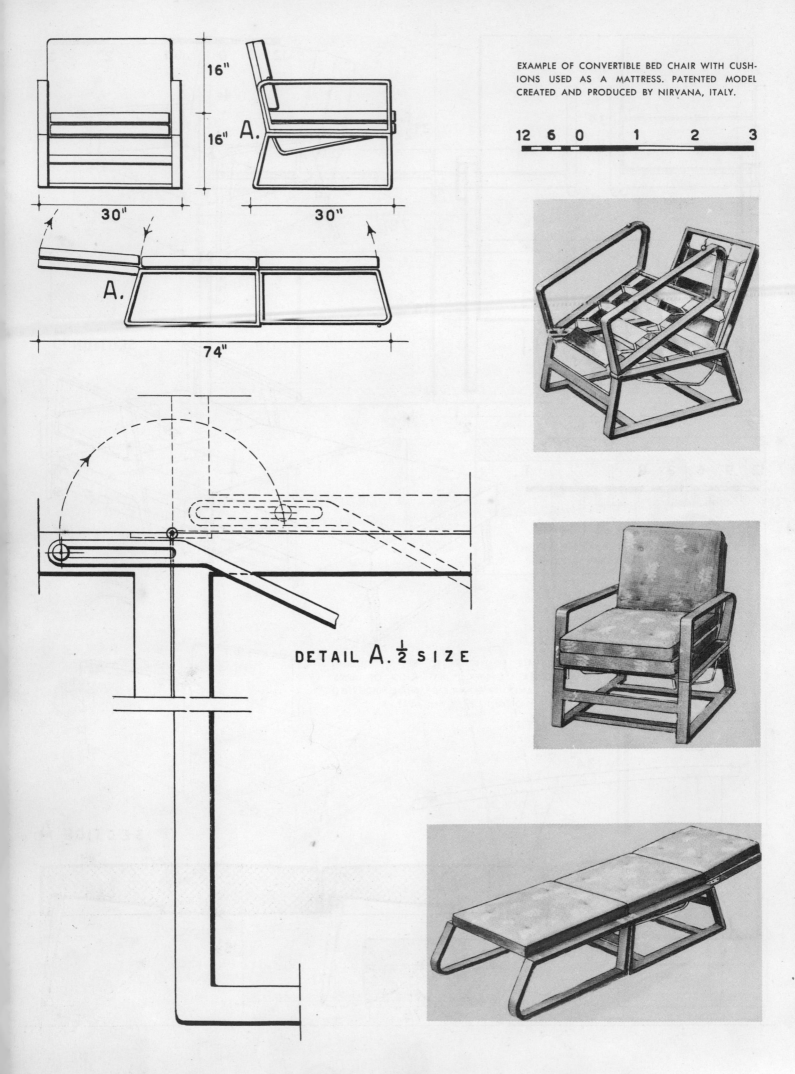

16"

16"

A.

30"

30"

A.

74"

EXAMPLE OF CONVERTIBLE BED CHAIR WITH CUSH-
IONS USED AS A MATTRESS. PATENTED MODEL
CREATED AND PRODUCED BY NIRVANA, ITALY.

12 6 0   1   2   3

DETAIL A. ½ SIZE

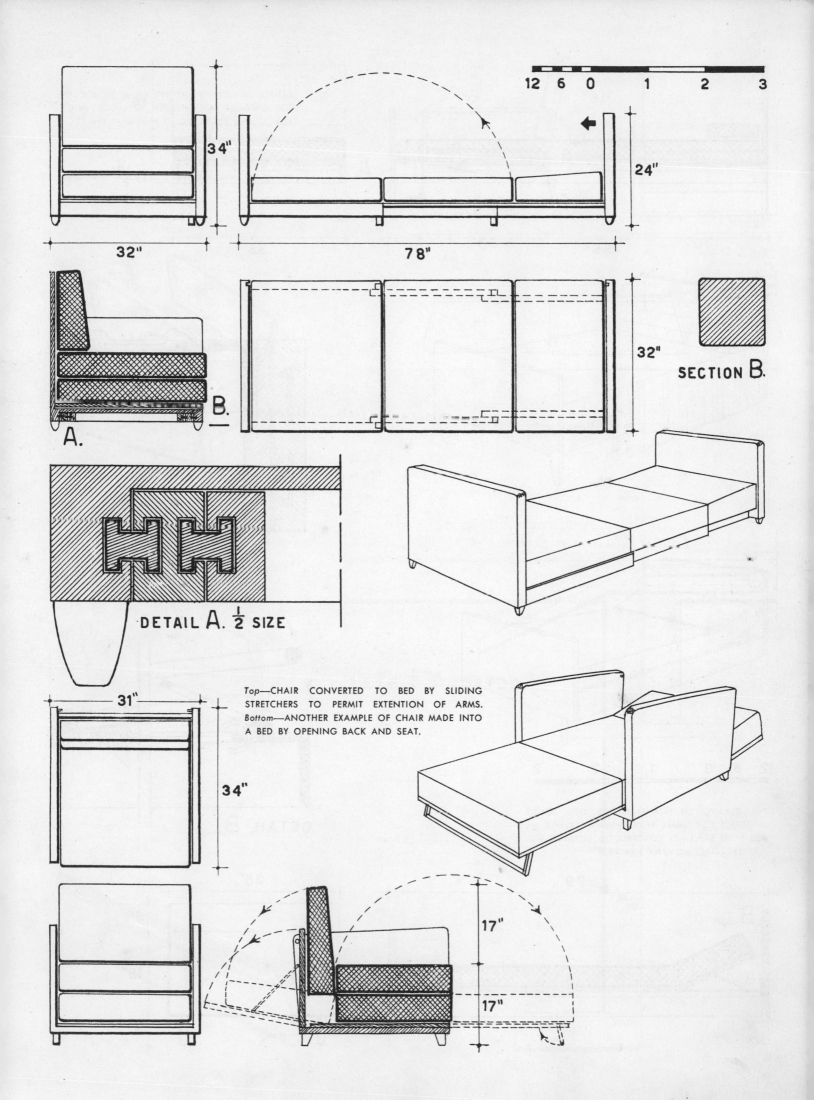

12 6 0 1 2 3

34"

24"

32"

78"

32"

SECTION B.

A. B.

DETAIL A. ½ SIZE

31"

34"

17"

17"

Top—CHAIR CONVERTED TO BED BY SLIDING STRETCHERS TO PERMIT EXTENTION OF ARMS. *Bottom*—ANOTHER EXAMPLE OF CHAIR MADE INTO A BED BY OPENING BACK AND SEAT.

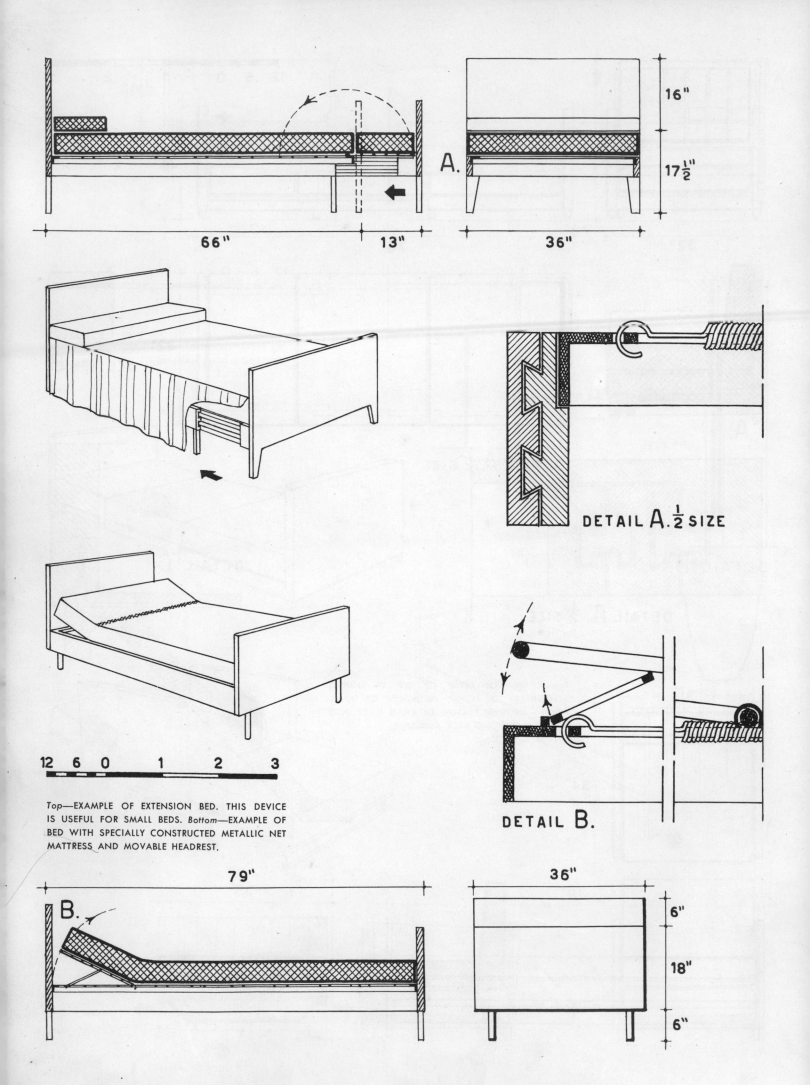

A.

66"   13"   36"   16"   17 1/2"

DETAIL A. 1/2 SIZE

DETAIL B.

12 6 0 1 2 3

Top—EXAMPLE OF EXTENSION BED. THIS DEVICE IS USEFUL FOR SMALL BEDS. Bottom—EXAMPLE OF BED WITH SPECIALLY CONSTRUCTED METALLIC NET MATTRESS AND MOVABLE HEADREST.

79"   36"   6"   18"   6"

B.

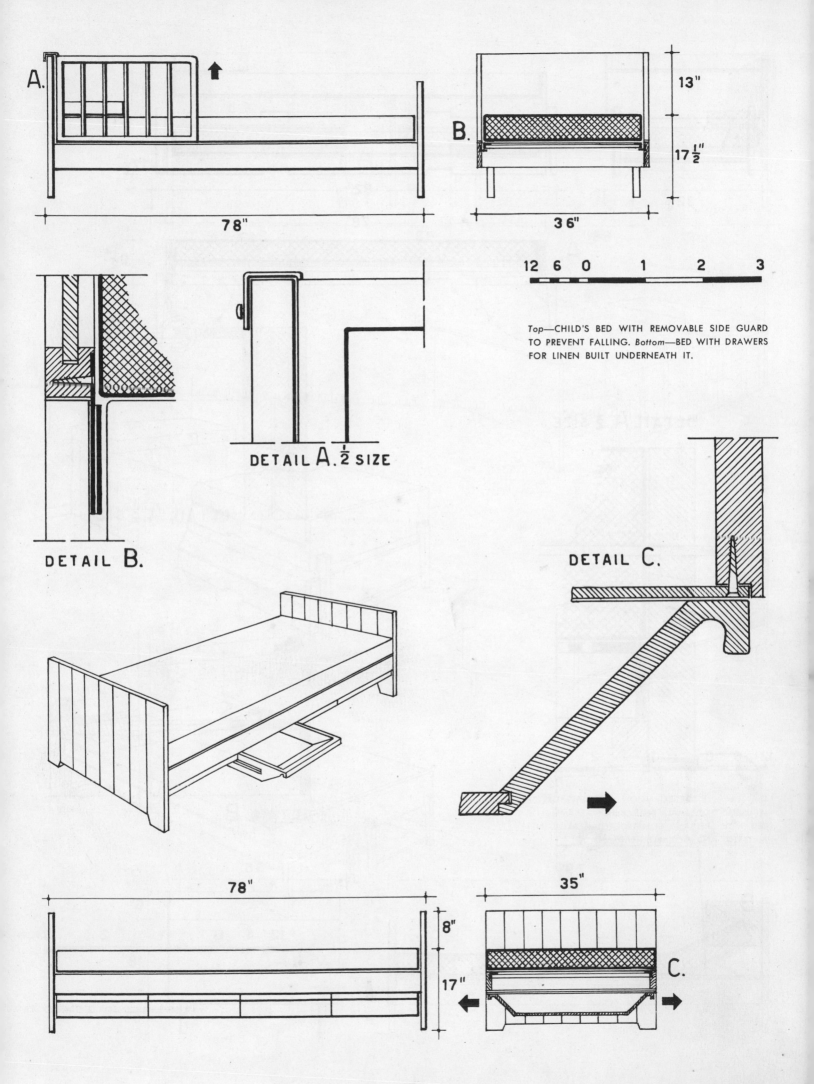

A.

78"

B.

13"

17 1/2"

36"

12 6 0 1 2 3

Top—CHILD'S BED WITH REMOVABLE SIDE GUARD
TO PREVENT FALLING. *Bottom*—BED WITH DRAWERS
FOR LINEN BUILT UNDERNEATH IT.

DETAIL A. 1/2 SIZE

DETAIL B.

DETAIL C.

78"

8"

17"

35"

C.

145

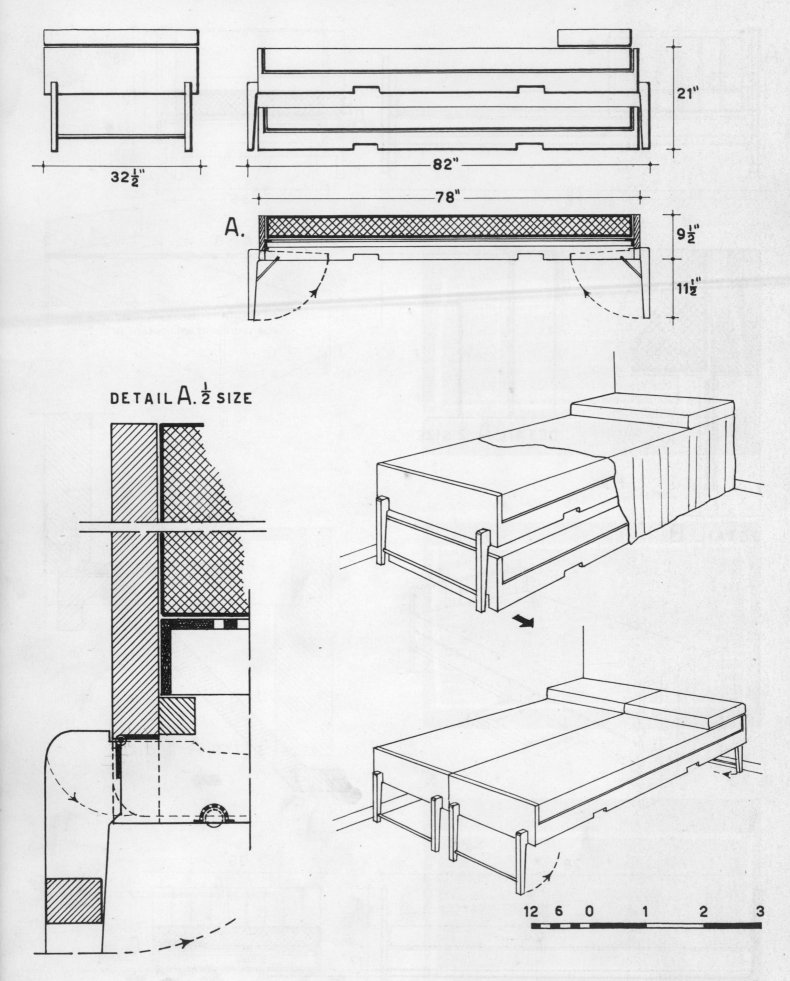

21"

82"

32½"

78"

A.

9½"

11½"

DETAIL A. ½ SIZE

12 6 0 1 2 3

BEDS WHICH MAY BE STACKED FOR STORAGE.

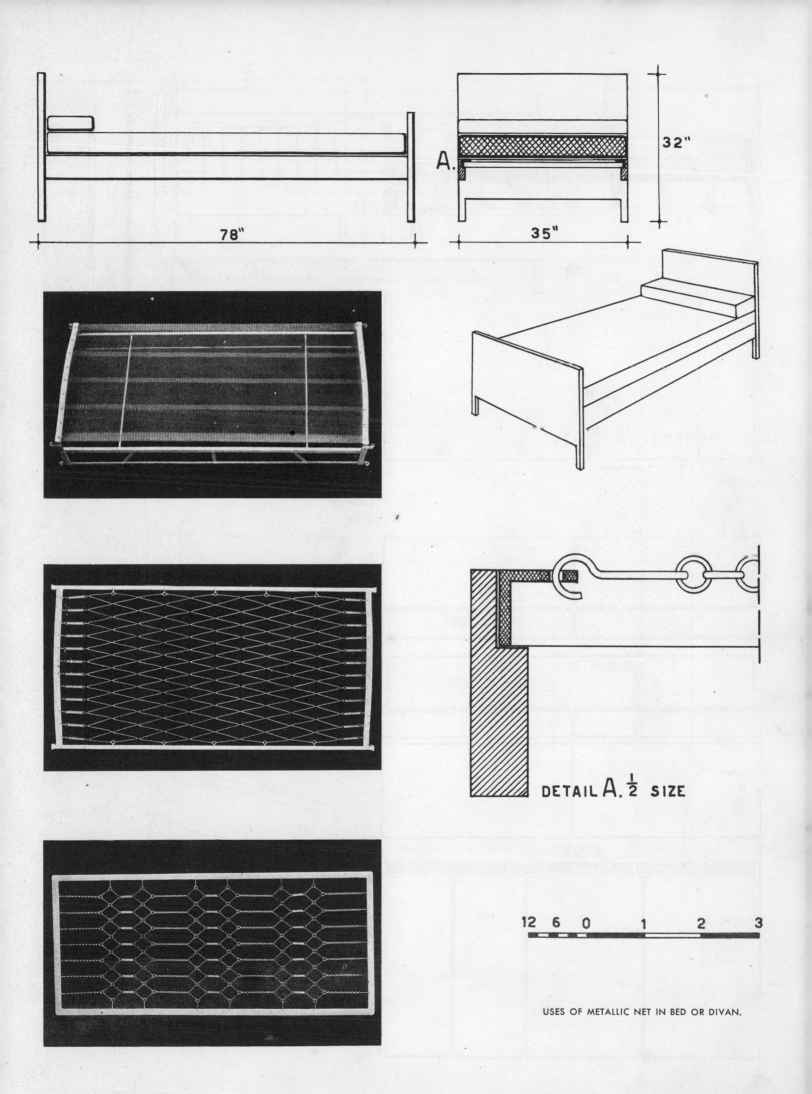

78"

35"   32"

A.

DETAIL A. ½ SIZE

12 6 0 1 2 3

USES OF METALLIC NET IN BED OR DIVAN.

147

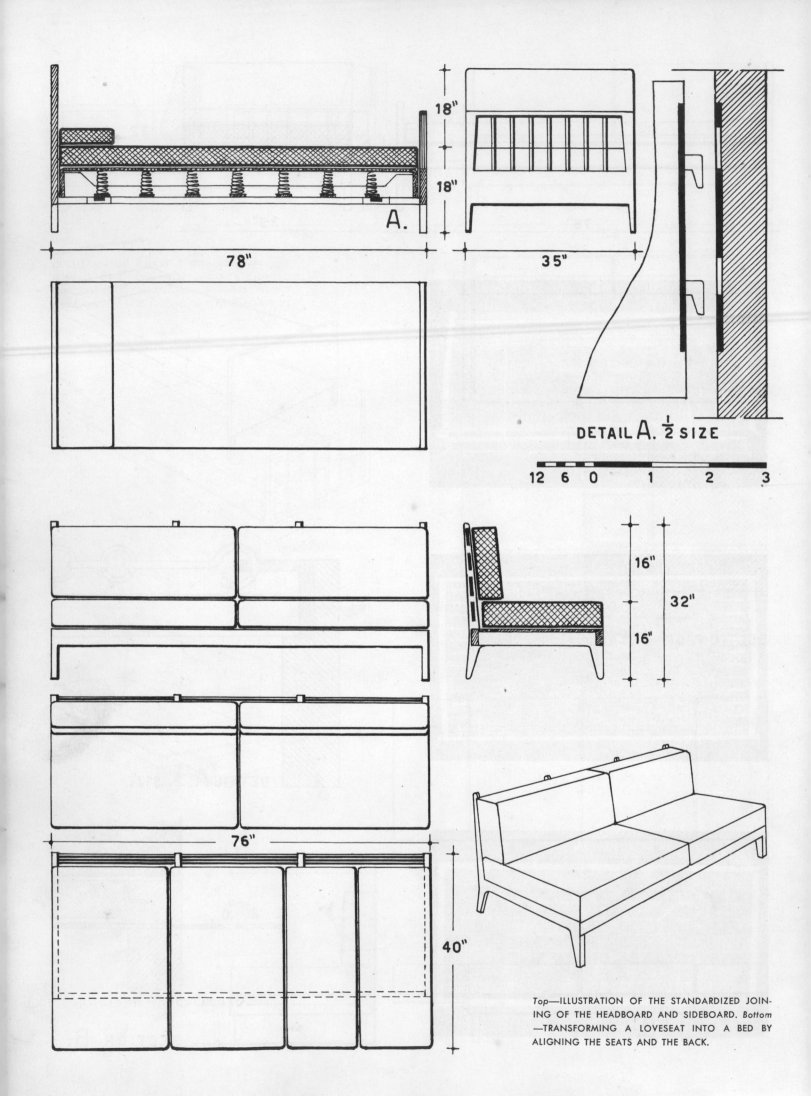

A.

18"

18"

78"

35"

DETAIL A. ½ SIZE

12 6 0   1   2   3

16"

32"

16"

76"

40"

Top—ILLUSTRATION OF THE STANDARDIZED JOIN-
ING OF THE HEADBOARD AND SIDEBOARD. Bottom
—TRANSFORMING A LOVESEAT INTO A BED BY
ALIGNING THE SEATS AND THE BACK.

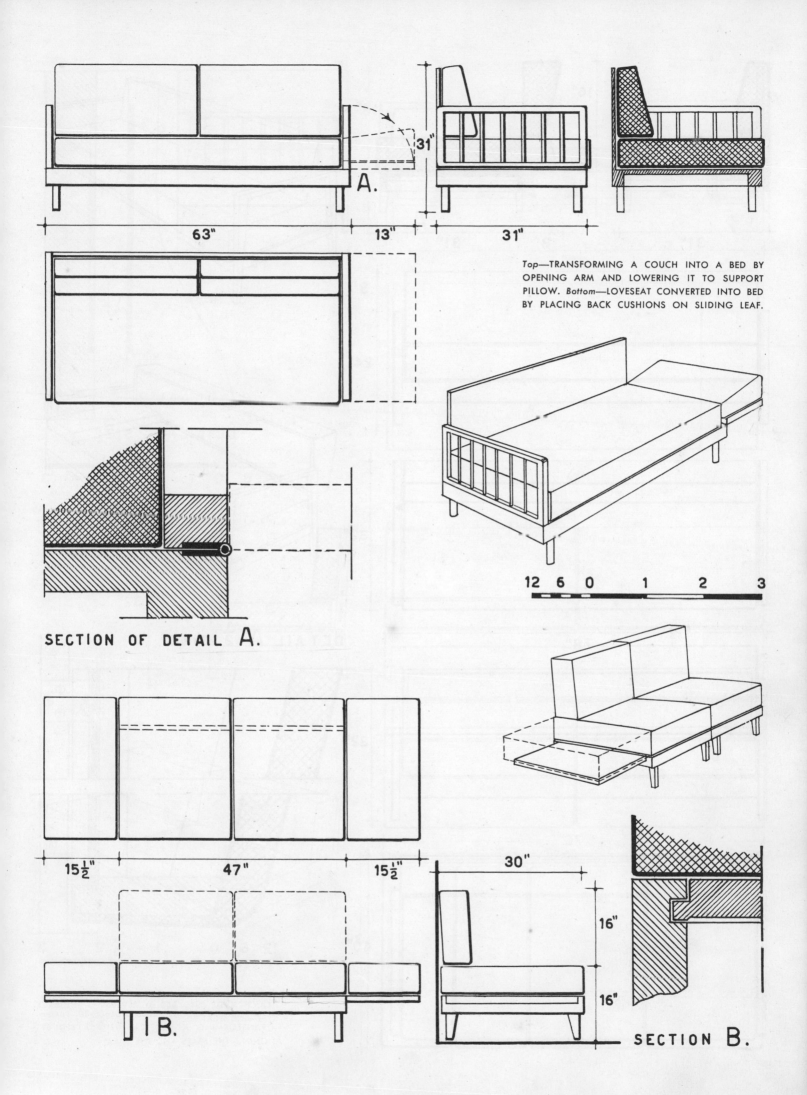

A.

63"   13"   31"   31"

Top—TRANSFORMING A COUCH INTO A BED BY OPENING ARM AND LOWERING IT TO SUPPORT PILLOW. *Bottom*—LOVESEAT CONVERTED INTO BED BY PLACING BACK CUSHIONS ON SLIDING LEAF.

SECTION OF DETAIL A.

12 6 0 1 2 3

15½"   47"   15½"

B.   30"   16"   16"

SECTION B.

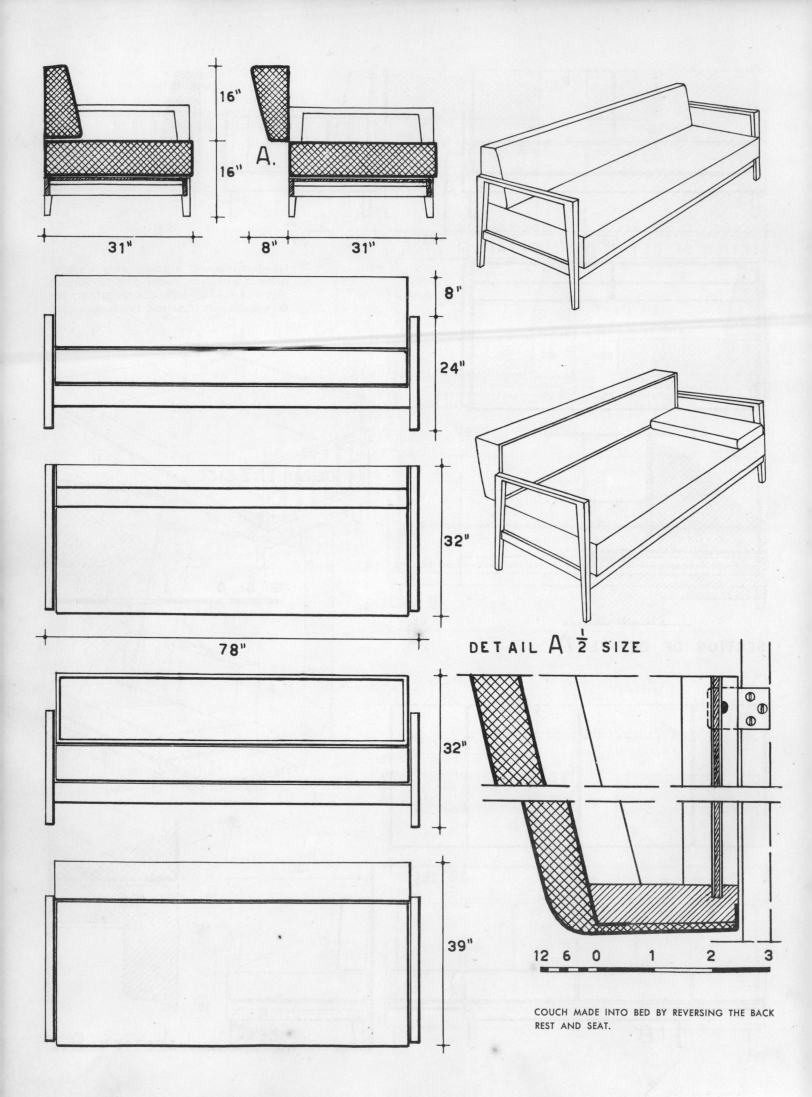

16"

16"

A.

31"

8"   31"

8"

24"

32"

78"

32"

32"

39"

DETAIL A ½ SIZE

12 6 0   1   2   3

COUCH MADE INTO BED BY REVERSING THE BACK
REST AND SEAT.

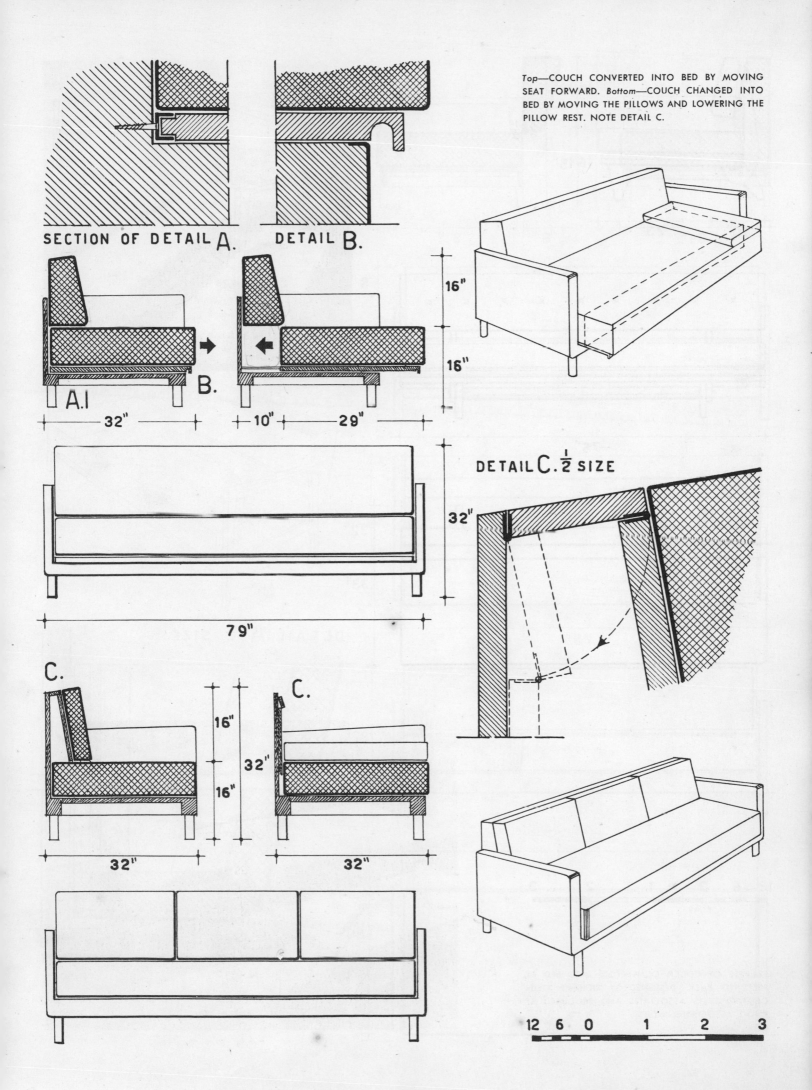

SECTION OF DETAIL A. DETAIL B.

A.I

B.

32"

10" 29"

16"

16"

79"

32"

C.

C.

16"

16"

32"

32" 32"

Top—COUCH CONVERTED INTO BED BY MOVING SEAT FORWARD. Bottom—COUCH CHANGED INTO BED BY MOVING THE PILLOWS AND LOWERING THE PILLOW REST. NOTE DETAIL C.

DETAIL C. ½ SIZE

12 6 0 1 2 3

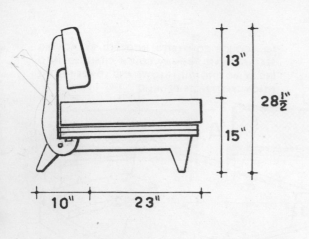

13"

28½"

15"

10"   23"

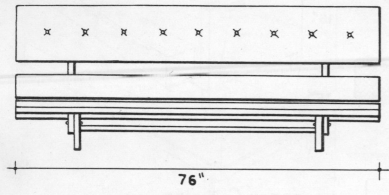

76"

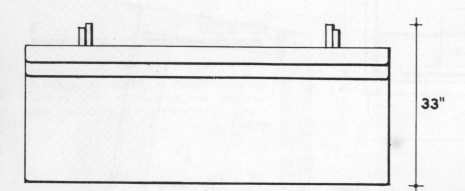

33"

12 6 0 1 2 3

EXAMPLE OF COUCH CONVERTIBLE INTO BED BY
RECEDING BACK. DESIGNED BY RICHARD STEIN
OF ARCHITECTS ASSOCIATES AND PRODUCED BY
KNOLL ASSOCIATES, INC.

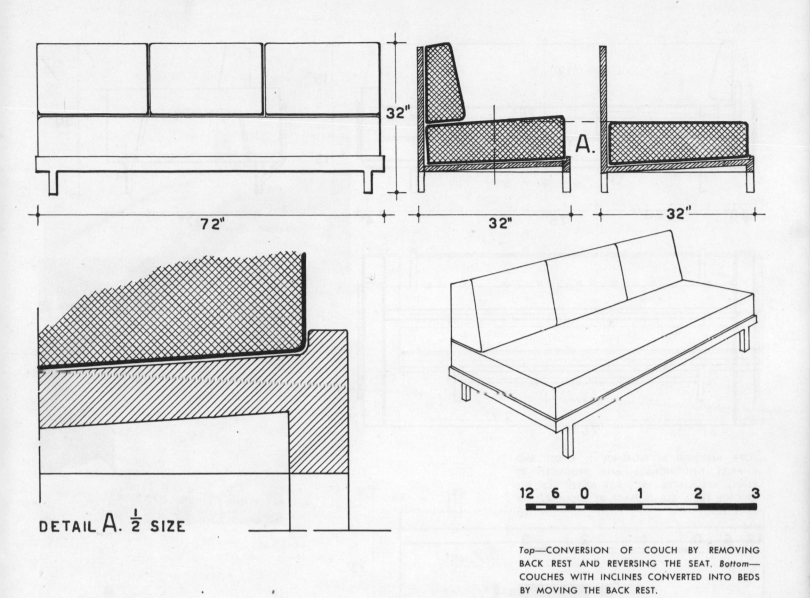

32"

72"

32"

32"

A.

DETAIL A. ½ SIZE

12 6 0 1 2 3

Top—CONVERSION OF COUCH BY REMOVING
BACK REST AND REVERSING THE SEAT. Bottom—
COUCHES WITH INCLINES CONVERTED INTO BEDS
BY MOVING THE BACK REST.

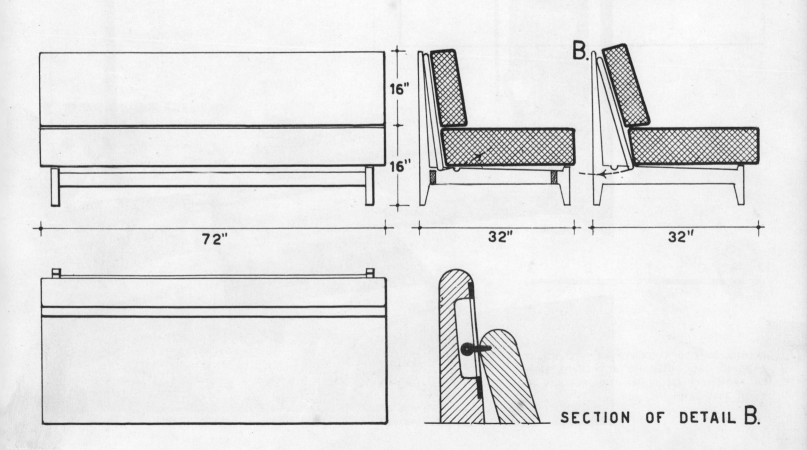

16"

16"

72"

32"

32"

B.

SECTION OF DETAIL B.

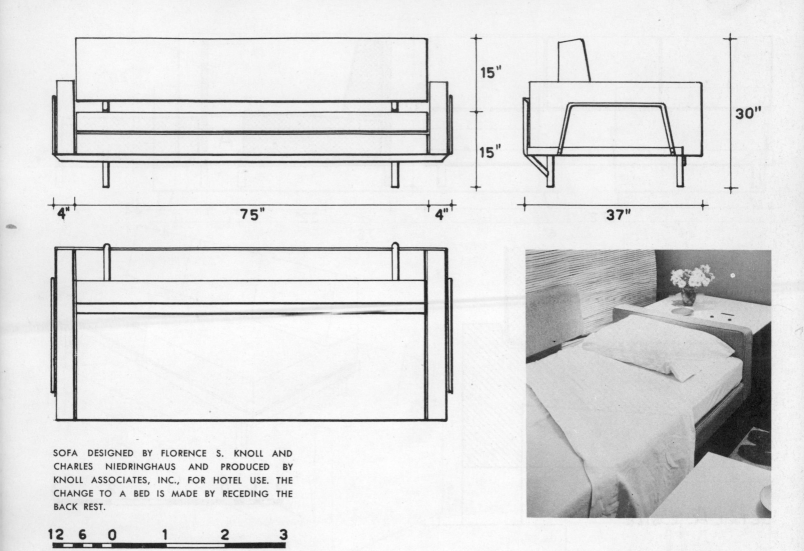

15"

15"

4"   75"   4"

30"

37"

SOFA DESIGNED BY FLORENCE S. KNOLL AND
CHARLES NIEDRINGHAUS AND PRODUCED BY
KNOLL ASSOCIATES, INC., FOR HOTEL USE. THE
CHANGE TO A BED IS MADE BY RECEDING THE
BACK REST.

12 6 0   1   2   3

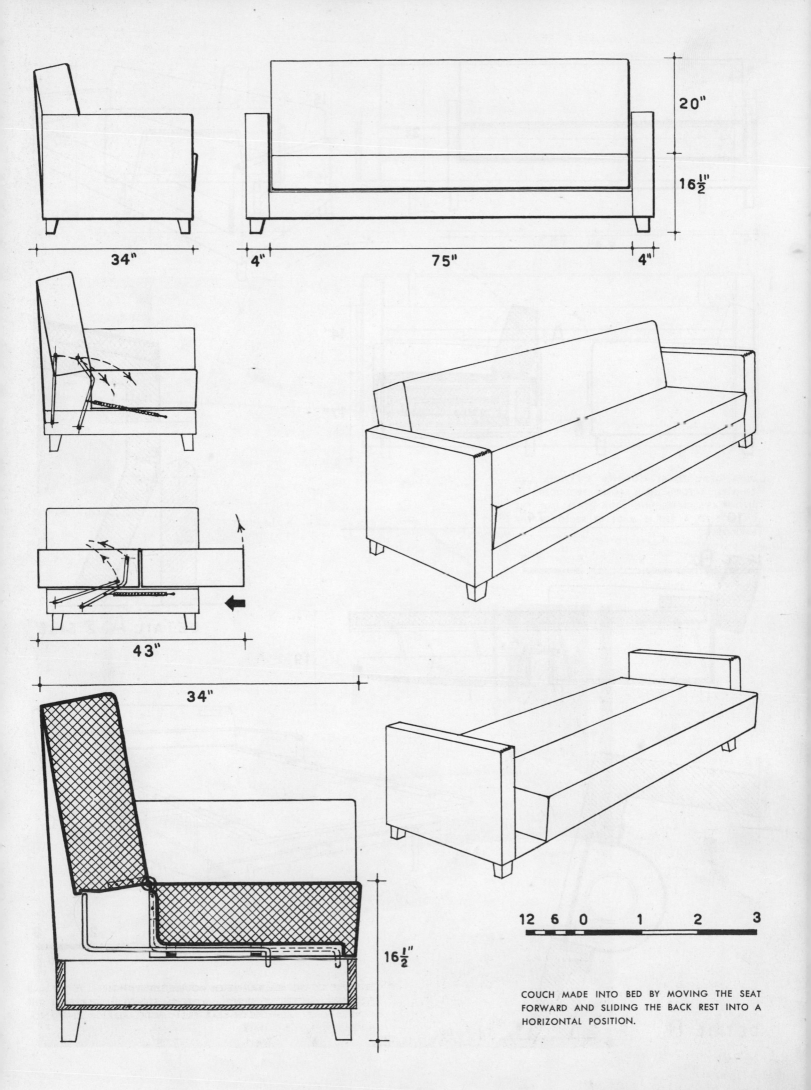

20"

16 1/2"

34"

4"   75"   4"

43"

34"

16 1/2"

12 6 0   1   2   3

COUCH MADE INTO BED BY MOVING THE SEAT
FORWARD AND SLIDING THE BACK REST INTO A
HORIZONTAL POSITION.

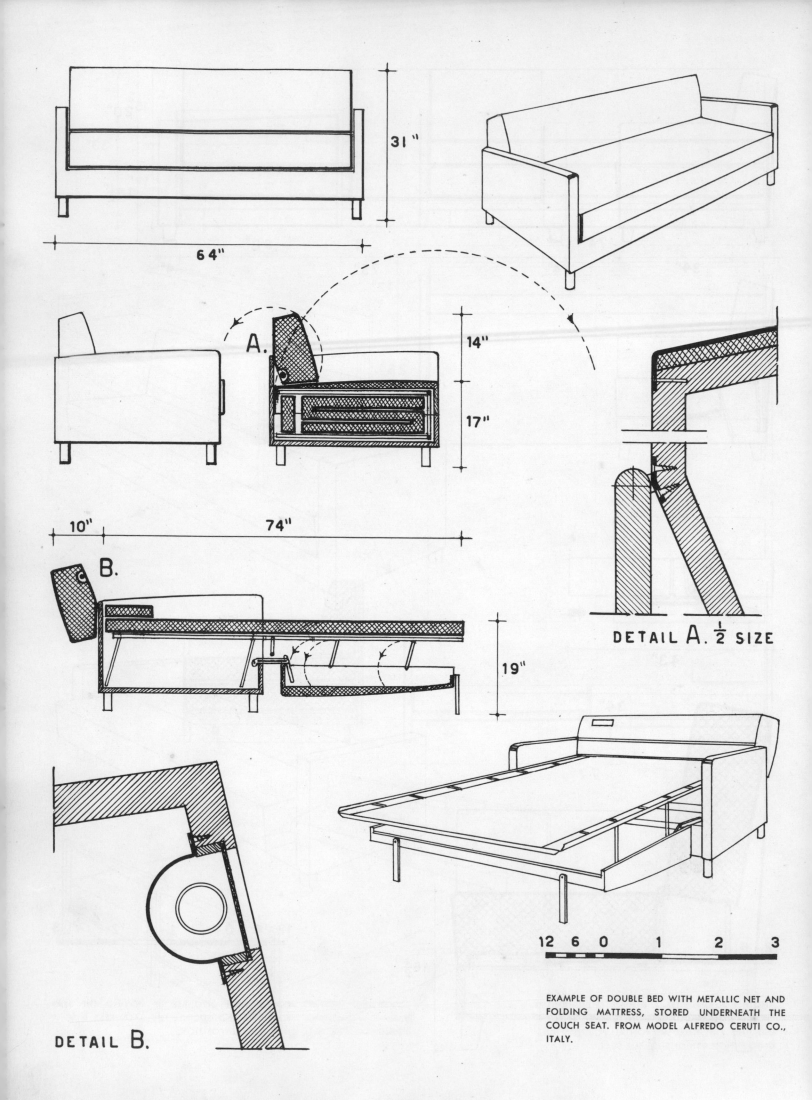

31"

64"

A.

14"

17"

10"

74"

DETAIL A. ½ SIZE

B.

19"

DETAIL B.

12 6 0 1 2 3

EXAMPLE OF DOUBLE BED WITH METALLIC NET AND FOLDING MATTRESS, STORED UNDERNEATH THE COUCH SEAT. FROM MODEL ALFREDO CERUTI CO., ITALY.

156

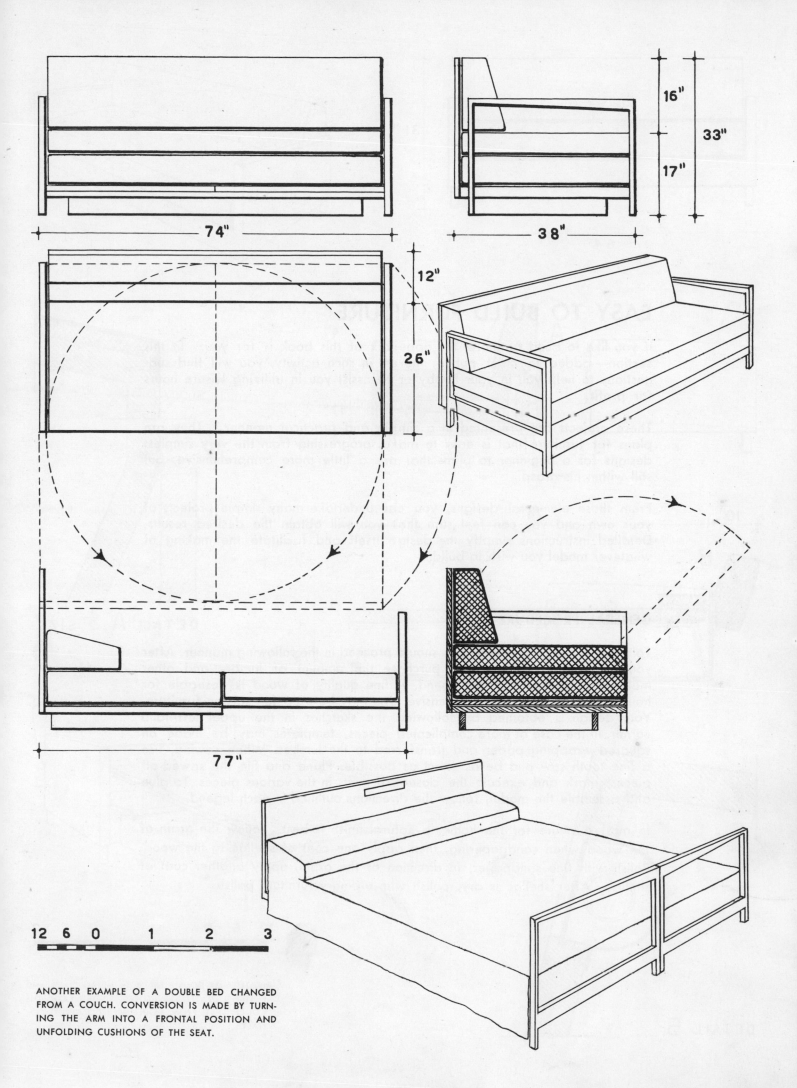

16"

33"

17"

74"

38"

12"

26"

77"

12 6 0 1 2 3

ANOTHER EXAMPLE OF A DOUBLE BED CHANGED
FROM A COUCH. CONVERSION IS MADE BY TURN-
ING THE ARM INTO A FRONTAL POSITION AND
UNFOLDING CUSHIONS OF THE SEAT.

EASY TO BUILD FURNITURE

If you like to build furniture, the appendix of this book is for you. In this section—added to meet public interest in such activity, you will find suggestions to help you in your hobby or to assist you in utilizing leisure hours for profit.

These projects are presented in a simple and practical manner. They are plans for furniture that is easy to make, progressing from the very simplest designs for a beginner to plans that are a little more comprehensive, but still within his grasp.

From these elemental designs, you can undertake many simple projects of your own and you can feel sure that you will obtain the desired results. Detailed instructions simplfy the design itself and facilitate the making of whatever model you wish to build.

GENERAL PROCEDURE

To make a selected model, you should proceed in the following manner. After you have chosen the design, purchase the amount of lumber and other material as specified in the legend. A fine quality of wood is desirable for house furniture, but a less expensive type may be used for garden furniture. Your design is obtained by following the sketches in the upper left-hand corner. In the case of more complicated pieces, templates may be made on squared wrapping paper and transferred to the lumber. When sawing, use a fine tooth saw and be as exact as possible. Plane and file the sawed-off pieces, mark and execute the closure of joints in the various pieces. To glue and assemble the model, follow the directions outlined in each legend.

In most furniture for the home, a natural finish is best. Follow the grain of the wood when sandpapering, then apply one coat of shellac to the wood. Polish with fine sandpaper, in direction of the grain, apply another coat of shellac. After shellac is dry, polish with ordinary furniture polish.

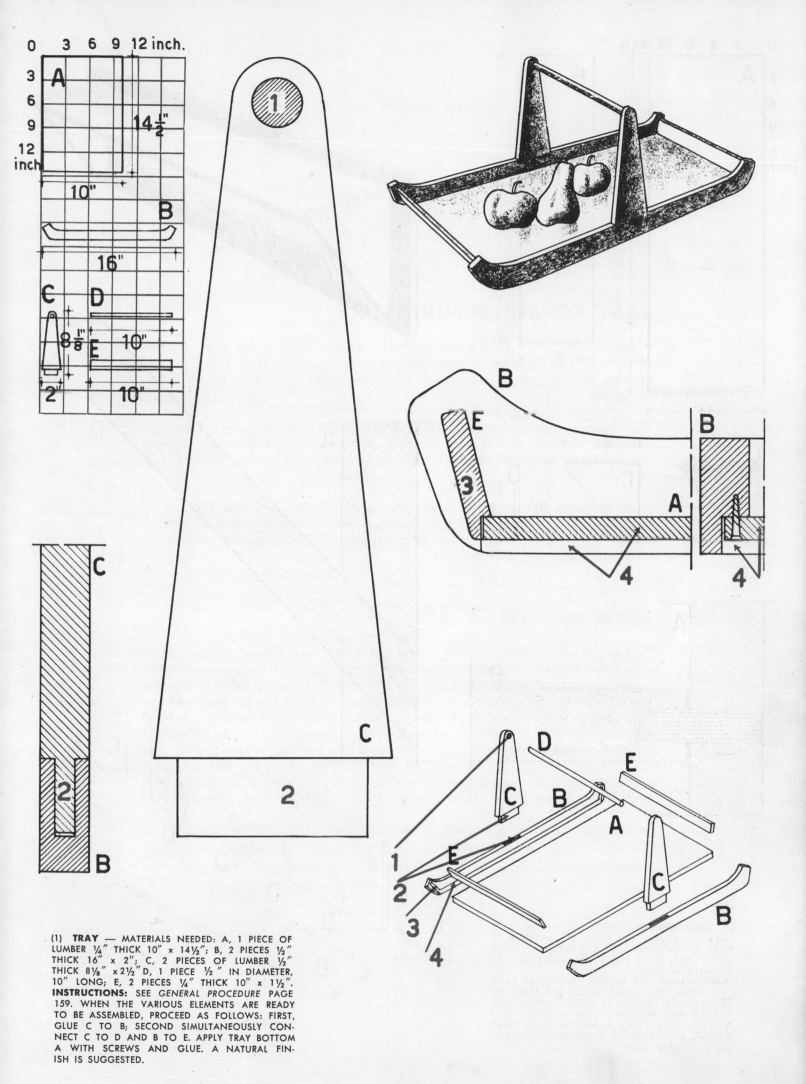

0 3 6 9 12 inch.

A

14½"

10"

B

16"

C   D

8⅛"   E   10"

2"   10"

C

2

B

C

1

C

2

B   E

3   A

B

4   4

D

C   B   E

A

1   E

2   C

3   B

4

(1) TRAY — MATERIALS NEEDED: A, 1 PIECE OF LUMBER ¼" THICK 10" x 14½"; B, 2 PIECES ½" THICK 16" x 2"; C, 2 PIECES OF LUMBER ½" THICK 8⅛" x 2½"D, 1 PIECE ½" IN DIAMETER, 10" LONG; E, 2 PIECES ¼" THICK 10" x 1½". **INSTRUCTIONS:** SEE *GENERAL PROCEDURE* PAGE 159. WHEN THE VARIOUS ELEMENTS ARE READY TO BE ASSEMBLED, PROCEED AS FOLLOWS: FIRST, GLUE C TO B; SECOND SIMULTANEOUSLY CONNECT C TO D AND B TO E. APPLY TRAY BOTTOM A WITH SCREWS AND GLUE. A NATURAL FINISH IS SUGGESTED.

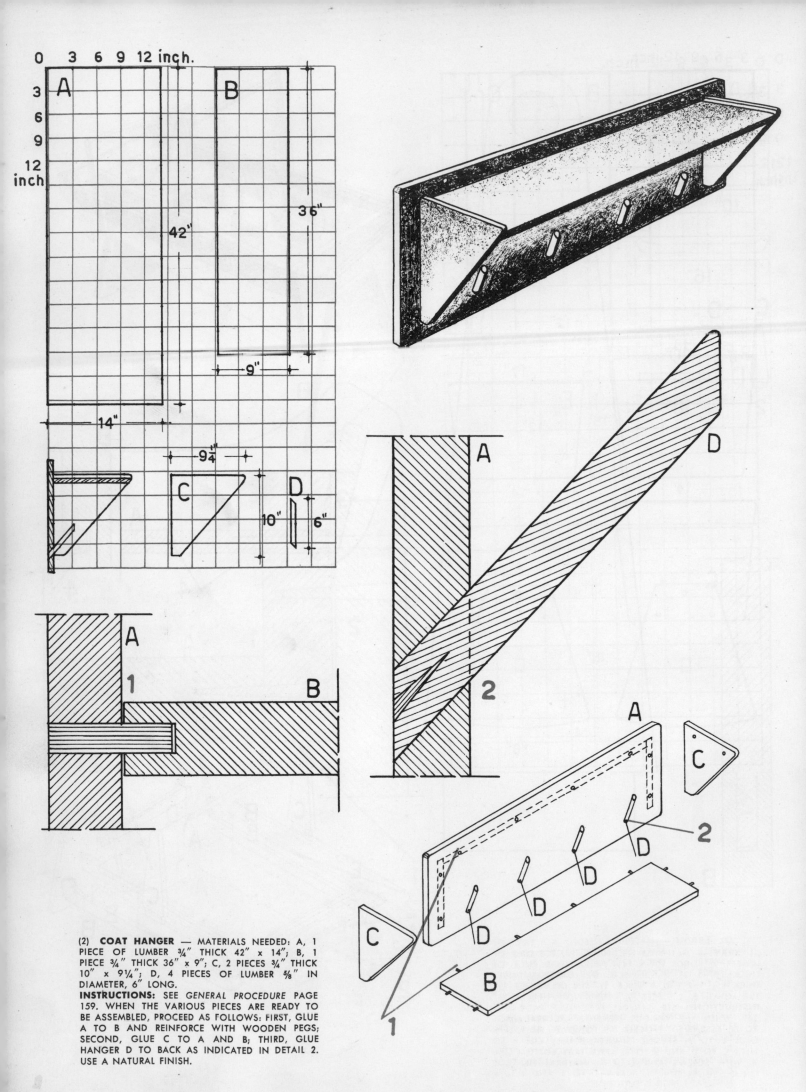

0 3 6 9 12 inch.

3 A

6

9

12

inch

B

42"

36"

9"

14"

9¼"

C

D

10"

6"

A

1

B

A

2

D

A

C

D

2

D

D

D

C

B

1

(2) **COAT HANGER** — MATERIALS NEEDED: A, 1 PIECE OF LUMBER ¾" THICK 42" x 14"; B, 1 PIECE ¾" THICK 36" x 9"; C, 2 PIECES ¾" THICK 10" x 9¼"; D, 4 PIECES OF LUMBER ⅝" IN DIAMETER, 6" LONG.

INSTRUCTIONS: SEE GENERAL PROCEDURE PAGE 159. WHEN THE VARIOUS PIECES ARE READY TO BE ASSEMBLED, PROCEED AS FOLLOWS: FIRST, GLUE A TO B AND REINFORCE WITH WOODEN PEGS; SECOND, GLUE C TO A AND B; THIRD, GLUE HANGER D TO BACK AS INDICATED IN DETAIL 2. USE A NATURAL FINISH.

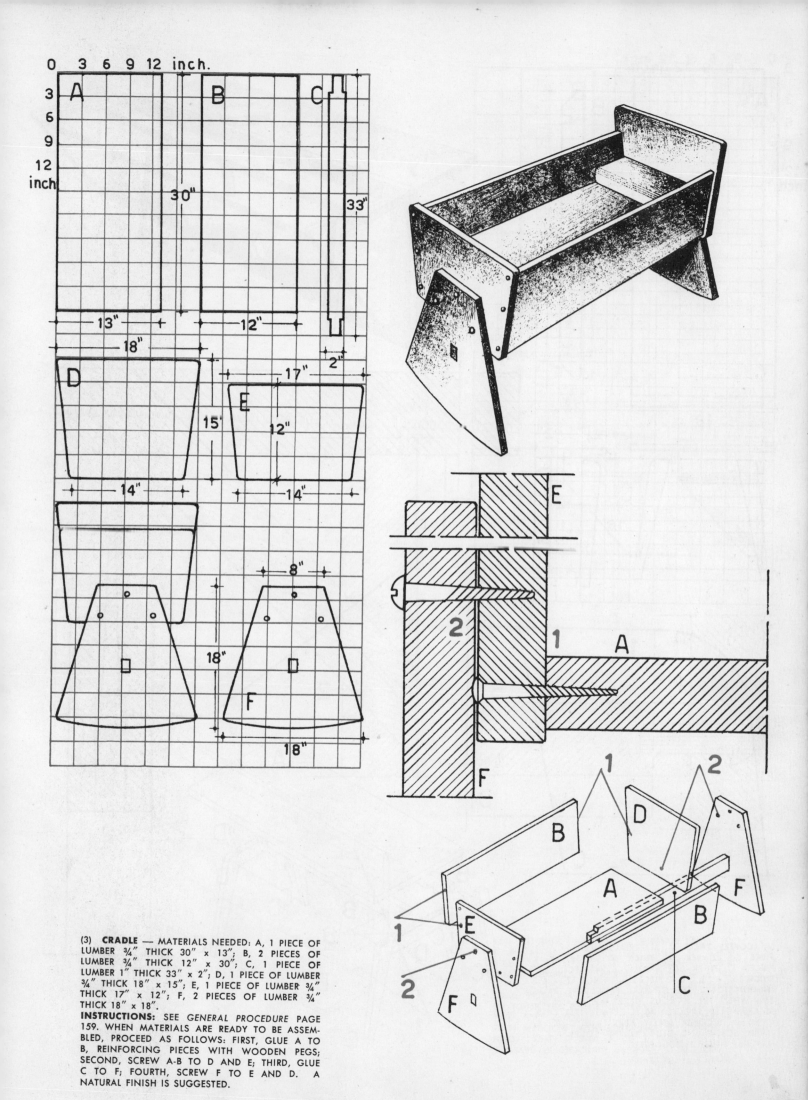

0 3 6 9 12 inch.

A 30" 13"

B 12" 18"

C 33" 2"

D 15" 14" 17"

E 12" 14"

8"

18" 18"

E

2 1 A

F

B

D 2

A

1 F

E B

2 C

F

(3) **CRADLE** — MATERIALS NEEDED: A, 1 PIECE OF LUMBER ¾" THICK 30" x 13"; B, 2 PIECES OF LUMBER ¾" THICK 12" x 30"; C, 1 PIECE OF LUMBER 1" THICK 33" x 2"; D, 1 PIECE OF LUMBER ¾" THICK 18" x 15"; E, 1 PIECE OF LUMBER ¾" THICK 17" x 12"; F, 2 PIECES OF LUMBER ¾" THICK 18" x 18".

INSTRUCTIONS: SEE *GENERAL PROCEDURE* PAGE 159. WHEN MATERIALS ARE READY TO BE ASSEMBLED, PROCEED AS FOLLOWS: FIRST, GLUE A TO B, REINFORCING PIECES WITH WOODEN PEGS; SECOND, SCREW A-B TO D AND E; THIRD, GLUE C TO F; FOURTH, SCREW F TO E AND D. A NATURAL FINISH IS SUGGESTED.

3

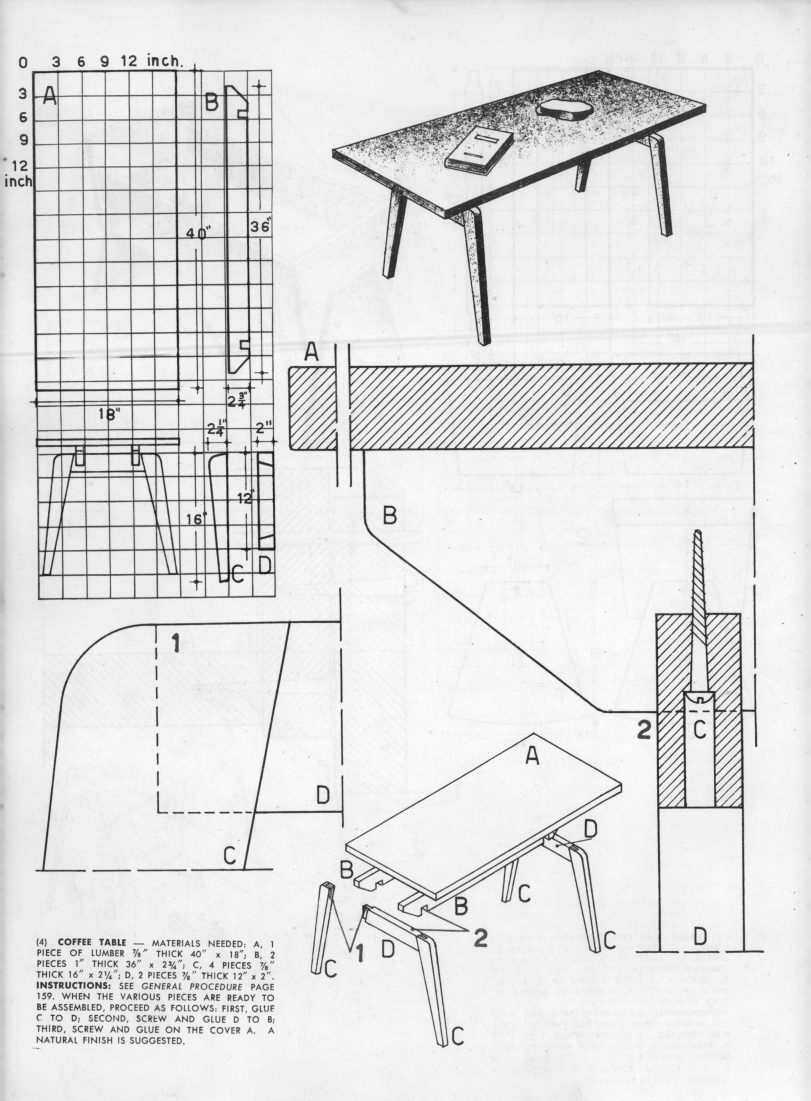

0 3 6 9 12 inch.

3 A   B

6

9

12

inch

40"   36"

18"

2 3/4"

2 1/4"   2"

16"   12"

C   D

1

2   C

A

D

B   B

C

D   2

C

1   D

C

C   D

(4) COFFEE TABLE — MATERIALS NEEDED: A, 1
PIECE OF LUMBER 7/8" THICK 40" x 18"; B, 2
PIECES 1" THICK 36" x 2 3/4"; C, 4 PIECES 7/8"
THICK 16" x 2 1/4"; D, 2 PIECES 7/8" THICK 12" x 2".
INSTRUCTIONS: SEE *GENERAL PROCEDURE PAGE
159.* WHEN THE VARIOUS PIECES ARE READY TO
BE ASSEMBLED, PROCEED AS FOLLOWS: FIRST, GLUE
C TO D; SECOND, SCREW AND GLUE D TO B;
THIRD, SCREW AND GLUE ON THE COVER A. A
NATURAL FINISH IS SUGGESTED.

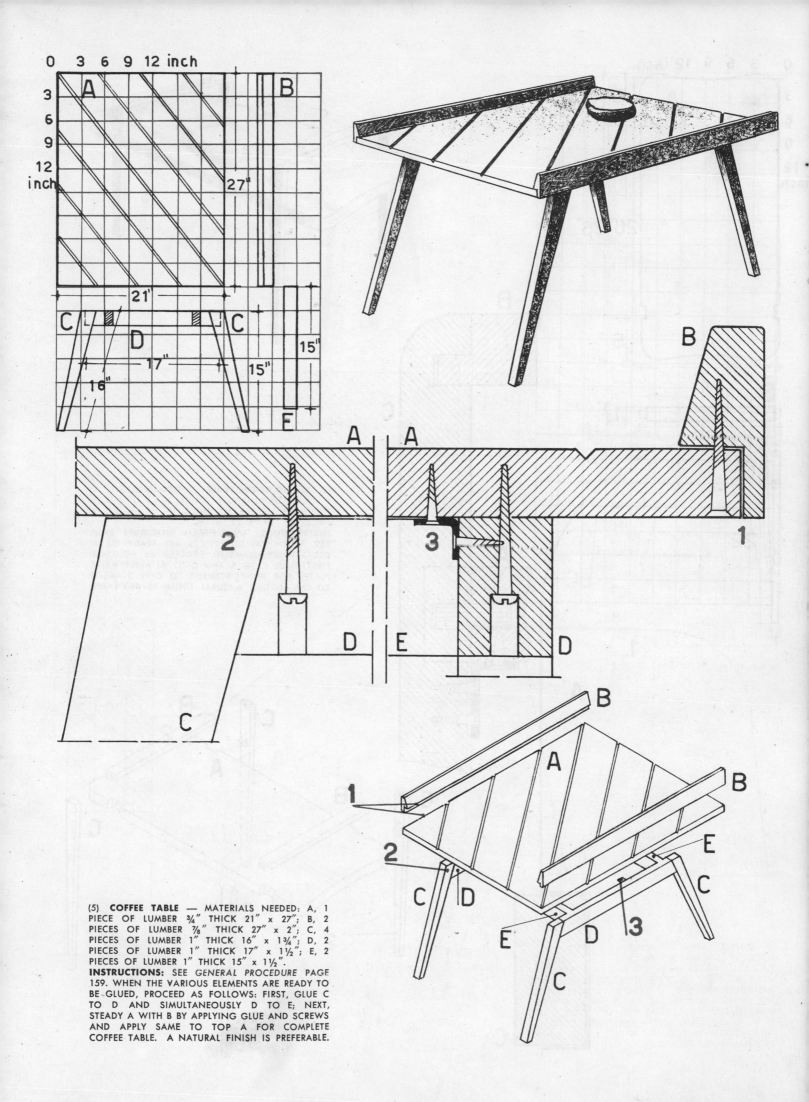

0 3 6 9 12 inch

A   B

27"

21'

C   C
D
17"
16"   15"   15"

E

A   A
B

2   3   1

D   E   D

C

1
2
B
A
B
E
C
D
C
E   D   3
C

(5) **COFFEE TABLE** — MATERIALS NEEDED: A, 1 PIECE OF LUMBER ¾" THICK 21" x 27"; B, 2 PIECES OF LUMBER ⅞" THICK 27" x 2"; C, 4 PIECES OF LUMBER 1" THICK 16" x 1¾"; D, 2 PIECES OF LUMBER 1" THICK 17" x 1½"; E, 2 PIECES OF LUMBER 1" THICK 15" x 1½".
INSTRUCTIONS: SEE *GENERAL PROCEDURE* PAGE 159. WHEN THE VARIOUS ELEMENTS ARE READY TO BE GLUED, PROCEED AS FOLLOWS: FIRST, GLUE C TO D AND SIMULTANEOUSLY D TO E; NEXT, STEADY A WITH B BY APPLYING GLUE AND SCREWS AND APPLY SAME TO TOP A FOR COMPLETE COFFEE TABLE. A NATURAL FINISH IS PREFERABLE.

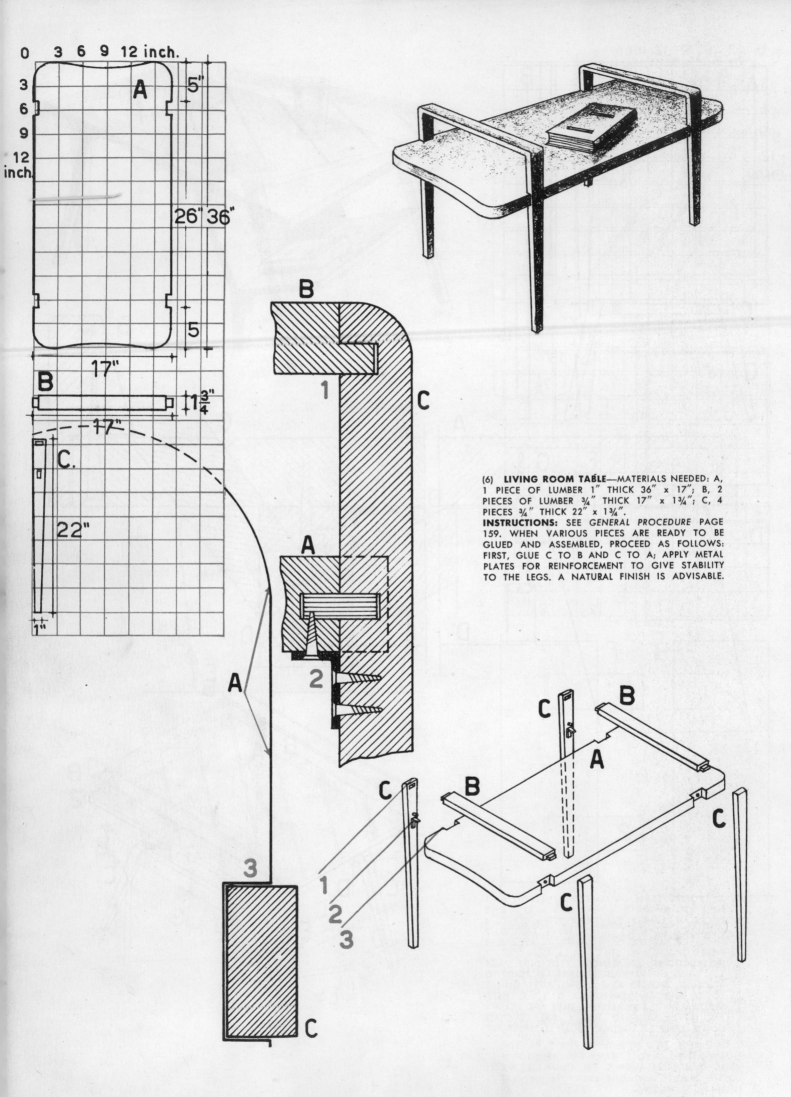

0 3 6 9 12 inch.

A

5"

3
6
9
12 inch.

26" 36"

5

17"

B

1 3/4"

17"

C.

22"

1"

B

1

C

A

2

A

3

C

(6) **LIVING ROOM TABLE**—MATERIALS NEEDED: A, 1 PIECE OF LUMBER 1" THICK 36" x 17"; B, 2 PIECES OF LUMBER 3/4" THICK 17" x 1 3/4"; C, 4 PIECES 3/4" THICK 22" x 1 3/4".
INSTRUCTIONS: SEE GENERAL PROCEDURE PAGE 159. WHEN VARIOUS PIECES ARE READY TO BE GLUED AND ASSEMBLED, PROCEED AS FOLLOWS: FIRST, GLUE C TO B AND C TO A; APPLY METAL PLATES FOR REINFORCEMENT TO GIVE STABILITY TO THE LEGS. A NATURAL FINISH IS ADVISABLE.

C **B**

A

C **B**

1
2
3

C

C

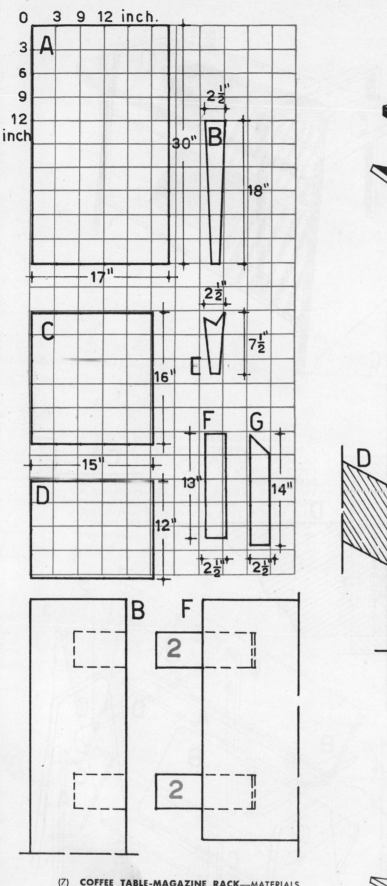

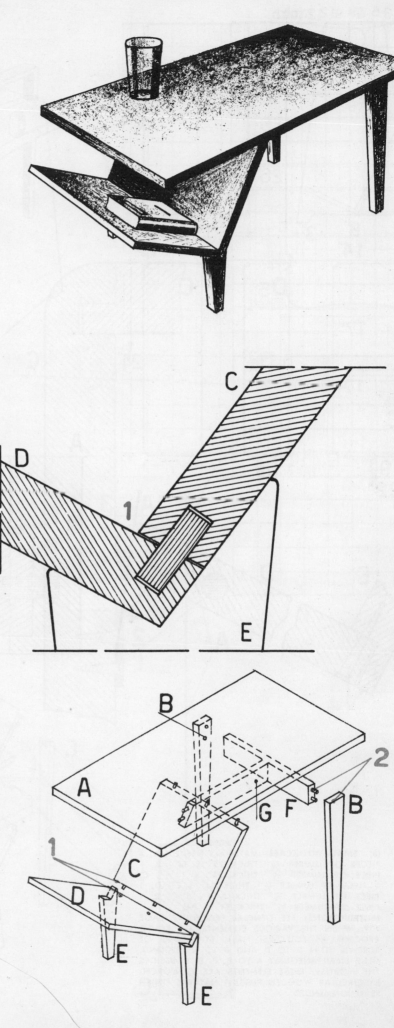

0   3   9   12 inch.

A

B   30"   18"   2½"

C   16"   2½"

E   7½"

D   15"   13"   F   G   14"

12"   2½"   2½"

17"

15"

B   F

2   2

2   2

(7) **COFFEE TABLE-MAGAZINE RACK**—MATERIALS NEEDED: A, 1 PIECE OF LUMBER ¾" THICK 17" x 30"; B, 2 PIECES OF LUMBER 1" THICK 18" x 2½"; C, 1 PIECE OF LUMBER ¾" THICK 15" x 16"; D, 1 PIECE ¾" THICK 15" x 12"; E, 2 PIECES OF LUMBER 1" THICK 7½" x 2½"; F, 1 PIECE OF LUMBER 1" THICK 13" x 2½"; G, 1 PIECE OF LUMBER 1" THICK 14" x 2½".
INSTRUCTIONS: SEE GENERAL PROCEDURE PAGE 159. WHEN THE VARIOUS ELEMENTS ARE READY TO BE GLUED, PROCEED AS FOLLOWS: FIRST, GLUE C TO D; SECOND, D TO E; THIRD, B TO F; FOURTH, F TO G; FIFTH, G TO C. APPLY THE TABLE TOP A WITH GLUE AND SCREWS TO COMPLETE THE COFFEE TABLE - MAGAZINE RACK. A NATURAL FINISH IS SUGGESTED.

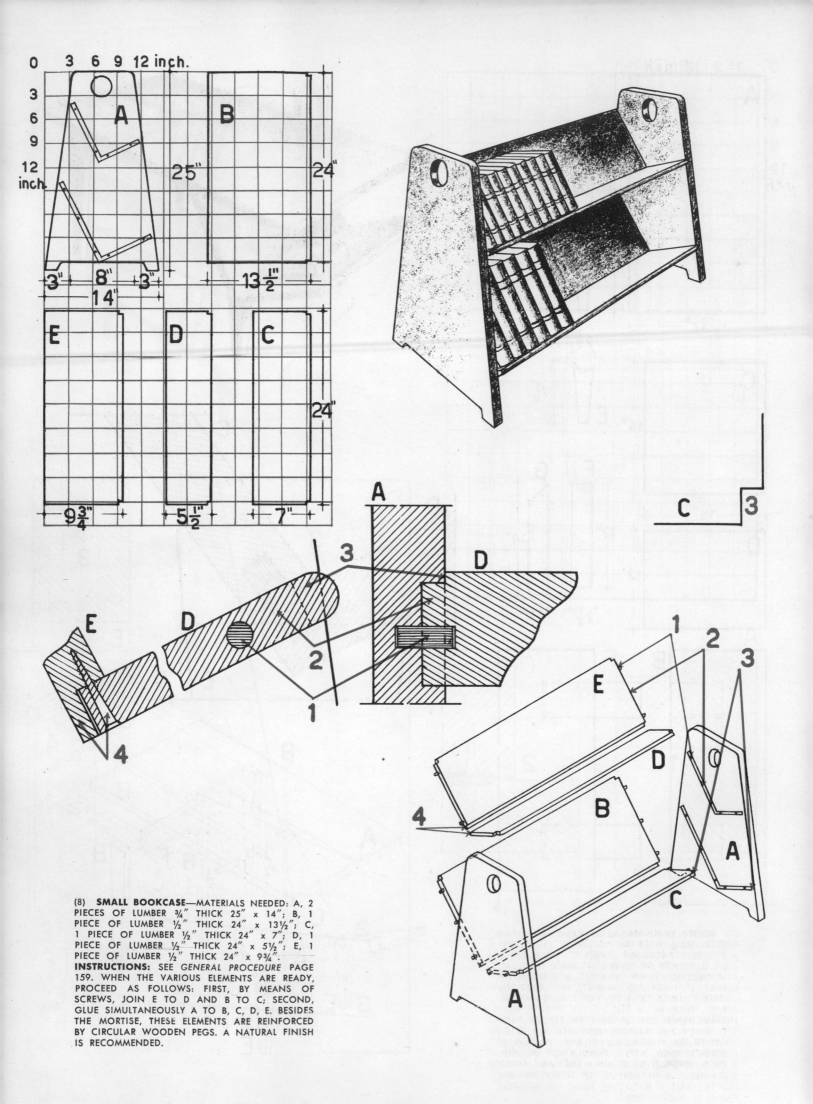

0 3 6 9 12 inch.

25"

24"

A

B

3"   8"   3"

14"

13 ½"

E   D   C

24"

9¾"   5½"   7"

C   3

A

3

D

E

D

2

1

4

E

D

B

A

C

1 2 3

4

A

(8) **SMALL BOOKCASE**—MATERIALS NEEDED: A, 2 PIECES OF LUMBER ¾" THICK 25" x 14"; B, 1 PIECE OF LUMBER ¼" THICK 24" x 13½"; C, 1 PIECE OF LUMBER ½" THICK 24" x 7"; D, 1 PIECE OF LUMBER ½" THICK 24" x 5½"; E, 1 PIECE OF LUMBER ½" THICK 24" x 9¾". **INSTRUCTIONS:** SEE *GENERAL PROCEDURE* PAGE 159. WHEN THE VARIOUS ELEMENTS ARE READY, PROCEED AS FOLLOWS: FIRST, BY MEANS OF SCREWS, JOIN E TO D AND B TO C; SECOND, GLUE SIMULTANEOUSLY A TO B, C, D, E. BESIDES THE MORTISE, THESE ELEMENTS ARE REINFORCED BY CIRCULAR WOODEN PEGS. A NATURAL FINISH IS RECOMMENDED.

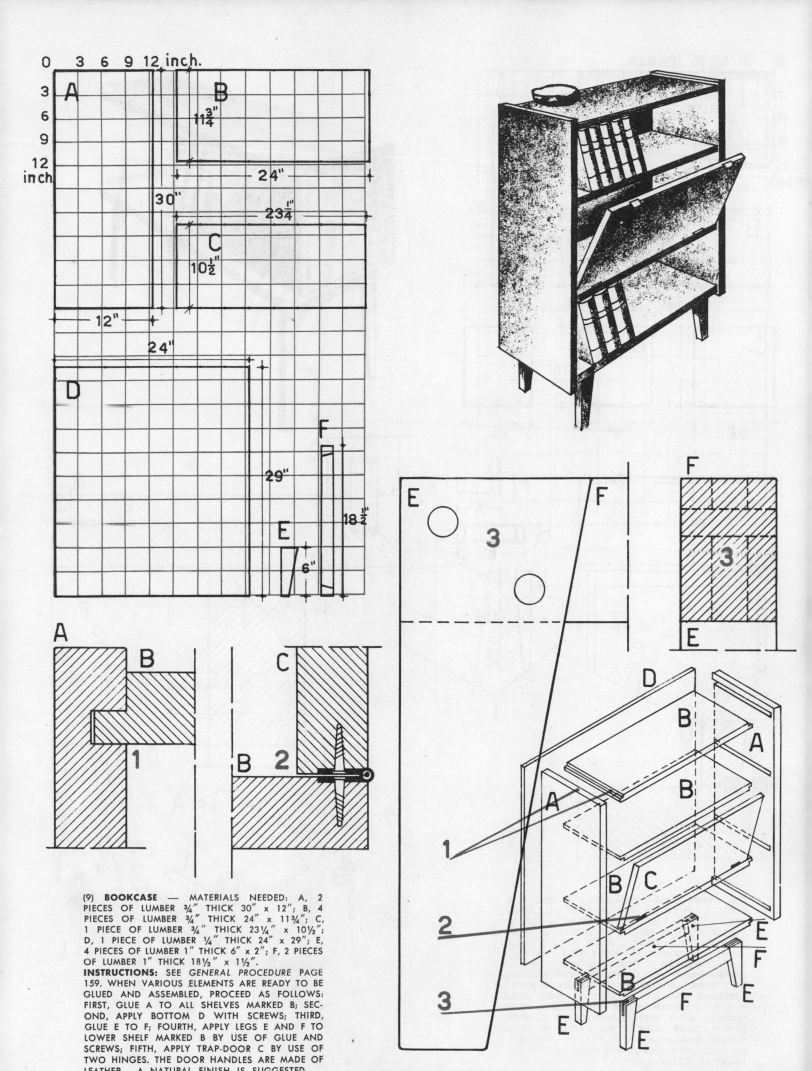

0   3   6   9   12 inch.

A

B

11¾"

24"

30"

23¼"

C

10½"

12"

24"

D

29"

F

18½"

E

6"

A

B

1

C

B

2

E

3

F

F

3

E

D

B

A

B

A

B

C

1

2

E

F

3

B

E

F

E

E

(9) **BOOKCASE** — MATERIALS NEEDED: A, 2 PIECES OF LUMBER ¾" THICK 30" x 12"; B, 4 PIECES OF LUMBER ¾" THICK 24" x 11¾"; C, 1 PIECE OF LUMBER ¾" THICK 23¼" x 10½"; D, 1 PIECE OF LUMBER ¼" THICK 24" x 29"; E, 4 PIECES OF LUMBER 1" THICK 6" x 2"; F, 2 PIECES OF LUMBER 1" THICK 18½" x 1½".
INSTRUCTIONS: SEE *GENERAL PROCEDURE* PAGE 159. WHEN VARIOUS ELEMENTS ARE READY TO BE GLUED AND ASSEMBLED, PROCEED AS FOLLOWS: FIRST, GLUE A TO ALL SHELVES MARKED B; SECOND, APPLY BOTTOM D WITH SCREWS; THIRD, GLUE E TO F; FOURTH, APPLY LEGS E AND F TO LOWER SHELF MARKED B BY USE OF GLUE AND SCREWS; FIFTH, APPLY TRAP-DOOR C BY USE OF TWO HINGES. THE DOOR HANDLES ARE MADE OF LEATHER.   A NATURAL FINISH IS SUGGESTED.

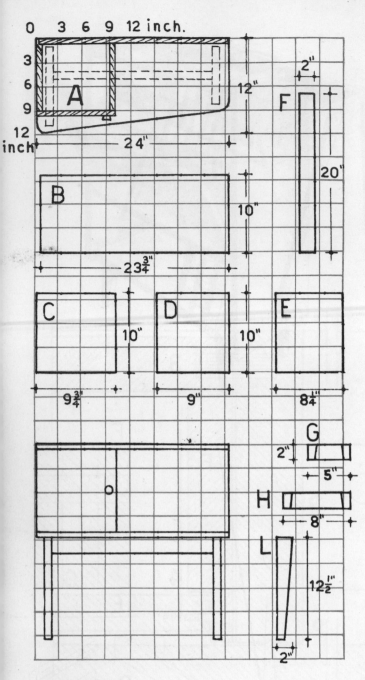

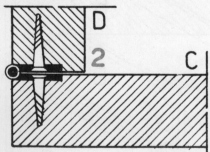

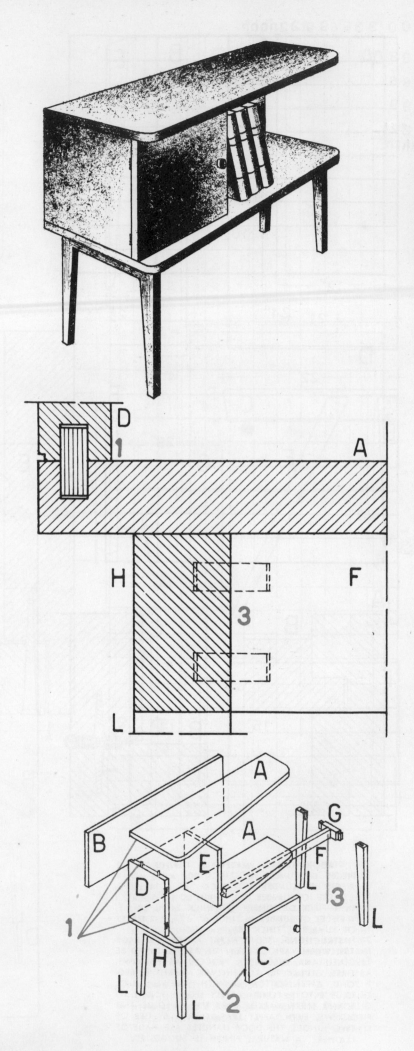

(10) **NIGHT TABLE** — MATERIALS NEEDED: A, 2 PIECES ¾" THICK 24" x 12"; B, 1 PIECE ¾" THICK 23¾" x 10"; C, 1 PIECE ¾" THICK 10" x 9¾"; D, 1 PIECE ¾" THICK 10" x 9"; E, 1 PIECE ¾" THICK 10" x 8¼"; F, 1 PIECE 1" THICK 20" x 2"; G, 1 PIECE 1" THICK 5" x 2"; H, 1 PIECE 1" THICK 8" x 2"; L, 4 PIECES 1" THICK 12½" x 2".

INSTRUCTIONS: SEE *GENERAL PROCEDURE* PAGE 159. WHEN VARIOUS PIECES ARE READY TO BE ASSEMBLED, PROCEED AS FOLLOWS: FIRST, GLUE B, D, E, TO A REINFORCING WITH WOODEN PEGS; SECOND, APPLY SIDE D AND DOOR C WITH HINGES; THIRD, GLUE H TO L AND G TO L; FOURTH, GLUE H AND G TO F; FIFTH, JOIN LEGS OF TABLE WITH SCREWS AND GLUE. A NATURAL FINISH IS RECOMMENDED.

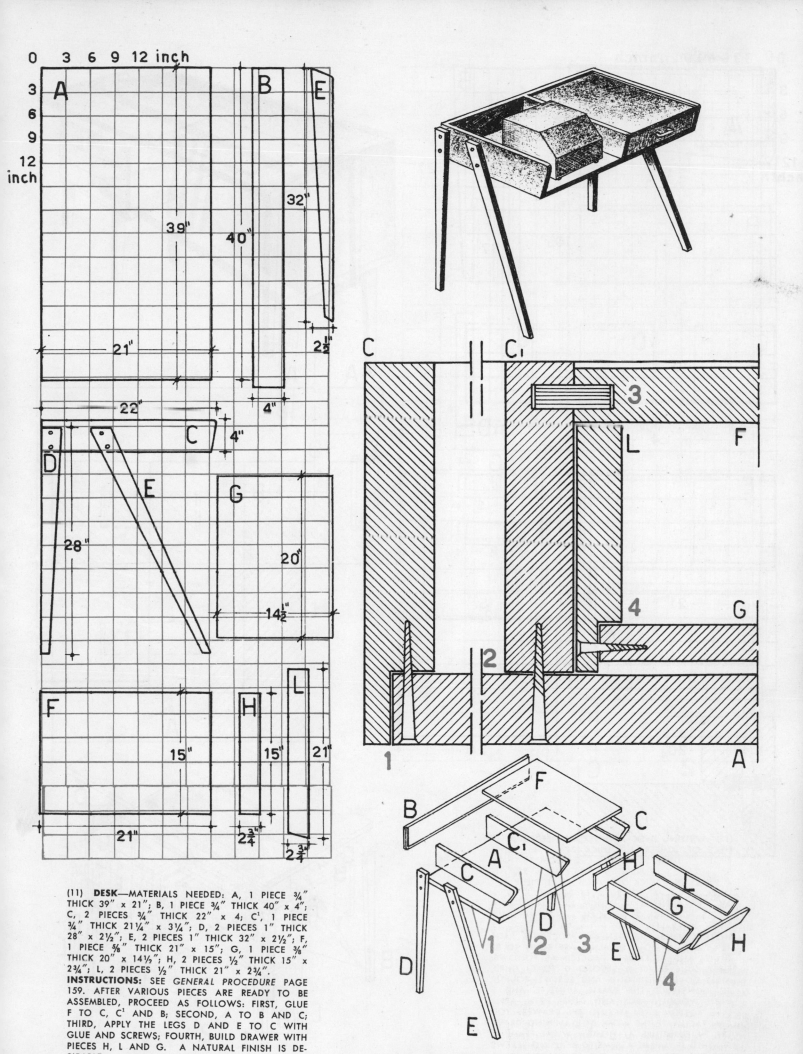

0 3 6 9 12 inch

A

B

E

39"

40"

32"

21"

2½"

22"

4"

C 4"

D

E

G

28"

20"

14½"

F

H L

15" 15" 21"

21" 2¾" 2¾"

C   C¹

3

L   F

4   G

2

1   A

B   F   C

C   C¹

A

H   L

D   L   G

1   2   3   E   H

4

D

E

(11) **DESK**—MATERIALS NEEDED: A, 1 PIECE ¾"
THICK 39" x 21"; B, 1 PIECE ¾" THICK 40" x 4";
C, 2 PIECES ¾" THICK 22" x 4; C¹, 1 PIECE
¾" THICK 21¼" x 3¼"; D, 2 PIECES 1" THICK
28" x 2½"; E, 2 PIECES 1" THICK 32" x 2½"; F,
1 PIECE ⅝" THICK 21" x 15"; G, 1 PIECE ⅜"
THICK 20" x 14½"; H, 2 PIECES ½" THICK 15" x
2¾"; L, 2 PIECES ½" THICK 21" x 2¾".
INSTRUCTIONS: SEE *GENERAL PROCEDURE* PAGE
159. AFTER VARIOUS PIECES ARE READY TO BE
ASSEMBLED, PROCEED AS FOLLOWS: FIRST, GLUE
F TO C, C¹ AND B; SECOND, A TO B AND C;
THIRD, APPLY THE LEGS D AND E TO C WITH
GLUE AND SCREWS; FOURTH, BUILD DRAWER WITH
PIECES H, L AND G. A NATURAL FINISH IS DE-
SIRABLE.

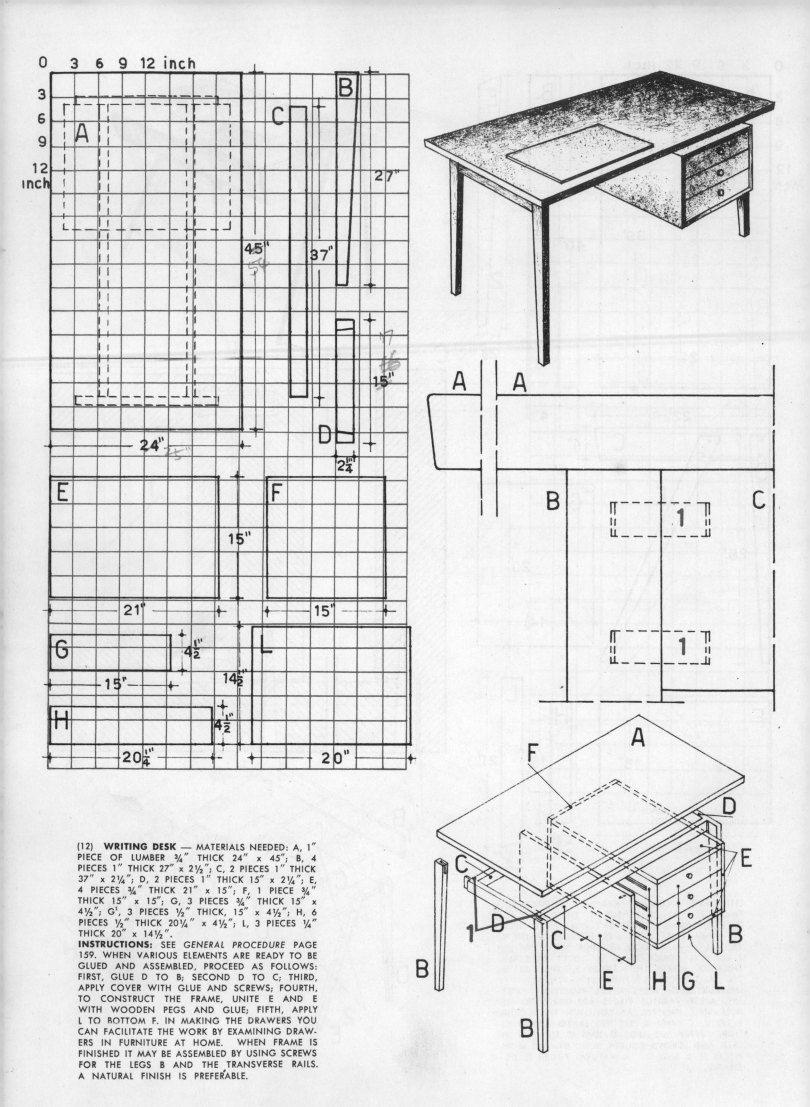

(12) WRITING DESK — MATERIALS NEEDED: A, 1" PIECE OF LUMBER ¾" THICK 24" x 45"; B, 4 PIECES 1" THICK 27" x 2½"; C, 2 PIECES 1" THICK 37" x 2¼"; D, 2 PIECES 1" THICK 15" x 2¼"; E, 4 PIECES ¾" THICK 21" x 15"; F, 1 PIECE ¾" THICK 15" x 15"; G, 3 PIECES ¾" THICK 15" x 4½"; G¹, 3 PIECES ½" THICK, 15" x 4½"; H, 6 PIECES ½" THICK 20¼" x 4½"; L, 3 PIECES ¼" THICK 20" x 14½".

INSTRUCTIONS: SEE *GENERAL PROCEDURE* PAGE 159. WHEN VARIOUS ELEMENTS ARE READY TO BE GLUED AND ASSEMBLED, PROCEED AS FOLLOWS: FIRST, GLUE D TO B; SECOND D TO C; THIRD, APPLY COVER WITH GLUE AND SCREWS; FOURTH, TO CONSTRUCT THE FRAME, UNITE E AND E WITH WOODEN PEGS AND GLUE; FIFTH, APPLY L TO BOTTOM F. IN MAKING THE DRAWERS YOU CAN FACILITATE THE WORK BY EXAMINING DRAWERS IN FURNITURE AT HOME. WHEN FRAME IS FINISHED IT MAY BE ASSEMBLED BY USING SCREWS FOR THE LEGS B AND THE TRANSVERSE RAILS. A NATURAL FINISH IS PREFERABLE.

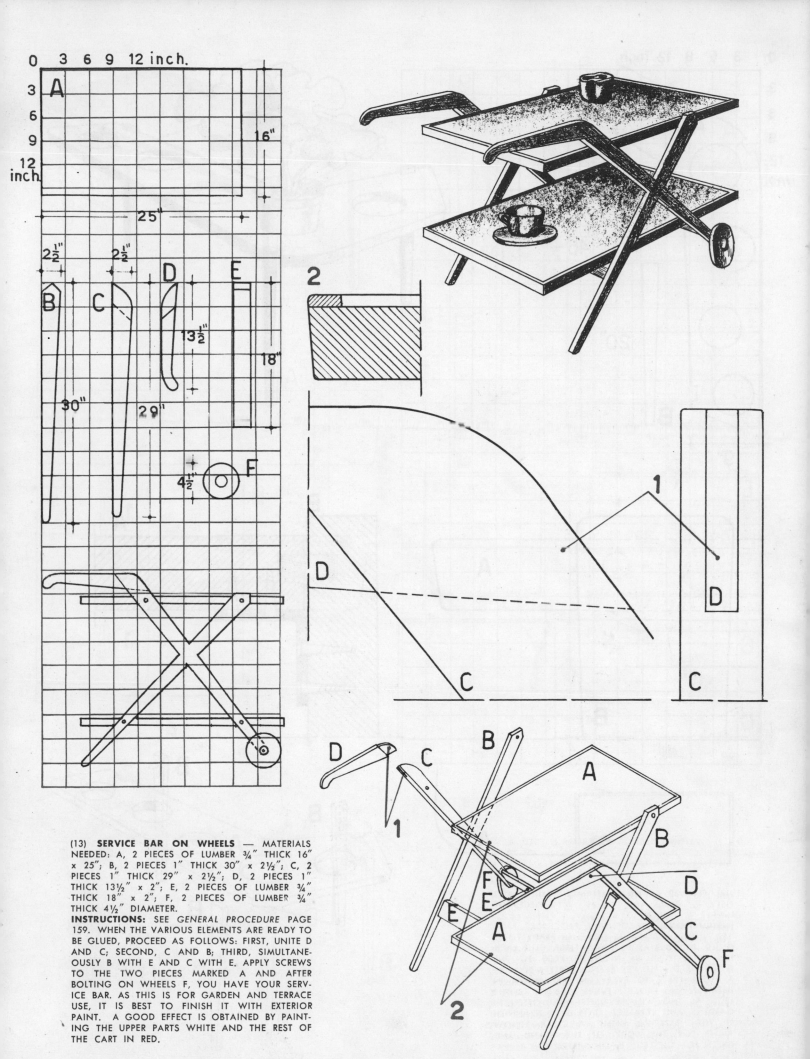

0 3 6 9 12 inch.

A

16"

25"

2½" 2½"

B C D E

13½"

18"

30" 29"

4½" F

2

1

D

C

D

C

D C B

A

1

B

F E A

E E A

D

1

C

F

2

(13) SERVICE BAR ON WHEELS — MATERIALS NEEDED: A, 2 PIECES OF LUMBER ¾" THICK 16" x 25"; B, 2 PIECES 1" THICK 30" x 2½"; C, 2 PIECES 1" THICK 29" x 2½"; D, 2 PIECES 1" THICK 13½" x 2"; E, 2 PIECES OF LUMBER ¾" THICK 18" x 2"; F, 2 PIECES OF LUMBER ¾" THICK 4½" DIAMETER.

INSTRUCTIONS: SEE *GENERAL PROCEDURE* PAGE 159. WHEN THE VARIOUS ELEMENTS ARE READY TO BE GLUED, PROCEED AS FOLLOWS: FIRST, UNITE D AND C; SECOND, C AND B; THIRD, SIMULTANE-OUSLY B WITH E AND C WITH E. APPLY SCREWS TO THE TWO PIECES MARKED A AND AFTER BOLTING ON WHEELS F, YOU HAVE YOUR SERV-ICE BAR. AS THIS IS FOR GARDEN AND TERRACE USE, IT IS BEST TO FINISH IT WITH EXTERIOR PAINT. A GOOD EFFECT IS OBTAINED BY PAINT-ING THE UPPER PARTS WHITE AND THE REST OF THE CART IN RED.

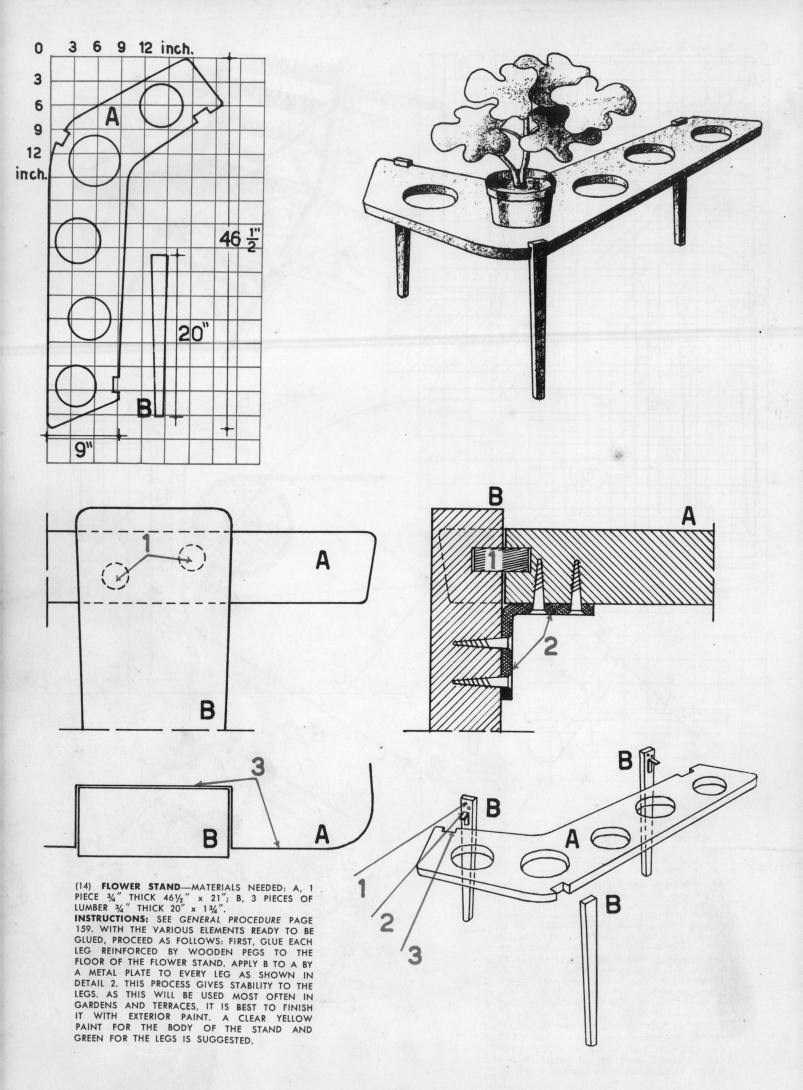

0 3 6 9 12 inch.

A

46 ½"

20"

B

9"

1

A

B

B

A

1

2

3

B

A

B

A

B

B

1

2

3

B

(14) **FLOWER STAND**—MATERIALS NEEDED: A, 1 PIECE ¾" THICK 46½" x 21"; B, 3 PIECES OF LUMBER ¾" THICK 20" x 1¾".
INSTRUCTIONS: SEE *GENERAL PROCEDURE PAGE 159.* WITH THE VARIOUS ELEMENTS READY TO BE GLUED, PROCEED AS FOLLOWS: FIRST, GLUE EACH LEG REINFORCED BY WOODEN PEGS TO THE FLOOR OF THE FLOWER STAND. APPLY B TO A BY A METAL PLATE TO EVERY LEG AS SHOWN IN DETAIL 2. THIS PROCESS GIVES STABILITY TO THE LEGS. AS THIS WILL BE USED MOST OFTEN IN GARDENS AND TERRACES, IT IS BEST TO FINISH IT WITH EXTERIOR PAINT. A CLEAR YELLOW PAINT FOR THE BODY OF THE STAND AND GREEN FOR THE LEGS IS SUGGESTED.